Entrepreneur MAGAZINE'S

LEGAL GUIDE

D1558582

Harassment and Discrimination

Additional titles in Entrepreneur's Legal Guides
Helen Cicino, Esq.
Managing Editor

Bankruptcy for Businesses: The Benefits, Pitfalls, and Alternatives

Business Contracts: Turn Any Business Contract to Your Advantage

Business Structures: How to Form a Corporation, LLC, Partnership, or Sole Proprietorship (Available December 2007)

Estate Planning, Wills, and Trusts

Forming an LLC: In Any State

Forming a Partnership: And Making It Work

Hiring and Firing

Incorporate Your Business in Any State

Intellectual Property: Patents, Trademarks, Copyrights, Trade Secrets

Principles of Negotiation: Strategies, Tactics, Techniques to Reach Agreements

The Operations Manual for Corporations (Available December 2007)

The Small Business Legal Tool Kit

Small Claims Court Guidebook (Available January 2008)

Tax Planning for Business: Maximize Profit, Minimize Taxes

Entrepreneur
MAGAZINE'S

LEGAL
GUIDE

Gavin S. Appleby
Attorney at Law

Harassment and Discrimination

And Other Workplace Landmines

- Prevent Workplace Problems
- Avoid Costly Lawsuits
- Protect Your Business

Editorial Director: Jere Calmes
Cover Design: Desktop Miracles, Inc.
Production: CWL Publishing Enterprises, Inc., Madison, Wisconsin,
www.cwlpub.com

Advisory Editor for the Entrepreneur Press Legal Guide Series: Helen Cicino, Esq.

This publication is designed to provide accurate and authoritative information in
regard to the subject matter covered. It is sold with the understanding that the publisher is not engaged in rendering legal, accounting, or other professional services. If
legal advice or other expert assistance is required, the services of a competent professional person should be sought.

> —From a Declaration of Principles jointly adopted by
> a Committee of the American Bar Association
> and a Committee of Publishers and Associations

ISBN 13: 978-1-59918-147-9
     10: 1-59918-145-2

Library of Congress Cataloging-in-Publication Data

Appleby, Gavin S.
  Harassment and discrimination : and other workplace landmines (with cd-rom) /
by Gavin S. Appleby.
    p. cm. — (Legal guide)
  Includes bibliographical references and index.
  ISBN 1-59918-145-2 (alk. paper)
  1. Sexual harassment—Law and legislation—United States. I. Title.
  KF3467.A965 2007
  344.7301'4133—dc22

                                              2007030406

Printed in Canada

11 10 09 08 07   10 9 8 7 6 5 4 3 2 1

Contents

Preface   xv

About the Author   xviii

Chapter 1   Introduction   1
             So Why Does This Happen?   3
             The Landscape Is a Complicated One   4
             So What's an Employer to Do?   6
             But Can You *Really* Avoid This Mess?   6

Chapter 2   Discrimination and the Law: What It Is
             and What It Does   9
             The Historical Difficulty of Creating Anti-
                 Discrimination Legislation   10
             The Evolution of the Law   11
             Early Cases Established the Path Forward   13
             Additional Laws and Categories
                 of Discrimination   14

Chapter 3   Legal Theories of Discrimination and
             Their Effect on You   17
             Providing a Legal Definition of Discrimination   18
             Disparate Treatment Cases in Real Life   19
             The Three Keys to Avoiding a Pretext Problem   20
             Understanding Disparate Impact Claims   24

	A Real Life Analysis of Disparate Impact Cases	25
	Are You a Statistical Disaster Waiting to Happen?	26
Chapter 4	**Unusual Situations: BFOQs, Retirement, RIFs**	**31**
	What on Earth Is a BFOQ?	32
	Don't Confuse a BFOQ with a "Customer Preference"	33
	Don't Confuse a BFOQ with a Sex-Based Protective Purpose	35
	The ADEA and Retirement Exceptions	37
	The Law Applicable to Reduction-in-Forces and Separation Agreements	38
Chapter 5	**Common Employer Mistakes, from Hiring to Firing**	**43**
	Tips in the Hiring, Promotion, and Pay Process	44
	Discharges	48
	Other Suggestions	53
Chapter 6	**A Wild and Crazy World—How Sexual Harassment Became Unlawful**	**59**
	The Awkward Nature of the Legislative Cure	61
	The World of Imperfect Legislation	61
	The "After-Thought" of Sex Discrimination	62
	So What Happened Next?	64
Chapter 7	**Round Pegs and Square Holes: Using Discrimination Law to Prohibit Harassment**	**65**
	Title VII and Its Applicability to Sexual Harassment	66
	The Square Peg–Round Hole Problem	66
	So What Do We Do About This Mess?	68
	And How Does All This Affect the Average Employer?	69
Chapter 8	**Reasonable Women, Welcomeness, and Other Early Concepts**	**71**
	Well, Everyone Knows What's Reasonable, Don't They?	72
	Are Reasonable Men Different from Reasonable Women?	73
	But Is It Fair to Say I'm Not Guilty Because She Welcomed My Neanderthal Behavior?	74
	Additional Early Complications Arose As Juries Came Aboard	78

Chapter 9   **It's Got to Be Severe or Pervasive, Whatever**
That Means   **81**

A Few Examples of Actions That Were Found *Not* to
Be Either Severe or Pervasive   82

Good Lord, Are There Any Bad Actions That *Are*
Covered by This Law?   83

So Why Did the Courts Create Such a Vague Standard
in the First Place?   84

Given Where the Courts Are, What Are Employers
Supposed to Do to Ensure an Effective Workplace
Based on Respect for the Individual?   86

The Danger of Defining "Inappropriate Behavior" Too
Firmly—the Problems of "Zero Tolerance" and
"Protected, Concerted Activity"   87

The National Labor Relations Act Poses a Second
Problem for a Policy Based on a Low-Level Limit of
Inappropriate Behavior   89

Advice to the Employer in Light of All This   91

Chapter 10   **The Wonders of E-Mail and the Internet**   **93**

What On Earth Does Porn Have To Do with This Book?   94

What Can You Do About the Internet?   94

Restricting E-Mail   95

Practical Ways To Deal with These Issues   96

My IT Guy Gave Me a 16-Page Electronics Policy,
So I Think I'm Covered   97

Chapter 11   **Stupid Manager Tricks: The Disaster of Quid**
Pro Quo Harassment and the Problem with
Hostile Work Environments   **99**

God, I Hate Latin, but Go Ahead and Tell Me What
Quid Pro Quo Is   99

How Much Quid and What Kind of Quo Does There
Have to Be?   102

Quids and Quos Aren't Always About Power, They
Also Can Be About Desperation   103

Since 1998, Quid Pro Quo Is Probably a Misnomer,
but It's Still Useful As a Training Concept   105

Chapter 12 Co-Worker Harassment: Party All the Time   **109**
Is This Sexual Harassment?   110
So What's the Danger? Don't Most Companies React
   Pretty Strongly to Harassment?   111
An Example   112
Good Grief, This Is All Quite Mad   114
Defining a Hostile Work Environment Is Not an Easy
   Thing to Do   115
Be Alert, Coach, Counsel, Discipline, and, Where
   Appropriate, Discharge   115

**Chapter 13 Building a Prevention System: Manager Harassment
and the *Faragher* Defense**   **119**
Manager Hostile Work Environment vs. Quid Pro Quo   120
How Much Trouble Am I in If My Manager Creates
   a Hostile Work Environment?   120
An Adequate System for Preventing and Effectively
   Dealing with Concerns of Sexual Harassment   121
Beware—the *Faragher* Defense Has Some Holes in It   122
Meeting the *Faragher* Standard—the Steps and
   the Requirements   123

**Chapter 14 Private Eyes: Investgating Allegations of
Harassment**   **129**
What Is a "Complaint of Harassment" Anyway?   130
Do We Really Need to Investigate Every Complaint?   130
Why Is It So Important to Investigate Every Complaint?   131
Who Should the Investigator Be?   133
What Steps Should Be Taken Before Conducting
   Interviews?   135
Who Should You Interview First and How Should
   the Interviews Be Conducted?   137
How Do You Conclude an Investigation?   139

**Chapter 15 Dealing with Witnesses, Credibility Issues,
and Clarence, Anita, Bill, and Paula
(the "He Said, She Said" Problem)**   **143**
The Business Judgment Rule: You Don't Have to Be Right   144
What Is a Good Faith Belief?   145

You Can't Assess Credibility If You Aren't There   146
Corroborate When Possible   147
Consider Motives   148
Recording Credibility Observations   148
In the Case of a Draw   149
Disciplining Witnesses Who Provided False Information   150

Chapter 16 **After the Investigation: Do We Fire All the Harassers?**   **151**
Here's Your Legal Obligation—and Don't Forget It   152
Some Obvious Watch-Outs and Some That Aren't   152
Tying the Remedy to the Level of Inappropriateness of the Behavior   153
Make Sure the Remedy Is Both Disciplinary and Proactive   156
Don't Be Afraid to Be Creative in Your Remedies   160
Be Results-Oriented in Your Thinking—Sometimes Discharge Is Appropriate Even If the Behavior Wasn't Over the Top   160

Chapter 17 **"Sensitivity School" for Those Who "Don't Get It"**   **163**
Why Is This So—Aren't These Smart People?   164
In What Ways Don't Highly Placed People Get It?   165
So Let's Fire the Idiots and Be Done with It   165
Dealing with These Things Quietly Sounds Suspicious and Even a Little Slimy   166
How to Make Someone "Get It"   166
"Sensitivity Training" Can Take Many Forms and It Can Be Effective   167
Can Higher-Level Executives Be Targets for Sexual Harassment Situations?   168

Chapter 18 **Dealing with the After-Effects: Building Bridges, Appropriate Documentation, and Closing the Loop**   **171**
If All Is Well, What's the Point?   173
The Cold Shoulder Sandra Got Was Not Sexual Harassment   174
What the Courts Are Doing with This Type of Issue   174
Faced with These Problems, What Should You Do?   175

**Chapter 19 Special Situations: Dating and Other Relationships—
Consensual Behavior Isn't Sexual Harassment** **181**
You Might As Well Face the Reality 182
This Must Mean Sexual Harassment Is All Over the Place 183
Why Is a Dating Break Up My Problem? I'm Their
  Employer, Not Their Mother 184
Handling the Relationship Gone Bad 186
What Should Happen with Calvin, Pam, Ginnie,
  and Antonio? 188
Can I Just Prohibit My Employees from Dating? 189

**Chapter 20 Fraternization Policies: "Love Contracts"
and Breaking Up Is Hard to Do** **191**
Efforts of Employers to Regulate Employee Relationships
  in the Workplace 192
Risks Posed to the Employer by Employee Relationships 193
Bye-Bye Love? Policy Choices for Regulating Dating
  and Other Intimate Relationships in the Workplace 199
What to Do When Evidence Suggests Employees Are
  Involved in a Relationship 202

**Chapter 21 Dealing with Managers with Bad Judgment
and the Implications of Having Alcohol
at Company Functions** **203**
Everybody Shows Bad Judgment Sometimes, So Why
  Pick on the Managers? 204
But, Expectations Aside, Managers Do Mess Up, Don't They? 204
You Really Can Make Better Hiring and Promotion Decisions 205
OK, You've Convinced Me, but What About This
  Alcohol Thing? 206
So Should We Banish Alcohol from Company Events? 209
Do We Have the Option of Serving Alcohol,
  If We're Careful? 210
Any Other Words of Wisdom? 211

**Chapter 22 Sexual Orientation, Same-Sex Issues, and
the "Because of Sex" Requirement** **213**
Not a Laughing Matter: How Same-Sex Sexual
  Harassment Can Arise in the Workplace 214

What Is Same-Sex Sexual Harassment?   215
Why Is Same-Sex Sexual Harassment Unlawful?   216
Addressing Same-Sex Sexual Harassment in the Workplace   218
Sexual Orientation Discrimination   219
But … Isn't Sexual Orientation Discrimination
   Against the Law?   220
Other Causes of Action   221
Muddying the Waters a Bit More: When Sexual
   Orientation Discrimination May Be Unlawful Under
   Federal Law   223
Addressing Sexual Orientation Discrimination
   in the Workplace   224

**Chapter 23 Customers, Vendors, and Other Nonemployees:
Thar Be Dragons Here, Too**   **225**
But These People Aren't Mine!   226
But What If I've Done Everything Right and
   They're Not Mine?   227
Liability for Customers   227
But What If the Customer Doesn't Want to Be Reasonable?   229
You May Have More Leverage over Vendors, Contractors,
   and Temp Agencies Than You Have over Customers   230
A Plan for Investigating and Dealing with Alleged Third-
   Party Discrimination or Harassment   231

**Chapter 24 Favoritism, Bullying, Nastiness, and Other
Potential Supervisor Landmines**   **235**
The Limits of the Concept of a Hostile Work Environment   237
What Constitutes an Equal Opportunity Jerk and
   Why He or She Isn't a Legal Problem   237
So If I Hire a Bully, I'm OK?   239
The Problem of Favoritism   240
Difficult Managers Who Do Not Behave Illegally   241
If Bullying Laws Get Passed, We'll Be Litigating Forever   243

Chapter 25 Training Requirements and Suggestions   **245**
California, Connecticut, and Maine: Mandatory Harassment
   Training Requirement   246
The Details of the California Training Law   247

Four Legal Landmines and How to Avoid Them
   Through Training   253
Mandatory Sexual Harassment Training Under
   Connecticut Law   256
Mandatory Sexual Harassment Training in Maine   258
Are Mandatory Training Laws Soon Coming to a
   State Near You?   259
Training As a Mandatory Part of the "*Faragher/Ellerth*
   Defense" to Workplace Harassment and
   the "*Kolstad* Defense" to Punitive Damages   259
Select the Training Platform—Some Training
   Is Better Than Others   261
Use Qualified Training Providers   263
Training Costs: Pay Now or Pay (More) Later   265

**Chapter 26 Beyond Sex: Race, Religion, and Many Other
Forms of Harassment   267**
Racial Harassment   268
National Origin Harassment   270
Religious Harassment   271
Disability Harassment   274
Age Harassment   277

**Chapter 27 The Relationships Among Discrimination,
Harassment, and Retaliation   279**
What Is Retaliation and Where Does It Come from Legally?   280
Retaliation Comes in Two Broad Forms   280
Many Harassment Cases Fall Under the "Opposition
   Clause" Rather Than the "Participation Clause"   282
Fair, but Worrisome   284
How the Retaliation Clause Affects Sexual Harassment Cases   284
The Reality of Retaliation   287
A Plan to Prevent Retaliation Claims   288

**Chapter 28 The Progressive Employer: Combining Respect,
Diversity, and Harassment Avoidance to Make
a Better Workplace   293**
With Dangers All Around, What Is the Best Course
   of Action?   294

Fairness As an Employment Concept   295
A Progressive Outlook Makes a Difference   296
Fair Compensation and Benefits   296
Effective Communications   297
Employee Empowerment and Loyalty   298
Consider the Concept of Change Management   299
Respect for the Individual   300
Diversity in the Workplace   301

Appendix A Glossary   **305**

Appendix B Talking Points: The Elements of Diversity **313**

Index   **321**

Preface

The purpose of this book is simple—to teach businesspersons how to avoid the problems that come from discrimination and harassment. The reality, however, is that some of those problems won't be of your own doing. Discrimination issues arise primarily through the actions of small-minded managers, and most of them don't disclose that particular weakness during the interview process. As for harassment concerns, both well-meaning individuals and employees who don't have a clue can get you in trouble. However, as this book describes, there are proactive steps that you can take to avoid at least some of the problems that can arise.

The book begins with an analysis of discrimination law. You really can't understand the world of harassment unless you have a good feel for the issues of discrimination. We're now living in the 21st century, and reasonable people might assume that discrimination doesn't occur much anymore.

However, that isn't the case. American society has generally moved away from intentional discrimination. The discrimination we see today comes from a lack of understanding of the implications of various behaviors. We're making progress, but issues definitely still exist. In addition, poor management and sloppy investigations and decisions can sometimes create the unintended appearance of discrimination. To make matters worse, judges and juries can find liability in discrimination cases simply because the employer mishandled the situation.

The second part of the book focuses on harassment issues. Again, the American workforce is far better than it used to be. However, people being people, sex still sells and sex occasionally still rules, even in the best workplaces. The problem, in part, is that sexual harassment doesn't always mean an inappropriate "come-on" or an abusive manager. It also covers situations where everyone but one co-worker seemed to be having a great, albeit bawdy, time. In addition, harassment isn't just about sex anymore—harassment issues also arise in regard to race, national origin, religion, sexual orientation, age, and disability, just to name a few.

The third part of the book analyzes topics that arise from discrimination and harassment. Included are discussions on some very important issues, including retaliation, training, and diversity. In fact, many of the later chapters of the book include proactive suggestions that can keep you out of court.

With that said, the most important aspect of this book can be found in every chapter—its practicality. If you're looking for high-level, technical legal analysis, you won't find it here. However, if you want to know what you can do to prevent, respond to, or defend yourself when there is an employment problem, please read on. Assuming you do keep reading, you'll also find a number of stories—some funny, some sad, all true. One great thing about being an employment lawyer—you don't have to make things up.

Hopefully the stories help. Legal learning to the businessperson comes best in a real life context. Spouting off about the law doesn't help very much.

Seeing what can happen in real life, however, and understanding how to prevent such problems in the first place, makes a difference.

Some of the practical advice in this book can be found in the inserts and boxes of information that periodically appear amid the text in each chapter of the book. However, don't just read the boxes. The rest of the text includes practical advice as well.

Finally, a number of forms and materials are included in the CD-ROM that accompanies the book. Feel free to use these forms and materials but, as the disclosure in the CD-ROM says, check with a reputable lawyer first—things change fairly quickly in the law, and you want to be up to date.

Acknowledgments

At the risk of sounding like an Oscar winner, I have a lot of people to thank, and I hope that I don't leave anyone out.

Initially, my utmost thanks to Jere Calmes and Inez Diaz for giving me the opportunity to write this book and for nagging me until I got it done. For those who are thinking about writing that long-planned book, it's a lot more work than you think, but it's definitely worth the effort.

Additional thanks to Ms. Diaz for assisting with the chapter on training, and for taking an over-the-top California statute and making it understandable to the common person. Similarly, my deepest appreciation to my colleagues at Littler Mendelson, Gina Cook and Angelo Spinola, for taking the time from their busy lives to draft several of the chapters in this book. Both did a great job, and it's nice to know that they, too, value humor in the midst of the law. Thanks as well to my dedicated and wonderful assistant, Sarah Allen, for working so hard to put the manuscript together—this book wouldn't have happened without her.

Finally, a special thank you to my family, especially Pattie and Chris. I appreciate the unbelievable understanding and patience you provided me. I realize I spent a lot of time hiding in the extra bedroom writing chapter after chapter. By the way, if you don't believe that's what I was doing back there, ask my favorite dogs, Dom and Daisy, who were at my feet the entire time.

About the Author

Gavin S. Appleby, originally from Pittsburgh, Pennsylvania, never intended to be a lawyer. He went to West Virginia Wesleyan College to play jazz and toured the U.S. and parts of Europe before realizing that getting a real job might be a good idea. Convinced by a friend to try law school, Gavin was fortunate enough to attend the University of Virginia School of Law.

Gavin spent several summers working in a steel foundry in Pittsburgh, joined the Steelworkers Union, and quickly realized that dealing with people and unions was far more fun than, say, writing real estate contracts. So deciding on labor and employment law as a specialty was easy. The area involves people and their actions, which makes it infinitely interesting.

Gavin started his practice in Florida, then moved to Atlanta, a center of employment law. He has spent most of his career working with large national firms, including Littler Mendelson, his current firm (and the largest employment law firm in the world). In the mid-1990s, Gavin took an in-house position, becoming the Chief Labor and Litigation Counsel for Kimberly-Clark Corporation.

As a representative of various employers around the nation, Gavin has handled over 800 litigation cases ranging from individual and class action discrimination cases to employment contract and other employee disputes. Gavin has successfully defended over 90 union campaigns, negotiated collective bargaining agreements, and tried or arbitrated over 150 matters. More importantly, he has enabled clients to avoid law suits through creative solutions to difficult problems and early intervention into employment law situations.

Described as one of the best employment law trainers in the country, Gavin has created numerous training programs and trained thousands of human resource professionals and operations managers across the country. He also has published articles on employment and labor law issues ranging from drug testing to dealing with problem employees. He is co-author of a published textbook on pre-employment testing. A member of the Tennis Anti-Doping Review Board, Gavin co-authored professional tennis's original anti-doping rules and successfully defended the ATP Tour and International Tennis Federation in international drug hearings.

The above accomplishments aside, Gavin is prouder of having coached some 200 great kids as a travel level and high school hockey coach. He also is proud of his son, Chris, who has become both a better musician and a better hockey player than his dad.

CHAPTER 1

Introduction

Want to quickly create chaos at your company? Just have one of your employees claim that one of your executives sexually harassed her at work. That complaint, whether accurate, exaggerated, or, significantly less likely, completely fabricated, will lead to some or all of the following reactions:

- an investigation, which includes a difficult interview with the accuser, whose feelings usually range from fear to relief, and whose expectations may vary from reasonable to outrageous
- denial, or sometimes an embarrassed admission, by the executive
- interviews of co-workers that may leave your employees talking about the situation for weeks or months to come
- difficult decisions about whether the allegations are true, false, or completely uncertain (does anybody remember Clarence Thomas and Anita Hill and the absolutely believable but totally inconsistent testimony they provided to Congress?)
- whether true or not, difficult decisions regarding what to do with both the employee and the executive
- a less than friendly letter from a plaintiff's lawyer demanding anywhere between $10,000 and $10 million
- a notice from the Equal Employment Opportunity Commission containing a charge of discrimination
- attorneys' fees needed to respond to that charge
- litigation if you can't get this mess to go away in some rational manner

In short, there are few employment problems that create more consternation than a sexual harassment claim. Absent a union campaign or a significant government investigation, however, few employment matters will have greater impact on your workforce.

What Can It Cost You?

Curious what a claim of sexual harassment can cost you? Let's assume federal law, which is more favorable to employers than state law. Here's one possible result, and not an outrageous one, where things didn't go so well for the employer: $100,000 in legal fees, $25,000 in actual damages, $75,000 in pain and suffering, $225,000 in punitive damages, and $120,000 in fees and costs paid to the prevailing plaintiff. Of course, a case can turn out much better than that as well, and much worse.

The same is only slightly less true if a claim of discrimination is brought against your company. As described throughout this book, that claim can cover many forms of discrimination. Here are just some of the myriad possibilities: race, sex, religion, color, national origin, age, disability, sexual orientation, marital status, veteran's status, "use of lawful agricultural problems" (e.g., tobacco), bankruptcy filing, and, in a few places, "personal appearance." And don't forget—discrimination claims can be brought by one person or a whole class of people. The current sex discrimination class action against Wal-Mart contains an estimated 1.6 million women. Whether big or small, the cost of defense in a discrimination case is significant.

So Why Does This Happen?

Well, to give you the lawyer's answer, it depends. Problems like race, sex, and religious discrimination are historically based. While the ugly and blatant discrimination of earlier times in the United States has largely gone away, discrimination problems remain. Amazingly, some very intelligent people still "don't get it." Additionally, those who grew up being taught that one race or sex is inferior to another may not easily lose such beliefs. Regrettably, some parents still teach such misguided values.

Much of the discrimination in today's business world is subconscious. When hiring and promotion decisions are based primarily upon the "fit" between the candidate and the company, the possibility of subconscious discrimination will always exist. In fact, as we will discuss in a later chapter, the issue of "subjective hiring practices" dominates most race and sex class actions.

Sexual harassment, including men behaving badly, affairs gone awry, and a simple failure to pay attention to the concept of political correctness, has been around for many, many decades. Sexual harassment legal claims, however, have existed only since about the mid-1970s. Such claims peaked in the 1990s, but the problem is still a significant one in the early part of the twenty-first century. At some point, a sexual harassment situation *will* happen in your workforce.

For many years, sexual harassment occurred largely due to this nation's history of sexism. In many workforces, men struggled with the introduction of women into "their" workplaces. The problem was at its worst in industrial environments, but no workplace seemed immune. To make matters worse, male managers sometimes had different expectations for female workers than male workers, ranging from "get me a cup of coffee, honey" to "have sex with me or you're fired." Fortunately, most (but not all) of the egregious cases have disappeared. However, as with discrimination, sexual harassment problems remain.

Today many sexual harassment cases involve the interactions of co-workers rather than the misdeeds of managers. There is a societal reason behind this situation too, but this particular phenomenon tends to be less sexist in its nature. For better or for worse, and as we will discuss throughout this book, people are people. Virtually all of us have sexual interests, sexual yearnings, and sexual habits. Those habits are carried to our workplace. Fortunately, so long as those interests and habits are shared by co-workers on a consensual basis, everything's legally ok. If conflicts in values or offensive communications occur among your employees, however, you've suddenly got yourself some serious employment problems.

Cutting to the chase, the law places the burden on an employer to prevent or, if not prevented, be responsive to concerns of discrimination and unlawful harassment. Whether employers deserve to be the principal bearers of all such societal burdens may be debated, especially with respect to co-worker harassment. Beyond question, however, are two certainties: (1) the law imposing duties on employers isn't going to go away, and (2) issues of discrimination and harassment will continue to arise.

The Landscape Is a Complicated One

The theory behind the anti-harassment and the anti-discrimination laws is beyond debate—people truly deserve to work in an environment that is free of both discrimination and unwanted sexual, racial, and any other form of unlawful harassment. When it comes to issues like sex, however, our society inadvertently creates an awkward double standard. Our television screens broadcast sex on a nearly constant basis. Radio hosts warble on about sexuality and tell sexually stimulating stories every morning as we drive to work.

And, for the coup de grace, the Internet gets used on a virtually never-ending basis for searches about sex and nudity. However, the minute we turn off the car radio, thereby cutting off Howard Stern's interview with stripper Misty May in mid-sentence, we're supposed to straighten up and play right. All that talk of sex simply isn't allowed to make an appearance at the office.

Unfortunately, many of your workers are unable to make the transition from Howard Stern and Misty May to "you can't talk about it at work." Sometimes your workers just can't help themselves, that is, they simply *have to* discuss that sex scene on TV last night, they absolutely *must* tell that great sexual joke they heard on the radio, or they just *can't help but* pass along that sexual e-mail they received this morning on their work computer.

Other workers see the workplace as an environment simply swarming with dating opportunities. More innocently, workers meet, find each other interesting, and sometimes fall in love. In fact, depending on whose numbers you believe, approximately 15–35% of Americans are married to someone they met at work. However, if the co-worker dating scene turns bad or if that affair between the boss and her subordinate falls apart, the law expects the employer to step in and solve the problem. What a deal, and what a challenge.

The possible ramifications of all this sexual stuff are endless. No wonder some employers want to replace people with robots. Properly programmed, the robots will think about sex only when they have safely returned home and begun excitedly firing up the Technology Channel. People, by contrast, are often unable to activate the tiny, little "off switch" that comes with their sexual wiring. Consequently, problems at work are going to arise.

What About Robots?

So can you actually hire robots? Not really, but they have replaced some humans in some capacities. But do the robots also have standing to sue? Not yet, but rest assured that some plaintiff's lawyer somewhere is currently working to fix that problem.

So What's an Employer to Do?

First, read the rest of this book. It explains why the law is what it is, and why good employers should abide by the law. More importantly, it provides numerous ways to establish employment systems that lessen the possibilities of both chaos and legal liability.

Most significantly, smart employers not only establish the right policies, they send the right messages. Good employers don't stop with just writing a policy that prohibits discrimination and inappropriate behavior, they properly communicate to employees about their expectations. They also respond effectively when problems arise. In addition, they establish human resource systems through which to limit their risk and they train managers and employees both on how to implement and abide by those systems.

The best employers even go beyond the above preventative devices and the limits of the law. They encourage an environment of dignity and respect. Additionally, they seek out diversity and work to eliminate any existing "good old boy" or "good old girl" networks. They set the expectation of professionalism from the top, and they're straightforward and sincere about that expectation. You, too, can create that type of environment, whether you're a small, large, or medium-sized employer or a start-up company. The last chapter in this book tells you how to do it, but don't skip to that chapter yet. To understand "best practices," one should be aware of "worst cases."

But Can You *Really* Avoid This Mess?

The answer, regrettably, is "probably not," at least in entirety. Fortunately, blatant discrimination can be eliminated. Subconscious discrimination is more of a challenge, but it can be limited through education as well as appropriate hiring and promotion systems. It's almost inevitable, however, that a sexual harassment problem of one type or another is eventually going to arise in your workplace. Think of the possibilities that come up in even the best of companies:

- People date. Dating relationships end. Some of them, in fact, end quite poorly.

- Affairs occur, with frightening frequency, including between bosses and subordinates.
- Sexual jokes and e-mails *will* make the rounds, and someone *will be* offended.
- The firewall *can be* avoided, and some employee *will click in* to "www.sexhappensatwork.com" on his company computer.

In short, stuff happens, and some of it is pretty nasty.

All that said, there is hope for the employer that does the right things. The courts have told us what to do to correctly position ourselves to avoid liability. As a result, you can plan accordingly and, far more often than not, you can prevent liability (or at least the punitive damages that follow).

This book coaches employers about doing the right things. The reality is that while no employer can prevent people from getting stupid, a smart employer can limit its problems (and its risk) by taking proactive steps and responding to problems quickly and effectively.

This book not only discusses the law of discrimination and harassment, it provides specific ways to deal with the problems that are likely to arise. The chapters that follow discuss everything from effective training to appropriate policies to dealing with individuals about a variety of issues. The book provides employers with quick and practical solutions to problems that occur.

Unfortunately, what this book can't do is prevent Bob Jones, a married manager, from falling in lust with Janet Smith, his best salesperson. It can't even prevent Bob from expressing his ever-abiding love for Janet in highly descriptive e-mails and frequent invitations to go for drinks. It also can't keep Shanita Andrews from telling every co-worker she sees about what Brandi did to Gary last night on the hottest TV show of the week. However, it can tell you how to limit these potential problems and what to do about them when they do occur.

In short: read on, do what we say, and hope for the best.

CHAPTER 2

Discrimination and the Law: What It Is and What It Does

The history of humankind is a history of discrimination, often of the blatant variety. Racism and sexism in particular have been around since man first learned how to use fire. Amazingly, even the most brilliant thinkers of their time couldn't get beyond such historical biases. Authors like John Locke and Thomas Jefferson wrote tremendously insightful analyses about the rights of man, many of which still guide our laws today. However, their societal influences caused them to disregard entirely the rights of both women and people of color. For these great historical thinkers, "equal rights for all mankind" was intended to be taken literally in regard to sex and to exclude anyone that wasn't the right color.

In the United States, issues of race discrimination led to civil war, violence, murder, poverty, and a number of other significant problems. In a historical context, however, the United States still dealt with the legality of discrimination far earlier than most countries. Nevertheless, it is a legal and societal embarrassment that the Civil Rights Act of 1964 wasn't enacted until a century after slavery was abolished in this country.

Not Just Men

For early democratic thinkers, "equal rights for all men" was truly meant to be taken literally. Fortunately, the United States Constitution is a malleable document. Society changes and, amazingly, the 230-year-old Constitution has largely kept up (except, of course, for that amendment that protects against the forced housing of British soldiers). That said, if the original writers of the Constitution knew that "equal rights" under the law now applied to women, "colored people," persons of varying sexual persuasions, and others, they would honestly be astounded.

The Historical Difficulty of Creating Anti-Discrimination Legislation

Forward-thinking legal scholars pushed for equal rights and an end to discrimination many years before the law was changed in 1964 to prohibit race, color, sex, national origin, and religious discrimination. Passing a law, however, was no easy task. The states, particularly in the South, were not even remotely interested in a civil rights law that prohibited race discrimination. Consequently, that task fell to the United States Congress. However, Congress itself is obviously composed of representatives and senators from many different states and many different backgrounds. While many in Congress championed making discrimination illegal, others in 1964 believed vehemently that discrimination was an inherent right of the majority.

Passing the Civil Rights Act of 1964 was no easy task. The proposed law went through numerous gyrations before it was enacted. In fact, as discussed in a later chapter, the prohibitions against sex and religious discrimination were added virtually by accident. Amazingly enough, those *opposing* equal rights for African Americans actually amended the law to protect women with the hope that such an amendment would *prevent* the law from passing.

Ultimately the proponents of nondiscrimination were victorious in Congress. Passage of Title VII of the Civil Rights Act of 1964, however, was just the beginning. Many states, especially in the South, refused to enforce the new legislation. State governors claimed the law was an abomination and many state judges ignored its mandate. The tide turned only after years of federal court decisions, marches and demonstrations, deaths and beatings, and the work of many brave souls, both black and white.

Living History

Not old enough to remember the fifties and the sixties? Go read some history. Better yet, listen to the White House tapes (available through a number of sources) during the Kennedy and Johnson era. The discussions among Martin Luther King, Jr., Bobby Kennedy, and Lyndon Johnson are nothing short of fascinating. Listening to them, one quickly realizes how far we've come in the last 43 years.

The Evolution of the Law

The Civil Rights Act of 1964 covers many areas of discrimination, from voting to education. The employment chapter of the law is Title VII, which prohibits discrimination in all areas of employment, based upon race, color, sex, national origin, and religion. The law applies to employers of 15 employees or more (amazingly, in most states in America, a small employer can still discriminate to its heart's content). Title VII also applies to employment agencies and unions. In fact, many early class actions were brought jointly against both the employer and the union that represented its employees.

Not surprisingly, most of the early Title VII cases dealt with race discrimination. It wasn't hard to prove discrimination in most of those cases. The facts were often blatant and ugly. Numerous employers had created "black jobs" and "white jobs." Unions maintained "colored locals" and "white locals."

The evidence of discrimination was sometimes so strong as to be repulsive—imagine a photograph of collective bargaining where the six company men and union men on each side of the negotiating table were white, while the three men sitting at the card table in the corner of the room were black. Those men were the representatives of the "colored local." Their job progression at the time was limited to three lower-level positions at the large paper mill in question. By contrast, the white lines of progression began at the first step above the highest-level "colored job."

Equal or Not So Equal

The paper mill case referenced in the text was real, and, amazingly, it wasn't tried until 16 years after the Civil Rights Act of 1964 was passed. Furthermore, the real obstacle to change in that case was the union, not the employer. Some unions now call themselves the protectors of equal rights. There are unions that can sincerely make such a statement. There are others that can't.

The situation was so bad that Congress took the almost unprecedented step of not permitting jury trials in Title VII cases. The thought of a Southern jury "meting out justice" in a race case was frightening not only in 1964 but for years afterwards. As a result, the enforcement of Title VII was left to federal judges, a few of whom were murdered for their valiant efforts to change the world.

As for women, lawsuits raising concerns of sex discrimination were far less common than race cases until the 1970s. Ultimately, however, the battle for equal rights for women also was waged. Fortunately, the viciousness of that fight was significantly less than the war over race discrimination. However, it still took years to change people's minds about the role of women in the workplace. In fact, the battle still continues at many levels. Historically, the proposed but never achieved Equal Rights Amendment was a meaningful catalyst for change, but Title VII ultimately served as the biggest weapon in the battle for equality.

In the early days, national origin and religion claims were substantially fewer in number than either sex or race claims. National origin cases are far more common in today's world than they were in the beginning days of Title VII. Similarly, religious cases in the early days were more about accommodating an employee's religious needs than they were about blatant discrimination. In the 1960s and 1970s, America was still largely a black-white world and the elephant in the courtroom was race discrimination. The diverse country that is now the U.S. was to come later, and it brought with it cases about more refined issues, such as gender identity discrimination, ethnicity matters, and religious harassment.

Title VII also prohibits color discrimination. Congress apparently included the terms "race" and "color" in an attempt to cover all bases for discrimination against African Americans. Since then, however, the term "color" has been used more broadly. That includes serving as the basis for liability in cases within the African American community where, for example, a darker-skinned African American allegedly discriminated against a lighter-skinned African American. Unfortunately, such situations continue to arise, although the number of cases employing such theories of liability has been fairly small.

Early Cases Established the Path Forward

Few statutes are written in a manner that fully establishes how cases under that particular law are to be handled. While Title VII broadly prohibited discrimination and created a federal agency (the Equal Employment

---

Anti-Discrimination Agencies

The EEOC is mentioned on numerous occasions throughout this book. You should realize, however, that numerous other anti-discrimination agencies exist. Nearly every state has one. Some are more aggressive than others, and some are more capable than others. All mean well, but a few can be difficult in the manner that they deal with even the best of employers. Check with your lawyer to get a better feel for the agency that may be investigating a claim against your organization.

Opportunity Commission) to investigate and evaluate claims, the courts rather than the legislators ended up developing the specific manner in which cases should be evaluated.

The U.S. Supreme Court was quite active in the early days of Title VII. In a seminal case, the court separated discrimination cases into two categories—disparate treatment and disparate impact. Those important categories, which are discussed in detail in the next chapter, remain largely unchanged from the early days. Consequently, there still exist two ways in which employers can violate the law—purposely, but also by accident.

The early Supreme Court decisions also established the way that burdens of proof were to be applied to discrimination cases. As a result, both the plaintiff and the defendant have standards to meet in most Title VII cases, although the ultimate burden of proving discrimination is on the plaintiff. Title VII also addresses who pays for discrimination cases. After some interpretation by the courts, the rule is that employers who lose discrimination cases must pay the plaintiff's attorneys' fees. By contrast, plaintiffs who lose are *not* required to pay the employer's fees unless their claims were found to be frivolous. As a result, plaintiffs rarely have to reimburse an employer for its attorneys' fees although plaintiffs often are assessed a limited amount of litigation costs if they lose. Such costs, however, are not usually collected because doing so typically isn't worth the defendant's effort—something about "getting blood out of a turnip."

Additional Laws and Categories of Discrimination

Only three years after Title VII was passed, Congress realized that it needed to add to the list of prohibited categories of discrimination. The Age Discrimination in Employment Act was passed in 1967 to deal with the increasing problem of age bias. Age discrimination, however, wasn't as easily categorized as race and sex. Initially, Congress decided that those in the 40–65 age range should be protected. Later the upper level of that bracket was adjusted to age 70. Currently the federal law applies to those who are 40 and above, without a cap. However, certain high-level executives and decision-makers can still be forced into retirement at age 65.

Congress also has passed two statutes to deal with the problem of discrimination against disabled persons. The first of those laws, the Rehabilitation Act of 1974, prohibited discrimination by federal contractors against "handicapped persons." The law was not particularly effective due to a variety of legal limitations. The Americans with Disabilities Act (ADA), however, passed in the early 1990s, has done an imperfect but better job of dealing with disability discrimination. Among other things, the ADA changed the applicable terminology from "handicapped" to "disabled." Appropriate political correctness caused that change—the word "handicapped" derives from the historical English term for beggar.

Too Limiting?

The Rehabilitation Act is still law but is rarely used. Most plaintiffs' lawyers find it very limiting. The current debate in the disabled community is whether the ADA is too limiting as well. Great disagreement exists over that issue. Some states, most notably California and Washington, have greatly expanded the definition of a disabled person, perhaps to the point of chaos. In California, one can argue that a broken toe makes someone a disabled person for at least some period of time.

Many state and local discrimination laws have been passed as well, covering numerous bases of discrimination, including marital status, sexual orientation, and even "appearance discrimination." The result of this patchwork quilt is that the law in general now varies greatly from state to state and city to city. That can complicate the efforts of multi-state employers. What is unlawful in one state may be permitted in other states *if* there is no federal law requiring nationwide compliance.

Here are just some of the anti-discrimination laws that now exist in various states and cities:

- age discrimination without reference to age limits (you can violate the law for not promoting someone because he or she is "too young," although "too inexperienced" is a valid defense in most cases)

- marital status and parental status
- sexual orientation
- lifestyle status
- use of lawful agricultural products, including tobacco
- genetic make-up
- personal appearance
- transgender and/or transsexual status
- filing of bankruptcy

In addition, all or nearly all of the above laws prohibit retaliation against someone who has raised a claim under those laws. But more about the difficult issues of retaliation in Chapter 27 of this book.

So, you know that you don't want to discriminate for both legal and ethical reasons. However, you're a little worried about understanding what constitutes discrimination and what doesn't, especially given the "personal appearance" ordinance that San Francisco and a few other cities have passed (aren't beauty and ugliness both dependent upon the eye of the beholder?). Well, to know how to avoid liability, one must know how the law actually operates. And that, of course, is the topic of the next chapter.

CHAPTER 3

Legal Theories of Discrimination and Their Effect on You

Common sense suggests that discrimination problems should be easy to avoid. Treat people the same despite their differences and everything should be fine. However, common sense and law aren't always on the same page. Sometimes they're not even in the same universe.

According to the law, discrimination is usually intentional. However, it can also be illegal to discriminate even if no discrimination was intended. That is the difference between disparate treatment discrimination (which requires intent, although "intent" can be "subconscious" as well as "conscious") and disparate impact discrimination (which doesn't require any type of intent at all). To protect your business, you need to understand both theories of legal liability.

Providing a Legal Definition of Discrimination

After Title VII was passed, the courts were quick to deal with the most pressing issues of obvious discrimination. Many of the early cases focused on "direct discrimination," where racist or sexist statements were made or blatant discriminatory actions were taken. Where proof of direct discrimination exists, the case is pretty simple to analyze and the employer is typically in deep trouble.

As time moved on, fewer and fewer cases involved direct evidence of discrimination. Still, a meaningful number of employers were continuing to discriminate, but in less obvious ways. To deal with cases in which no direct evidence of discrimination existed, the courts developed "indirect methods" for evaluating discrimination claims. The "indirect method" varies depending upon whether the situation involves disparate treatment or disparate impact.

To provide some definition to this legal morass, disparate treatment cases require direct or indirect proof of intentional discrimination. By comparison, disparate impact cases don't involve intended discrimination at all. Under a disparate treatment analysis, one or more individuals are treated differently from other individuals based on a protected category, such as sex, disability, or age. In disparate impact cases, a "tool, rule or policy" is used by the employer and, while neutral on its face, that "tool, rule or policy" negatively impacts one group more than another.

Disparate treatment is easy enough to understand. A woman is held to higher performance standards than a man. A 59-year-old manager is fired because of a perception that older people are less able to be effective than younger people. While disparate treatment cases can be decided based on nuances, the concept of unequal treatment is pretty straightforward.

Disparate impact discrimination is harder to comprehend. To understand disparate impact, consider the following example: Studies suggest that taller people are statistically more likely to be successful salespersons than shorter people (honest, studies really do suggest that). Knowing of these studies, the CEO of ABC Shoes decides to hire only people who are at least six feet tall. The CEO does that not because she wants to discriminate against anyone (except, perhaps, short people who, by the way, aren't protected by federal law except perhaps in extreme cases involving disabilities), but because she wants to increase sales. However, the impact of the CEO's hiring rule is that at least three protected groups are statistically affected in a negative manner: females, Asians, and Hispanics. Consequently, the hiring rule is likely to be found to violate Title VII even though it wasn't created with the intent to discriminate based on a protected characteristic.

The Subjectivity of Height

Do consumers really prefer to buy from tall people? Yes, but only to a degree. Height is less meaningful for a female salesperson and, for men, the positive impact wears away as the person gets "too tall," that is, about 6'5" or above. Attractive people also outsell unattractive people, and thin salespersons outperform overweight salespersons. Given these phenomena, do you really think we're past the issue of discrimination in our society?

Disparate Treatment Cases in Real Life

Most cases involve disparate treatment rather than disparate impact. To prove disparate treatment, a claimant must show either direct or indirect evidence of discrimination. Direct discrimination cases have already been discussed. As for the more common, indirect discrimination case, the following analysis of proof occurs:

1. The claimant must establish something called a prima facie case. How that occurs varies depending upon whether the case is about hiring, firing, pro-

motion, or some other action. In a hiring case involving age, for example, the claimant must show that (a) he is protected by the law (i.e., he is over 40), (b) he was qualified for the position in question, (c) the employer did not hire him, and (d) the employer continued to consider other candidates or hired a candidate who was meaningfully younger than the claimant.

2. If the claimant establishes a prima facie case of discrimination, the employer must then articulate a legitimate, nondiscriminatory business reason to justify its failure to hire the claimant.

3. Even if the employer can articulate a legitimate, nondiscriminatory business reason for its decision, the claimant can still prevail if he can show that the employer's reason is pretextual. "Pretext" essentially means that the employer's reason, when carefully analyzed, is not worthy of belief.

4. Throughout this process, the claimant retains the ultimate burden of establishing discrimination based upon a *protected* classification. Proof of discrimination based upon some non-protected consideration (such as being a Pittsburgh Steelers fan) doesn't count.

Most disparate treatment cases rise or fall based upon the third step above. Many claimants can establish a prima facie case and employers can almost always articulate a legitimate, nondiscriminatory business reason for their actions. As a result, the court battle typically focuses on the question of pretext.

It's Subtle Now

The reason that pretext is so meaningful is that there now exists relatively little blatant discrimination in the United States. Pretext issues are the way to dig deeper and undercover less obvious discrimination.

The Three Keys to Avoiding a Pretext Problem

In regard to discrimination issues, the best practical advice that this book can offer any employer is *evaluate potential employment decisions by considering whether proof of pretext exists*. Most of the time that can be done through consideration of the three following principles.

Principle 1: Treat Similarly Situated People in a Consistent Fashion

The easiest way for a claimant to establish pretext is to show lack of consistency. Assume that a Latino worker is fired for attendance. The employer can certainly articulate a legitimate basis for the discharge, that is, the claimant missed too many days of work. However, if the claimant can show that there are three white employees in his department who missed more work than the claimant but were not fired, pretext is established. In short, consistency is crucial.

In most cases, lack of consistency is the most common way for a claimant to establish pretext. However, an employer need not be consistent to the degree of absurdity. Recognizing that total consistency may make no business or common sense, the courts require only that an employer treat "similarly situated" persons in a consistent manner. If a 30-year employee makes a performance error and a 30-day employee makes the same mistake, the 30-day employee can be fired while the 30-year employee is given a written warning. If both employees threaten to assault a co-worker, however, their length of service may not be so significant (although it wouldn't be irrelevant either).

In recent years, the courts have largely permitted employers to define who is and who isn't similarly situated. However, that analysis must be made fairly and straightforwardly. The employer must be prepared to rationally and credibly explain why one person was considered to be in a different set of circumstances than another. If it can do that, most judges will defer to the employer's judgment.

Principle 2: Avoid Stupid Statements

Plaintiffs' lawyers thrive on human stupidity. In the world of discrimination, human stupidity includes dumb statements made by managers, whether such statements are truly discriminatory or not.

Initially, a statement that "this isn't a job for women" isn't just stupid, it constitutes direct evidence of discrimination. As discussed earlier, such cases are almost over before they start, as mounting a reasonable defense is virtually impossible. However, other stupid statements do not necessarily constitute evidence of direct discrimination, although they may be evidence of pretext.

The line between direct evidence and pretextual stupidity is a fine one. A manager can call an employee "an old fart" but could still decide that such an employee is the best candidate for a promotion. Nevertheless, use of terms like "old fart," "old man," "babycakes," "hot mama," "Afroman," "midget," "brownie," "spic," bitch," "wetback," and "retard" may well provide the basis for a finding of pretext. But they also may not.

Inappropriate Nicknames

Americans are regrettably good at teasing by inappropriate nicknames. All the terms above are from actual cases. Where some of them came from is quite unclear—an "old fart" but not a "new fart?" An "Afroman" is evidence of discrimination while an "African-American man" obviously is not? Racial terms in particular can be complex for someone not in a particular racial category. Sensitivity is smart, even if you are honestly uncertain why a "colored person" is a horrible insult but a "person of color" is a welcome characterization. The differences are real and they are meaningful, so respect them.

The courts have struggled with stupid statements that aren't clearly discriminatory. If the statement didn't relate to a negative decision, it effectively doesn't count. The same is true of a stupid statement made by someone who was not involved in the hiring, firing, or promotion situation. Further, even a stupid statement made by a decision maker could be considered "only a stray remark," if the decision otherwise seems legitimate. Nevertheless, employers should not only train managers to avoid moments of stupidity, they should ask about the presence of stupid statements before taking actions such as a discharge.

Principle 3: Evaluate the Believability of Your Reasons for Acting

The third issue of pretext is arguably becoming the most tested of the three principles. It can be expressed in one question—is the alleged legitimate, nondiscriminatory business reason believable under the circumstances?

A couple of examples make the point. First, think about Fred, an older employee who has been with the company for 20 years. Although never a great worker, Fred has always been a nice guy. Consequently, his managers have consistently rated him as "meets" or "exceeds" expectations even though his performance has never been anything but just above marginal. Twenty years later, however, Fred's marginal ways catch up with him and he is fired for lack of performance. Unfortunately for the company, Fred has aged over the last 20 years and he is 55 when he is fired. He sues, claiming age discrimination.

In its defense, the company asserts "lack of performance" as its legitimate business reason for terminating Fred's employment. However, Fred's lawyer claims that the company's reason isn't believable. As proof, he offers as exhibits Fred's last five performance appraisals, all of which are labeled "meets expectations" or "exceeds expectations." In addition, Fred received meaningful "merit increases" during the last few years. As a result, the company's motion for summary judgment is denied and the jury awards Fred $400,000 in damages.

Be Careful with Appraisals

So why was Fred given good appraisals when he was a mediocre worker? Because he was a nice guy. In addition, his manager didn't like to give bad news. Train your managers to avoid this crucial weakness—and read Chapter 5 very carefully.

The second example raises a different problem of believability. Francine is turned down for a promotion that is given to Jim, her less experienced coworker. Frustrated with the situation, Francine brings a claim of sex discrimination. Crucially, when the company explained to Francine why she wasn't chosen for promotion, they told her that it was because of her lack of education and her insufficient computer skills. In its response to Francine's charge of discrimination, however, the company asserts that it based its decision on Francine's lack of computer skills and her attendance record. Further, in the deposition of Francine's manager, he states that he based the decision not on computer skills or educational background, but on Francine's lack of leadership ability.

The problem with the company's defense to Francine's claim is that its reasons for not promoting Francine keep changing. For better or for worse, the courts have concluded that inconsistent justifications create a believability problem. Thus the judge denies the company's motion for summary judgment and the jury awards Francine $275,000. The company then fires Francine's former manager for not having his act together, but that action comes too late to avoid having to pay Francine for the company's errors.

The good news is that a smart employer can evaluate the issue of believability in advance. The most common risk lies with the lack of cohesiveness between the company's performance records and its discharge decision. As explained in detail in Chapter 28, no employee should ever be surprised to be fired. Similarly, performance communications should be tactful but honest. In short, if its communications are credible and consistent, an employer should be able to avoid believability problems. Thus it also should be able to avoid losing disparate treatment cases.

Understanding Disparate Impact Claims

The burdens of proof related to disparate impact claims are different from those in disparate treatment cases. That is true for two primary reasons: (1) disparate impact is usually unintentional rather than purposeful discrimination and (2) disparate impact issues affect a class of people rather than one individual. In fact, disparate impact cases often are brought as class actions, which are words that no employer is ever anxious to hear.

The Supreme Court has established the burdens in a disparate impact claim as follows:

1. The plaintiff must show that the employer uses a rule, tool, policy, or practice that statistically impacts a protected group in an adverse manner.
2. The employer can argue that the adverse impact is not statistically meaningful or it can show that the rule, tool, policy, or practice is required by business necessity.
3. If the employer establishes business necessity, the plaintiff can still prevail if he or she shows that a less discriminatory alternative exists that would meet the employer's business needs.

As one can imagine, proving "business necessity" is difficult. Consequently, many disparate impact cases focus on whether the statistical

disparity is sufficiently meaningful and whether such disparity was actually caused by the tool, rule, policy, or practice.

Bad Defense

"Business necessity" is a difficult burden because no one knows what it means. Is a tool or policy OK if the absence of that tool or policy will cause the company to go under? Good luck proving that one. In reality, employers have not won many cases relying on the business necessity defense.

A Real Life Analysis of Disparate Impact Cases

Class actions often arise from issues of disparate impact. The inherent nature of these cases is that they involve a protected group rather than a protected person. As a result, class actions under Title VII often involve thousands of employees and/or applicants for employment. A sex discrimination class action brought against Wal-Mart allegedly covers 1.6 million women. And size matters—class action employment cases often settle for tens of millions of dollars or more.

What's a Tool, Rule, Policy, or Practice?

It's not always easy to define a tool, rule, policy, or practice. For example, the height requirement discussed earlier is a rule or policy that is applied to the selection process. However, even a hiring preference based upon employee referrals in a mostly white company could be an unlawful practice since it

Choose the Right Test

Most modern-day pre-employment tests are not unlawful. They usually do not create meaningful adverse impact and they are typically far more job-related than the tests of the past. In fact, such tests, used properly, can limit discrimination by adding a selection tool that is more objective than manager discretion. However, avoid old-fashioned tests like the MMPI and generic psychology tests like Myers-Briggs.

tends to screen out minority candidates. Use of a pre-employment test that creates meaningful adverse impact also is a tool that may lead to a disparate impact case.

The "policy or practice" that is at the center of most disparate impact class actions is the alleged subjectivity of an employer's hiring, promotion, or pay system. If such unfettered discretion leads to a statistical imbalance based on race or sex, a disparate impact problem arises. In fact, this type of case has been brought against some of America's biggest companies, including Wal-Mart, Cintas, Coca-Cola, and Home Depot.

Are You a Statistical Disaster Waiting to Happen?

Disparate impact cases focus heavily on statistics. If employers are statistically balanced, they are a less tempting target for a disparate impact class action. Creating a system where individual decisions are based upon keeping a racial or sexual balance, however, are illegal on a disparate treatment basis. So, caught between a rock and a hard place, what's an employer to do?

Federal contractors are required to create affirmative action programs that include statistical analyses. The purpose of such statistical exercises is to determine if the employer's workforce is representative of the qualified and available labor force. If the answer is "no," federal contractors are required to take steps to improve their numbers. Some federal contractors also use the affirmative action statistical process to evaluate their risk of a disparate impact claim.

Non-federal contractors are unlikely to be assessing their representational status on a regular or even a semi-regular basis. That may be a mistake. Statistical audits can be both complex and dangerous (they can create good or bad evidence, depending upon the facts). However, they can be used to perform self-assessments that, if focused upon, could lead to better hiring and promotion practices. Through such a methodology, meaningful statistical imbalances may be addressed and avoided. Such proactive analyses are addressed in part in Chapter 28, which discusses diversity programs and other means to be a world class employer.

The Proper Use of Testing

Many of the early disparate impact cases involved the use of pre-employment tests. The granddaddy of all disparate impact cases is *Griggs v. Duke Power*. There the Supreme Court ruled that the use of pre-employment tests was unlawful if the tests were not job-related and they created a meaningful adverse impact.

Lest any employer who reads this be concerned about pre-employment testing, the employer in *Griggs* was not using sophisticated pre-employment tests in a job-related manner. In fact, the company was giving IQ tests to job classifications as low as janitors, thereby excluding African Americans at a larger rate than Caucasians. The Supreme Court's use of a disparate impact analysis in these circumstances was justified, but the *Griggs* decision gave pre-employment tests in general a bad name.

As previously noted, modern day pre-employment tests bear little resemblance to the testing that was the subject of *Griggs*. Effective test publishers now have created job-related tests that often are specific to particular job skills and duties. In addition, adverse impact is less significant of a problem than once was the case, both as to sex and race. In short, rather than shying away from testing, many good employers now welcome that approach as a means of making decisions that are more predictive and job-related than would otherwise be the case.

Men's and Women's Jobs in the Workplace

Another element of some disparate impact class actions is whether an employer seems to have segregated women and men into different jobs. At first glance, sex segregation in the twenty-first century seems highly implausible. However, some businesses experience such situations even in this day and age, albeit often unintentionally.

Walk into a grocery store. Where are the women? If you answered "they're cashiers," think more carefully. Most deli and bakery workers also are women—it's almost like some unseen guide leads a female candidate into the grocery store and says "why you're a woman, surely you must like to bake?"

By contrast, where are the men? Well, doing manly things, of course—stocking, loading groceries, and cutting meat!

The same problem arises in a Home Depot or a Lowe's store. Where are the women? Beyond being cashiers, they're often found in home décor and gardening. And the men? Once again involved in manly endeavors—cutting lumber, selling tools, and working in plumbing.

So are Home Depot, Lowe's and the bulk of the nation's grocers discriminatory employers? Generally, no. Rather, much of the sex segregation that occurs in these and other businesses arises from self-selection. Home Depot, for example, has created systems through which women have opportunities to go into different parts of the business, including "the manly areas." Sometimes, however, women choose gardening and décor instead.

In cases like the above, where sex segregation flows from self-selection, the issue arises as to whether the employer is guilty or whether society is guilty. On its fact, Title VII doesn't require an employer to change society. However, to avoid disparate impact cases, the smart employer needs to understand the risk of not diversifying. At a minimum, employers should evaluate whether they have inadvertently created "women's" and "men's" jobs. If so, they should make efforts to broaden interest in those jobs, if for no other reason than to create a way to defend against a disparate impact case.

Subjectivity vs. Objectivity

The large disparate impact class actions discussed above often focus on the issue of subjective decision making, combined with statistical imbalances. The issue is whether subjectivity led to the statistical problem of placement or pay of either men versus women or black versus white. The courts also somewhat inconsistently say, however, that employers are entitled to apply some subjectivity to their hiring and promotion processes. In fact, criteria such as initiative, leadership, and judgment are unavoidably somewhat subjective in nature.

That aside, employers should try to avoid undue subjectivity. Some do so through the use of job-related pre-employment tests and carefully articulated standards of quality and quantity of work. Others add objectivity through behaviorally based interviews, that is, have you ever had a problem with a boss—

how did you handle it? Behavioral analyses are less subjective since they focus on actual examples of positive and negative behaviors and whether the employee employed a positive rather than a negative approach to a specific situation.

What employers most want to avoid is the completely subjective concept of "fit." While some analysis of corporate cultural symbiosis is ok, "fit" is a problem if it is consciously or subconsciously based on "how much is this job candidate like me?" Thus an interview where the primary topic of discussion is Saturday's USC–Notre Dame football game doesn't say much about a candidate's qualifications, yet such discussions occur all the time in interviews. Should they? Well, some small talk is ok, but at some point the selection process needs to focus on job-related matters.

Train your managers to make job-related decisions using valid criteria. Combine such training with statistical audits and you should significantly reduce the risk of disparate impact cases. For a better idea about training options, take a look at Chapter 25. Otherwise, let's discuss a few more legal nuances, and then we'll consider the mistakes that most employers make that lead to discrimination claims.

CHAPTER 4

Unusual Situations:
BFOQs, Retirement, RIFs

Before we get to the fun stuff, including how not to inadvertently create a million-dollar lawsuit, we need to discuss a few more legal concepts. These don't come up as often as disparate treatment and disparate impact issues. However, they can be important, particularly if you own a Hooters' franchise or you have always wanted to be a Chippendale dancer.

Despite the sex-segregated job problems we covered in Chapter 3, there are a few employment positions where sex and age may make a difference. Those jobs arise from something called a bona fide occupational qualification, or "BFOQ." In addition, some odd nuances arise in regard to retirement issues and reductions in force. Each of these subjects is addressed below.

What on Earth Is a BFOQ?

A BFOQ, or bona fide occupational qualification, is essentially a validation of what otherwise would be unlawful discrimination. The courts have held in limited circumstances that a certain sex or age and, in far more limited circumstances, race and national origin, can be required for particular jobs. Some of the jobs in question are no-brainers—one must be a male to be a Chippendale dancer and one must be black to play the role of Ray Charles in the movie "Ray." The acting profession, in fact, is replete with sex-, race-, and age-based roles. Obviously it would silly to require equal opportunity in a profession that seeks to show real life scenarios.

Other BFOQs are less obvious. Debate has long raged, for example, as to whether guards in prisons must be the same sex as those they guard. Experiments in which female guards were placed in male prisons and male guards in female prisons have not always gone so well. The courts, however, remain split over this particular BFOQ.

Other BFOQs that have stood for many years but still remain the subject of debate relate to age. Categories where age has been considered a BFOQ include airline pilots, firefighters, police officers, and judges. Laws or policies requiring that persons in these jobs must retire at certain ages have been upheld with surprising regularity. The fundamental belief behind each of these situations is that the aging process inherently limits an older person's ability to effectively perform the duties of his or her position in a safe or satisfactory manner. Consequently, commercial pilots, for example, must retire at certain ages, which vary depending upon the type of plane being piloted.

The problem with age-based BFOQs is that they are somewhat based on fact and somewhat based on stereotype. And the problem with stereotypes is that they are somewhat (*and only somewhat*) based on reality. Certainly, it is true that the aging process makes it less likely that a 60-year-old firefighter, compared to a 40-year-old firefighter, can carry an unconscious person down a ladder. The problem with the complete ban created by a BFOQ, however, is that there are 60-year-old firefighters that can perform the over-the-shoulder body carry while there are 40-year-old firefighters that can't. Nevertheless, instead of testing each individual's ability to perform, a universal ban, called a BFOQ, is often created and is sometimes accepted by the courts.

Perhaps BFOQs, if established carefully based on facts, are the easier way to deal with these issues. How often would we have to test firefighters to ensure that age hasn't caught up with them yet? Still, age-based BFOQs are patently unfair to some percentage of the population. However, these BFOQs continue to receive judicial blessing in a limited number of positions.

Don't Confuse a BFOQ with a "Customer Preference"

Both in the past and now, some employers have created a demographic requirement for some jobs. These usually have been based upon sex. In a sense, the sex-based requirement looks like a BFOQ, but it really is a policy driven by real or perceived customer preference.

The early poster child for this strategy was Southwest Airlines. Years ago, Southwest and virtually every other airline employed "stewardesses," not "flight attendants." Further, these stewardesses were almost always women—the apparent perception being that this simply wasn't a job for men. To complicate things further, Southwest created an interesting uniform for its stewardesses—hot pants. If you're too young to recall hot pants, think Daisy Dukes with a little more class (but the same amount of leg). The phenomenon was powerful enough at one time that the late Godfather of Soul, James Brown, had a hit song entitled, simply enough, "Hot Pants."

In any event, someone eventually suggested that Southwest's strategy was entirely sexist. A lawsuit followed, seeking to permit men to become stewardesses, or perhaps stewards, as the case may be. (Frankly, it isn't clear whether the men in the lawsuit wished to wear hot pants, but conceptually, a sex-neutral uniform requirement would be permitted by Title VII). In any event, Southwest decided to defend the case. It did so in part by asserting a "customer preference" defense, that is, that its customers simply would refuse to fly Southwest if they couldn't be attended to by women wearing hot pants.

Not surprisingly, Southwest's customer preference claim didn't fare very well in court. Nor have other defenses based on sexual stereotypes. As a result, we now live in a country where stewardesses have become flight attendants and men as well as women are eligible for such jobs. Further, hot pants have largely gone out of style (although they periodically make comebacks). Customer preference defenses, in the meantime, have largely gone the way of the dinosaur. The latter is fortunate, as a complete "customer preference defense" would enable companies to remain sexually and perhaps racially segregated in some jobs for years.

The Flaws in Customer Preference

If customer preference were a legitimate defense to a discrimination claim, Title VII never would have gotten us to where we are today. Employers in Georgia in 1965 might have said "our customers won't buy clothes from us if these black people have to wait on them." Fortunately, we didn't extend such a defense to those types of employers. These issues get complicated, however, when it comes to items such as women's makeup, which perhaps understandably is straightforwardly marketed to "women with a pale complexion," and "women of color."

The above legal developments aside, America's infatuation with sex continues to create situations where customer preference exists, whether legal or not. Discerning readers already may have asked themselves, "well, where does Hooters fit into all this?" In fact, Hooters is essentially doing the same thing that Southwest Airlines did. Consequently, the Equal Employment Opportunity Commission went after Hooters a number of years ago. In response, Hooters defended itself more through a public relations effort rather than a legal campaign. Hooters dressed up a somewhat portly, heavily mustachioed man in an orange "Hooters girl" outfit and placed him on billboards across America. The billboards asked: "Washington, don't you have better things to do?"

Amazingly, Hooters' PR campaign worked. The case with the EEOC was settled for relatively small dollars, but the concept of the "Hooters girl" remained unchanged. There apparently exists a difference between an airline and a restaurant that specializes in hot wings. The same is true of an airline and strippers (male and female), a variety of interesting jobs in Las Vegas, and many positions that are used by companies to sell a product by selling sex. Whether legal or illegal, good or bad, America as a whole believes that some sex discrimination in selling is ok. Don't, however, call these scenarios BFOQs—they're not. Men can, in fact, competently wait on customers who want beer and wings.

Don't Confuse a BFOQ with a Sex-Based Protective Purpose

Another area where BFOQs get confusing involves "protective legislation" and "protective policies." Protective legislation used to abound in the United States. State legislatures once sought to ensure that "the weaker sex" was treated accordingly. Statutes commonly restricted the number of hours that women could work, how long women could stand up before they had to be given a chair, and how long women could go without taking a break.

State protective statutes have slowly gone the way of the dinosaur. A still few exist but they are rarely used or enforced. In today's world, such laws seem silly. Only a few decades ago, however, they were considered absolutely sensible.

A more difficult issue is posed by a few employer "protective policies." Employers have sometimes restricted women from performing certain "heavy" jobs and also have prevented women from working in certain areas of a facility. Some of these restrictive policies were based on plain sexism and thus were clearly unlawful. Others, however, were more difficult to assess.

One of the cases dealing with protective employer policies actually worked its way to the U.S. Supreme Court. In that case, Johnson Controls took the position that women of childbearing age could not work in an area of the facility that contained lead. Rather than based on pure sexism, Johnson Controls had taken this course of action due to studies that found that lead can create birth defects. Nevertheless, Johnson Controls was sued for sex discrimination.

In a case that poses some very complicated issues, the Supreme Court concluded that, well-intended as the company's policy might be, it was discriminatory. Among other things, birth defects arguably also could arise from men who worked in the area of lead. More significantly, however, the Supreme Court essentially concluded that the choice as to whether to work in the lead area should be that of the female employee rather than the company.

Candidly, the result in Johnson Controls, while correct under Title VII, puts a company in a difficult position. Should a baby be born with birth defects because of lead in the workplace, a negligence and/or a workers' compensation case may arise. In short, the employer is placed in a no-win situation. As a result, employers facing this type of danger in the workplace should educate employees about risks and options in a nonsexist, straightforward, and factual manner. Otherwise, they may have limited defense to whatever type of case is brought against them.

Protective policies aside, the courts have permitted a few policies to be "male and female" in nature. These, however, have been more societal and, somewhat surprisingly, more customer-based in nature. A great example is a 2006 case involving Harrah's Casino. Harrah's, seeking to improve its image, established a new dress code policy. Much of the policy was sex-neutral, but part of it was sex-specific. Among other things, female workers were required to wear makeup while male workers were prohibited from wearing makeup.

A female bartender at Harrah's refused to comply with the Casino's makeup requirement. She claimed that Harrah's sex-specific policy constituted gender stereotyping, which many courts recognize as a violation of Title VII. The case was eventually heard by the entire U.S. 9th Circuit Court of Appeals, which ultimately upheld the dress code policy as legitimate from a business perspective.

Confused by all these sex-specific, customer-concerning, sometimes sexual stereotyping issues? To some degree, so are the courts. At its core, the problem is: at what point must an employer change society's expectations of men and women? The answer, unfortunately, is anything but clear.

The best strategy for employers is to avoid sex-based rules and policies wherever possible. For employers that deal with the public, however, especially in regard to retail, restaurant, gaming, and hotel environments, some sex-based policies may be viable. Certainly such employers are permitted to "put on their best face" for the public. Whether that includes adding makeup may still be a bit uncertain.

The ADEA and Retirement Exceptions

A much simpler exception to the general rule of nondiscrimination arises under the Age Discrimination in Employment Act. While that law broadly prohibits age discrimination beginning at age 40, forced retirements are still permitted in some positions.

When the ADEA was passed, some in Congress raised concerns about business strategy and the ability of a business to plan for and implement leadership changes. Worried that an age 40–70 (or, now, forever) cut-off point could create succession planning and leadership change problems, Congress elected to permit companies to require certain executives to retire at age 65. These forced retirements were (and are) limited to high-level executive managers and policymakers.

Interestingly, the high-level executive manager and policymaker rule has not been significantly challenged nor has it led to much litigation. In fact, most companies do not seek to mandate these retirements and some may be blissfully unaware of this exception to the age discrimination law.

For a company wishing to force the retirement of certain executives, consideration must be given to who is and who isn't a high-level executive manager or policymaker. In general, those terms have not been well-defined. However, this exception to the law clearly was meant to be limited in nature. Further, most companies don't fire high-level executives because they get old. Rather, these executives may be given a healthy severance package and they often go away happily.

Ageism Today

The world of age discrimination is slowly undergoing an interesting transformation. Discrimination still occurs. At the same time, however, some employers are now trying to convince some Boomers to delay retirement due to a shortage of persons in some skill areas.

The Law Applicable to Reduction-in-Forces and Separation Agreements

One final set of nuances revolves around the world of reductions-in-force and individual or group circumstances in which employees are offered separation agreements. For those not familiar with the latter issue, some employers offer workers severance pay, but only if the worker signs an agreement waiving any legal claim he or she has against the company. Such agreements can arise in the discharge of an individual worker or in a group reduction-in-force. Done correctly, such agreements are enforceable.

First with respect to reductions-in-force, the courts have generally concluded that they should not be attempting to run the employer's business. The courts therefore, at least as a matter of discrimination law, will not prohibit an employer from implementing a workforce reduction. In addition, absent proof of discrimination, courts will not tell the employer how or on what basis to implement the cutback in headcount. As many courts have stated, their role is not to serve as some "super-powered human resources function" that seeks to tell the employer how to run its business. Rather, they will simply judge whether discrimination has occurred.

In reductions-in-force, the most common discrimination concern is age. Whether employers are truly attempting to get younger as a result of such reorganizations is uncertain, but often workforce reductions seem to be weighted toward older employees. Aware of that fact, many employers now do demographic assessments as part of their reorganization process, primarily to ensure that they are not discriminating. Nevertheless, some managers seem more comfortable with letting older workers go in workforce reductions, sometimes because they are seen as outdated and sometimes because they may already be eligible for retirement. Thus the impact of the job loss will affect them less. Either way, discrimination arises.

While the courts are willing to defer to employer business needs related to reductions-in-force, employers should train their managers to avoid age and other unlawful decisions in connection with reductions-in-force. Further, employers should perform demographic assessments, essentially by comparing the pre-reorganization workforce with that which would exist after the cutback to see if age and other forms of discrimination have occurred. In large reductions-in-force, that may entail some sophisticated statistical analysis. In smaller reorganizations, the employer should simply evaluate the pool of persons it has considered letting go versus the pool that is being let go to determine if a fair comparison exists. If not, the employer may be setting itself up for a difficult case of alleged discrimination.

Employers considering reductions-in-force also should be aware of three laws that may impact how such reorganizations are done: (1) the Worker Adjustment and Retraining Notification Act (WARN), (2) the Older Workers Benefit Protection Act (OWBPA), and (3) various related state laws. Each of these legal issues is discussed below.

The Worker Adjustment and Retraining Notification Act

WARN has been loosely referred to as the "plant closing law." That is a misnomer. The statute requires the employer to provide 60 days' notice before discharging employees in three situations: (a) where a single site of employment is closing, affecting at least 50 workers, (b) where a layoff or reduction-in-force is occurring at a single site of employment, affecting at least 50 workers and 1/3 of the workers at the site (in other words, 50 workers must be let go and the number who are let go must be at least 1/3 of the total number of workers at the site), and (c) where a mass layoff or reduction-in-force occurs at a single site (i.e., where at least 500 persons are let go even if the number of affected workers does not make up 1/3 of the workforce at the site).

The WARN law is complicated. It is far too complex to be discussed in detail in a book that is focused on discrimination and harassment matters. For now, focus on the above applications of the law and be aware that there are limited exceptions to the WARN requirements. In addition, be aware that the law requires certain notices be given to affected employees and others before the 60-day period commences. Finally, and most significantly, be alert to the fact that if you are going to undertake a reduction-in-force that fits within WARN, you should first and foremost seek legal advice.

The Older Workers Benefit Protection Act

Congress was aware when it passed OWBPA that some employers were weighting reductions-in-force toward older workers and were demanding that employees sign cheap and sometimes unconscionable separation agreements. To combat such abuses, it passed the OWBPA and established standards under which employees could be asked to waive their age discrimination rights. Oddly, Congress limited the law to age discrimination. Consequently, employers can act differently (and less favorably) toward younger workers than those over 40 in setting up separation agreements.

For reductions-in-force involving a "group" of workers (a group, by the way, is "more than one" person), employers comply with the OWBPA only if they do each of the following:

a. provide monetary or other consideration in return for a valid release of claims
b. include in the release language a statement that the release includes a waiver of claims under the Age Discrimination in Employment Act
c. inform the individual that he or she has the right to have a lawyer review the agreement
d. provide 45 days in which the individuals can consider whether to sign the agreement
e. provide 7 days in which the individual can change his or her mind after having signed the agreement (the individual can waive the 45-day period and sign whenever he or she wants, but the 7-day period cannot be waived);
f. explain in general terms what criteria were used for the reduction-in-force
g. attach an exhibit to the agreement, which includes two columns: (a) one setting forth by job title and age the names of those considered but not

chosen for the workforce reduction, and (b) one setting forth by job title and age the names of those chosen for the reduction-in-force.

As one can imagine, the OWBPA is technically detailed and compliance can be something of a pain in the neck. Further, if one of the above requirements is missed or done incorrectly, the release of the age claims is not valid (although the release of all claims other than age still could be enforceable). However, on top of the technical compliance pieces set forth above, *any* release of claims must be generally willful and voluntary.

An employer that provides severance pay as part of a reduction-in-force should use a release form that includes a valid waiver of claims. Think of it as an insurance policy—by providing severance, you should receive assurance that you won't be sued. Additionally, by using a carefully written release agreement, you can (among other things) limit disclosure of the agreement, protect confidential information, obtain a "no future employment relationship" guarantee, and get an agreement that the individual will not disparage the company and its agents. However, *it is very easy to mess up these agreements.* Don't just talk to a lawyer about this exercise, *talk to a lawyer who specializes in employment matters.*

Related State Laws

Not to be outdone by the U.S. Congress, numerous states have passed their own versions of WARN and have enacted statutes that add requirements to separation agreements and releases. As with all situations, check with a lawyer about the requirements of the laws of the states in which employees will be impacted.

States Differ

The complications of state laws affect employers in many ways. State laws vary greatly in regard to everything from payroll practices to minimum wage. No longer can a multi-state employer use a singular policy in many of its practices. However, many employers remain surprisingly oblivious to such facts.

Finally, employers should be aware of the impact of the Older Workers Benefit Protection Act on individual situations where an employee is discharged but offered severance pay if he or she will sign a waiver of claims. Sub-parts (a)–(e) above apply to an individual release as well as to a group release. In an individual situation, however, the time period for considering the agreement is 21 days instead of 45 days. Once again, call a lawyer before setting up a separation agreement.

CHAPTER 5

Common Employer Mistakes, from Hiring to Firing

Before tackling the legal issues related to sexual and other forms of unlawful harassment, let's add a section on practical advice related to the law on discrimination. Despite the best efforts of many employers, mistakes happen. Some of those mistakes are the product of a manager who is truly biased on one basis or another. More often, however, employers lose cases not due to a discriminatory manager but because of a poorly managed decision. Ineptness and insensitivity can come across as discrimination even if no discrimination was intended.

Some potential employer errors have already been addressed, especially in Chapter 3. That is particularly true in regard to claims of disparate treatment and issues related to alleged pretext. Set forth below, however, are a number of additional mistakes as well as suggestions for avoiding such errors.

In reviewing this chapter, please don't think that every possible employer mistake is covered. People can be incredibly creative and managers can be creatively inept—in short, mistakes can occur that the rest of us haven't even thought of yet. If you follow the advice below, however, you should be safe from liability (although let's face it, this is America—you can do everything right in this country and still get sued, and sometimes even lose).

Uncertainty

Afraid of getting sued and losing even if you didn't do anything wrong? In reality, that doesn't happen as much as you think. Employers win more cases than they lose, and many other cases settle for relatively small figures. However, bad stuff can still happen, and an employer can honestly lose a case in which it technically did nothing wrong.

Tips in the Hiring, Promotion, and Pay Process

Create a Process

Most employers have figured out that recruiting shouldn't be a haphazard process. The days are gone when all one did was ask one's current workers if they had any competent friends who needed jobs (a system, by the way, that often led to inadvertent discrimination in, say, an all white workforce). Done correctly, recruiting involves a system. So does promotion and so does pay.

Establishing a recruiting, promotion, and pay system goes well beyond the scope of this book. However, numerous options exist. Aspects of some of those possibilities are discussed below.

Give Managers a Plan

Make managers part of the system, but only if they understand the system. That means giving them a plan and ensuring that they are acting in accordance with the plan and not in reference to their own whims. Many of the problems that arise in discrimination law are the result of managerial biases or incompetencies.

By "a plan," tell managers what to look for, give them tools to enable then to make better decisions, and evaluate them on their ability to meet the requirements of the plan. Companies should know what they need in terms of skills and abilities. They should evaluate pay using a system. Based upon that data, managers should be able to make decisions that are consistent with the company's business rather than some personal preference.

Focus on Objective Criteria

Subjectivity continues to reign in regard to hiring and promotion decisions. The most common factor expressed by most employers is whether a candidate "fits" the employer's culture. Legally, this type of system creates risk, particularly for employers that are big enough to be the subject of a class action.

Some subjectivity is not only inevitable, it is legally permitted. To a meaningful degree, an employer is entitled to subjectively determine if a candidate is likely to enjoy the type of business culture presented by the employer. If "fit" is the primary factor, however, subjectivity combined with a statistical imbalance can create a disaster, as we discussed in Chapter 3. To reduce the role of "fit," a company should consider stated and verifiable needs as well as criteria to assess whether a candidate can fit those needs. The more the analysis focuses on qualifications, skills, and experience, the less subjective a decision will be. That said, if two candidates both meet the employer's objective needs, an analysis of fit may be appropriate, but only if "fit" is defined in nondiscriminatory terms.

Focus on Job-Related Criteria

Part of reducing the impact of subjectivity is to focus on job-relatedness. Some managers spend an entire interview discussing last week's Raiders-Eagles game. Such an interview may show how much the candidate knows about professional football, but such information isn't job-related unless the opening is for a coach or a sports announcer. Interviews should evaluate a candidate's skills relative to the job in question.

Many companies now use a set of interview questions that specifically focus on the skills needed for a job. Such questions relate to how particular job issues are handled, how work-related concerns are identified and analyzed, and how workplace decisions might be made. These "targeted selection questions" are oriented towards job skills, real life work situations, and traits needed for success in the position. "Targeted" and "job-related" questions also help eliminate discriminatory decisions.

Perform Background Checks

The law in virtually every state permits an employer to do background checks of potential candidates. Doing so correctly requires that an employer obtain candidate authorizations under a technical law called the Fair Credit Reporting Act. The same law also requires an employer to give a candidate a chance to explain a problem in the report. However, the Fair Credit Reporting Act does not mandate that an employer actually excuse or not excuse something in a candidate's background report.

Background reports can provide a significant amount of data. In general, employers should focus only on job-related information. A marijuana conviction at age 19 is not likely to make a 35-year-old candidate unfit for a bookkeeping job. However, any employer that hires a driver with a DUI on his or her record is taking a risk of a possible negligence case if the individual later gets in a wreck in a company car after drinking three beers.

Background Check Services

Not sure how to do a background check? Call a company that specializes in the area. The same is true in regard to drug testing, which is discussed below. The costs of such tests are not outrageous. In many instances, it is well worthwhile to pay that cost.

Depending on the Job, Consider Drug Testing

For private sector employers, drug testing is legal unless a specific state law prohibits, restricts, or governs such testing. In general, while one should talk to a lawyer about particular state regulations, candidate testing is permitted, especially for safety sensitive jobs. Among other things, statistics suggest that drug testing reduces workers' compensation problems.

Consider Pre-Employment and Promotional Testing

As discussed in Chapter 3, pre-employment and promotion-related testing once was considered legally risky. Now, however, tests have become more sophisticated and job-related. In fact, capable testing companies now seek to increase the objectivity of an employment decision, not decrease it. Talk to some of the more credible testing companies like PreVisor and Hogan, and analyze your options. For many jobs, the use of testing will lead to better decisions, greater retention of new hires, and comparatively few legal issues.

Be Cautious about Interview Notes

Interview notes tend to be written in a hurried and sloppy manner. Most interviewers are simply trying to get some tidbits of information down on paper so they'll recall some specifics about the candidate once the interview has concluded. Somewhat as a result, interview notes have created legal issues.

Sometimes the notes are nothing short of stupid—"this one's pregnant" is a notable example. Other times they tend to focus on matters that aren't job-related—"good looking guy, seems likeable." In short, poorly written and often misleading interview notes can create serious legal problems. A word to the wise, the less written, the better, unless what's written is job-related. The use of an interview form helps, as does some training given to interviewers before they undertake their tasks.

Push for Diversity

In Chapter 28 of this book, the concept of diversity is discussed as a means of both broadening and bettering one's workforce. Most employers now serve a diverse public of potential buyers and users. In addition, diversity tends to lead to better decision-making. Consequently, seeking diverse candidates is a positive goal. Chapter 28 tells you how best to evaluate and address diversity as a concept.

Pay Equity Is Important

A variety of laws address the issue of pay equity from the perspective of discrimination. In general, an employer should pay equal wages for equal work. Even absent the concept of nondiscrimination, however, pay equity should be your goal. Like it or not, employees discuss their pay and salaries with each other and the National Labor Relations Act generally protects such discussions. Given that perceived favoritism will create a negative workplace, pay should correspond to job-related factors, such as qualifications, performance, and skills.

Discharges
Communicate about Performance

Nobody likes to tell someone that their performance resembles a Hoover vacuum cleaner. In fact, most managers went into management not to communicate with poor performers, but because the money was better and running an operation seemed like a good idea. Some managers can't sleep the night before giving a negative performance review, and most bosses use grade inflation to rate a "D" level performer as a "B-." No wonder people feel misled when they get fired for legitimately bad performance.

What employers fail to understand is that a failure to communicate in an effective and honest fashion can be portrayed as both ineptness and discrimination in court. Words to live by—be direct, tactful, and then a little more direct. Most managers are too tactful and way too indirect for everyone's good, often leaving the impression that the employee is performing satisfactorily when he's not.

Afraid to be direct, or don't know what to say? Script it out and, if you have to, read from the script—it might seem awkward, but at least you'll get the point across. You don't need to be Bobby Knight or Simon Crowell in your manner of criticism, but you shouldn't be Mr. Over-Sensitivity either. Remember—no one should ever be surprised to be fired, but surprised they will be if you don't give them fair criticism of their deficiencies as well as suggestions to overcome those deficiencies.

Remember the Pretext Issues—Consistency, No Stupid Statements, and Believability

As stated in Chapter 3, most discrimination cases come down to the issue of pretext. Before you make a decision, particularly a discharge decision, check the three primary questions of pretext: consistency among similarly situated people, stupid sounding and often discriminatory sounding statements, and believability.

Focus on the "Cause" of the Action

The employer's burden in a discrimination case is to articulate a legitimate, nondiscriminatory business reason for its actions. The more adeptly that one can articulate such reasons, the better the case for the defense. Be specific and don't rely on "slush" terms. Statements like he's a lousy performer or she had a bad attitude don't mean much in court. However, a statement that "he's a lousy performer because he lost the Jones' account and he failed to show up at two meetings" says a lot. The same specificity gives life to the words "bad attitude," if that problem is properly described as "she doesn't come to work on a regular basis, she can't get along with her teammates, and she doesn't get her assignments done on time."

Beyond being specific and staying away from slush words, be thorough. If there are five reasons why you fired an employee, list them all. The more specificity, the better. In addition, specific examples of inferior performance are difficult to counter. At the same time, don't overreach and pick on trivial problems when legitimate issues can be discussed instead.

Consider the Perception You Are Creating

Ever find yourself getting caught in the heat of the moment? Consider the perception you're creating when you're overreacting or mismanaging an issue. Both juries and arbitrators evaluate fairness as much as they do discrimination. While companies sometimes win cases using something called the "equal opportunity jerk" defense, juries don't like jerks (remember—all jurors have worked for at least one jerk at some point in their lives).

Technically, the law regarding discrimination in the United States is that a company doesn't have to be a smart employer or even a fair employer. It only has to be a nondiscriminatory employer. However, if the plaintiff starts telling stories at trial about her jerk-face boss, look out. If you observe the jury carefully, you'll actually see juror #5 elbow juror #6, saying "I had a boss like that once, and this may be my chance to exact a little vicarious revenge."

Be Patient

Occasionally employment lawyers get calls from clients at 3:30 p.m., asking for guidance as to a discharge discussion that is set to occur at 4:00 p.m. The appropriate legal response is to say, "Wow, you gave me 30 minutes for input—what did she do, punch somebody?" Unfortunately, the answer to that question is often, "Well, no, she's just being fired for bad performance." The appropriate follow-up question from the lawyer is "Well, how long has she worked there?" Regrettably, the answer may be something like "22 years."

Bad performance? Twenty-two years? And must be fired by 4:00 p.m. What's going on here? Answer: the manager in charge snapped and decided "that's it, she's gone."

Not surprisingly, a company gets points for doing things right. It loses points for snap decisions, especially emotionally driven decisions. Inexperienced managers often feel they must act quickly and definitively, while a more measured and carefully evaluated decision would have been better. Knee-jerk reactions just don't play well in court. Don't go there.

Don't Be Too Patient

On the other hand, too much patience is just as bad as having no patience at all. Too many employers let too many malcontented employees get away with too many things. Why? Because managers find it's easier to ignore the problem than do something about it. Hoping, however, that someone who is a pain in the posterior will eventually quit isn't much of a strategy, particularly when good employees are leaving because "I hate working with that idiot."

Ever wonder how many good workers have left due to your unwillingness to confront a problem child? In short, being afraid to make a decision isn't a good idea, particularly if the decision is overdue. Granted, firing the jerk could lead to a lawsuit, but perhaps he's going to sue you anyway. Go through the performance process and try to solve the problem—but, if it isn't going to get better, act. That approach sure beats dumping extra work on your best worker just because it's difficult to deal with your worst worker.

Treat Your Employees with Dignity and Respect

No matter what, don't get disrespectful. Even the malcontents deserve dignity and respect, and you'll risk punishment if you don't give that to them. Granted, you've inadvertently hired a few mud wrestlers in your organization. However, mud wrestlers really don't want to jump in the mud unless you'll jump in with them. Don't do it!

Fortunately, most managers know that they have to stay out of the mud. However, some just can't risk the temptation of reaching into the mud, grabbing a good clump of the goo, and letting it rip—usually in the form of an e-mail. Trust me, the recall button doesn't do any good. In a real case, a Human Resources director, delighted that her biggest problem child had just quit, sent an e-mail that started with the following words: "Ding, dong, the witch is dead!" Unfortunately, the witch later sued the employer, claiming that she was forced to quit, then in discovery sought every e-mail ever written about her. So how do you think "ding dong the witch is dead" is going to play in front of the jury?

Dignity and respect—don't forget. Whether they deserve it or whether they don't. In particular, don't use that exit interview to get everything off your chest. It just isn't worth it. In another true story, a manager spent over four hours conducting an exit interview of a worker he was firing, effectively rehashing and arguing over 21 years of working together. Amazingly, the manager called in lunch for himself and the worker in the midst of the exit interview. One can only imagine the conversation: "Bill, we're not done firing you yet, what do you want—ham and swiss or a chef salad?"

Think About "Triggers" and Invitations

Interestingly some employees actually invite you to fire them. What's amazing is how often managers turn down the invitation. It's always an interesting discussion in these situations: "Look at me, look at me—look what I did wrong today!" "Now, now, Jenny, sit back down. We're not going to fire anyone today."

When employees essentially ask to be fired, you should pay some attention to them. However, that isn't to say fire without cause. At the same time, the cause shouldn't be that the manager finally got tired of the employee's antics. Far too many discharges seem caused by the straw that broke the camel's back.

Give a poor performer enough rope and he'll do the inevitable. Knowing that, employers should look at performance and repeated lower-level discipline situations from two perspectives: (1) what did Kim do to get fired? and (2) what did she do today to cause the decision to occur when it did? Think about the triggering event—if it's petty and you're just tired of Kim, don't do it. One well-known company inadvertently created a problem for itself by repeatedly warning an employee about her attendance record. Finally, after some 15 warnings, the employee came in three hours late for work with no valid excuse. Instead of firing her, however, the manager gave her warning number 16, but apparently said to himself, if she does one more thing wrong, she's gone. Three days later, the employee was fired for being five minutes late to work. Great opportunity missed on Monday, bad opportunity taken on Thursday.

Consider Public Policy As Well As Nondiscrimination

Most states now require that a discharge decision be both nondiscriminatory and consistent with the public policy of the state. Firing someone because they refused to get out of jury duty looks and smells bad. Summarily discharging a whistleblower is a serious problem. If the reasons for the discharge don't pass the common sense test, they may not pass the state public policy test either. Be cautious, as the nature of the law is slowly expanding from issues of discrimination to matters of public policy.

Unfortunately, a state's public policies aren't usually listed anywhere. However, think back to the perception of the action concern addressed above. If you think a decision could be perceived as unfair, it will be so perceived.

Have a System to Eliminate Knee-Jerk Reactions

One crucial aspect of managerial decisions and discrimination avoidance is to eliminate the ability of one person alone to fire someone. If two managers must sign off, and particularly if a human resources person gets involved, the ability to claim discrimination is dramatically reduced. It's relatively easy to claim that one manager is ageist or racist, but it's much harder to argue that everyone in the management chain is discriminatory. Use a system, including an investigation piece to the system, before making decisions. The extra time and energy that you spend will be well worthwhile.

Other Suggestions
Call for Assistance

The law is complex and sometimes counterintuitive. Even employment lawyers don't know all the nuisances in the thousands of statutes that exist in the United States. Don't assume that you know more than they do.

Litigation costs tens and sometimes hundreds of thousands of dollars. Calling a capable employment lawyer is expensive too—rates of the better employment lawyers are in the $300–$600 range per hour, depending upon where you are in the country. However, litigation can often be avoided through a 30-minute telephone call, the cost of which is negligible compared to the lawsuit that was avoided. Pick up the phone and make the call.

Train, Train, and Train Some More

Managers usually have technical skills and, hopefully, leadership abilities. That doesn't mean they know how to respond to a worker's concern about racial harassment. Train them, in a way that's effective. Don't let a talking head or a videotape read them the law. Use a capable trainer who is adept at interactive training. People learn better by doing, not by listening.

Sexual harassment avoidance training is discussed in detail in Chapter 25, partly because such training helps create a defense and partly because some states now mandate such training. Other areas where training is highly recommended include (1) EEO decision-making, (2) dealing with the Americans with Disabilities Act, the Family Medical Leave Act, and related state laws, (3) understanding how liability arises under the nation's wage and hour laws, (4) analyzing risk in regard to human resource decisions, and (5) dealing with difficult employees.

Review and Simplify Your Policies

As the law has become more complex, policies have gotten longer and longer. Many employers, for example, now have a six- or seven-page anti-harassment policy. The problem with such detail is that it creates both an underdone and an overdone concern. No policy, irrespective of length, can anticipate every emanation of a problematic situation, so even the wordiest policies miss specific issues. At the same time, the long policy may be so confusing and detailed that employees don't really understand how it addresses an important topic.

The best approach is to simplify the longer policies and leave room for some flexibility. Harassment, for example, is really a form of inappropriate behavior. Rather than trying to define every aspect of harassment law, the better approach is to deal with inappropriate behavior, whether or not such behavior legally constitutes sexual harassment. In short, simple is good, but the law is such that the day of the one-paragraph policy is probably gone forever. Nevertheless, seven-page policies are just too long.

Don't Eliminate Common Sense

One plus with simple and flexible policies is that they leave room for common sense. Sometimes, despite the best efforts of a capable and knowledgeable writer, a specific application of a particular policy is just wrong. Common sense, while arguably a growing example of the ultimate oxymoron, has to have a place in dealing with people. Use it, but don't abuse it. Among other things, don't let "the need for total consistency" get in the way of common sense. The legal test is, as previously explained, consistency "among similarly situated persons," not total consistency.

Document Properly

Documentation has become more and more important in terms of dealing with legal issues. However, poor documentation is often worse than no documentation at all.

Let's break documentation down into two broad categories: documentation of facts and documentation of analysis. As for the former, detail helps, but some realistic sense of length should apply too. Think about writing down a "healthy summary of the facts." Then ask whether you have included enough detail of the most significant points. Finally, consider whether you have written the document such that you'll actually recall what happened two years later.

In terms of increasing the likelihood of recall, make sure to include some high points. If someone called someone a name, write the name down. If someone said something stupid or notable, consider quoting it in the document. Those are the types of things that bring back recall years later.

As for evaluation, keep it simple unless you're asked to write a recommendation from among a series of options. In discipline situations, start with a summary of the facts and conclude with a simple statement of what was decided and why: "We fired Mary today because she threatened to run over a coworker in her fork lift." Don't editorialize or equivocate. Saying "I never much liked Mary anyway" doesn't help, nor do comments like "We considered giving her a suspension instead of firing her, but the HR person said firing would be better." All editorial comments and equivocation will get you is a longer and more difficult deposition if litigation arises.

If your evaluative document includes an analysis of legal risk (i.e., could this be age discrimination?), talk with a lawyer. That is a document that you might consider protecting through use of the attorney-client privilege. In general, only analysis can be privileged—facts are still facts. Before discussing risk in writing, however, get legal help—otherwise, what you say can definitely be used against you.

Don't Save Everything Forever

Stuff gets old, but many companies never throw anything anyway. Documents that dealt with a performance problem in 1988 really don't mean much some 20 years later. Performance appraisals from five years ago are usually outdated by now. In fact, the employee you're considering firing today for poor performance may have "met expectations" five years ago, but not since then.

So why do you keep old documents? Because you don't know when to throw them away. In fact, there are laws regarding document retention, but most of them don't require retention beyond three years. Granted, five years may be safer, but anything beyond that doesn't mean much except for certain compliance records.

Consider creating a system. Appraisals get tossed after five years. Warnings last a year or two unless the problem keeps repeating. Many companies are moving toward the paperless office. Perhaps the electronic systems that maintain the "paperwork" for these offices will do a better job of throwing outdated stuff away.

Realize That the Nuances Are at the State Level

Thirty years ago, employment law was all about federal statutes. Today much of the action flows out of the myriad of state laws that now apply to the area. Realize that, and do something to see if the state you're in has a unique way of looking at a situation. Good lawyers can help in that regard—the national employment firms usually maintain state-by-state surveys on the law. Participation in state chambers of commerce or similar organizations also provides insight into state nuances.

Evaluate Comparative Risk

Most decisions assume that more than one answer exists. Don't always take the most conservative legal course—it isn't healthy for your business. Many managers are very good in particular at evaluating the risk of *acting*. What they aren't good at is evaluating the risk of *failing to act*. As stated previously, ask yourself how many good employees will quit because the deficiencies of a difficult person are being ignored. Work with your managers to help them evaluate comparative risk. They'll make better decisions that way.

Consider Appropriate Audits

In some areas of the law, you may be in violation without even knowing it. A great example is wage and hour law, where a group of employees may be classified as exempt when they should be deemed hourly (and thus subject to overtime pay). Other examples relate to EEO decision-making, analysis of OSHA compliance, and legality of one's immigration practices. Auditing those types of issues can uncover a problem before it's too late. If you need help in considering an audit, call a lawyer. In certain circumstances, you might even be able to protect some of aspects of the audit through the attorney-client privilege.

Find a Good Lawyer

This one isn't as easy as it sounds. Sure, they're everywhere, but the good ones are hard to find. Most importantly, don't settle for one that just tells you what you *can't do*. A good employment lawyer offers advice not just on the law, but on the applicability of the law to your business. Good lawyers are proactive rather than reactive, and they should provide a healthy measure of practical business advice that is legally related. And, remember, not every lawyer is a good litigator—ask about both the lawyer's litigation experience and his or her track record before handing out that million dollar case to the lawyer from the big firm with the high hourly rate. On the other hand, do *not* hire a lawyer to handle an employment case just because he is a business litigator. Employment cases are a different kind of horse.

CHAPTER 6

A Wild and Crazy World—How Sexual Harassment Became Unlawful

Most laws exist for a reason. They are intended to cure a real or at least a perceived problem with society. Title VII is certainly a law that needed to be passed to deal with a real societal concern—discrimination in the United States was a serious problem in 1964, the year the law was finally enacted. When Title VII was passed, the statute was intended to quickly end discrimination against various categories of people, including blacks and women. "Quickly," however, didn't happen. Title VII is still in the process of trying to accomplish the task of doing away with discrimination, although meaningful progress has clearly been made.

The positive nature of Title VII aside, one problem that existed in 1964 involving the working relationship between men and women was nowhere to be found on Congress's radar. It was a problem later dubbed "sexual harassment." That problem undoubtedly existed in 1964 but, compared to the larger issue of blatant race and sex discrimination, it was virtually invisible based on the mores of the time. Was there really an issue regarding sexual harassment that needed to be cured? You bet, and it was a big one.

If you were a woman in the 1970s and even the 1980s, the chances are good that you were being sexually harassed. The problem (which many people, unfortunately, didn't actually see as a problem) was rampant. Even though Howard Stern and Jerry Springer were still in their formative years back then, sexual banter was in the air. Sexual jokes abounded, even without the assistance of the Internet. Far worse, some managers' expectations of women who worked for them went well beyond what might have been set forth in a job description. Those expectations, in fact, sometimes included sexual favors, or at least sexual "come-on's." At a minimum, women as a whole were subject to sexual teasing, sexist comments, and inappropriate descriptions of their dress and their anatomies. Other women were subject to much worse—sexual demands, sometimes as a condition of employment.

If you've never seen the film or if you are too young to remember the 1970s, go rent the movie *9 to 5*. In it, you can see Jane Fonda, Dolly Parton, and Lily Tomlin exact revenge on their extremely sexist boss. By making light of the problem, the movie helped open eyes to the fact that *there was a problem*. However, despite the movie, revenge typically was *not* in the cards for the harassed woman. Rather, revenge was usually of a much different and far uglier type—women who did not play along were often retaliated against through insufficient pay raises, transfers, demotions, and even discharges.

The 1970s also were the days when "Human Resources" was more likely to be called "Personnel." Anti-harassment policies did not generally exist, and Human Resource professionals were not particularly attuned to the issues of sexual harassment. Let's look at a likely scenario.

Jill, a plant secretary, appeared in Personnel one day in 1978, and said "I don't know how to tell you this, but I'm being harassed because of my sex." In

all likelihood, the "Personnel man" may have responded by asking "Well, who's been picking on you, dear?" Jill replied by saying, "Joe Smith keeps teasing me by saying sexual things about my body." Unfortunately, the "Personnel man's" response may well have been "Joe? Joe Smith? Jill, you shouldn't complain about that—good grief, this isn't about you. Joe teases *everybody*. That's just Joe."

In short, when even the Personnel man doesn't get it, it was time for a law. However, needing a law and passing a law are very different things. The reality is that Congress has never passed a law intended to deal with the problem of sexual harassment. Instead, the courts have been forced to use a law that already was in place, even though that law really had little or nothing to do with issues of harassment. The law in question was Title VII, the federal anti-discrimination law passed in 1964.

The Awkward Nature of the Legislative Cure

The law that the courts have used to address the issue of sexual harassment is a tremendously important law. Title VII of the Civil Rights Act of 1964, as described in Chapter 2, is one of the most important laws passed in this country. Unfortunately, however, a desire to eliminate sexual harassment had nothing whatsoever to do with the development, creation, or passage of that law. The same can be said of most of the many state laws that also have been used to regulate issues of sexual harassment.

In short, in regard to the "law of sexual harassment," we're dealing with an imperfect world. There is, in fact, no federal legislation setting forth the definition of unlawful harassment and there are no legislative standards describing how employers should respond to such problems. In effect, the courts are making this anti-harassment stuff up as they go. A little history provides some needed perspective on this awkward legal situation.

The World of Imperfect Legislation

To begin with, the legislative process is ripe for dysfunctionality no matter what the subject. Political agendas, personal biases, and constant compromise create a perfect formula for imperfect legislation. The "law" of sexual harass-ment provides a very good example of this political reality.

To begin with, as noted above, virtually all laws are passed for the purpose of correcting a real or perceived wrong. However, due to the compromise inher-ent in the legislative process, the statutes that are enacted may or may not address that wrong in an effective or practical manner. Further, the vagueness of any given law can ultimately lead to an interpretation of the law that was entirely unforeseen and unimagined by the legislators that actually passed the law.

Good Law and Bad Politics

The legislative process really is a mess. To write a good law, politics are the first thing that have to be overcome. Beyond that, some of the drafting is done with the "assistance" of special interest groups or lobbyists. Then the amendment process takes place, and amend-ments can sometimes gut a good chunk of the underlying law. In short, it's sometimes amazing that anything effective gets done in Congress.

Finally, laws are largely drawn up in light of the environment of the era in which they were written. However, in regard to both people and business issues, things change quite quickly. Consequently, a law passed two decades ago may well already have become outdated, but such laws are rarely erased from the books. In fact, they are not often even amended to make them more adaptable to the changes that have occurred around them. Consequently, the courts are left to interpret the applicability of older laws to new situations, many of which were completely beyond the vision of the legislators who wrote the law 20 years earlier.

The "After-Thought" of Sex Discrimination

Perhaps the greatest legal embarrassment of the United States is that it didn't pass a specific law to broadly prohibit race discrimination for nearly 100 years after the end of the Civil War. That isn't to say that some legislators didn't try. In the early 1950s, a number of congressmen began working in earnest to deal with the problem of racism, but the laws that they introduced did not make it through Congress.

The crucial law that was finally passed by Congress to cure the problem of race discrimination was the Civil Rights Act of 1964. That statute, as we by now know, included a section entitled "Title VII." It is that part of the law that prohibits discrimination in the workplace. What the average person doesn't know, however, is that Title VII almost didn't happen, at least not in 1964. Numerous legislators fought to retain the existing two-tiered work system that discriminated blatantly on racial characteristics.

What even fewer people know is how discrimination against sex in the workplace became part of the Civil Rights Act of 1964. The huge fight at the time was over issues of race discrimination, even though women also were similar victims of discrimination. In any event, because the Civil Rights Act of 1964 as a whole focused on race, the employment aspects of the law did the same. In fact, for much of the time that Title VII of the Civil Rights Act of 1964 was being considered in Congress, it prohibited discrimination only on the basis of race, color, and national origin.

Amazingly, when it appeared likely that Title VII would ultimately pass, a number of white congressmen concocted a desperate plan to stop the legislation. That plan included numerous amendments and attempted changes to the language of the proposed statute. It eventually became clear, however, that such game playing was not going to be sufficient to stop passage of Title VII. Facing this reality late in the legislative game, a number of prosegregationist congressmen took a gamble. They offered an amendment to Title VII that would expand the prohibitions of discrimination to include sex and religion.

The theory behind the segregationists' amendment was that if the law protected women and religious rights, fewer congressmen would vote for it and Title VII might not pass at all. So strongly did these legislators feel about continuing the world of racial segregation that they were willing to offer a *broader* discrimination law, because they thought that breadth might prevent passage of *any* discrimination law. However, the efforts of the segregationists failed—Title VII passed despite their efforts, and it now prohibited discrimination in employment on the expanded bases of race, color, sex, national origin, and religion. One can only imagine the consternation of those who had been trying to hijack the legislation—"Oh my God, the blacks are covered and now the women too—what have we done?"

In any event, once sexual discrimination became unlawful, challenges by women who were not being promoted or hired due to their sex became fairly common and legally straightforward, at least as a matter of how the law came to operate. What was far less easy to challenge, and in fact to legally analyze, was the impact of Title VII on the world of sexual harassment. That, in fact, was a world that was far from the minds of the congressmen that passed this important anti-discrimination law. The reality is that in all likelihood, the issue of sexual harassment was never seriously considered by anyone in Congress at the time that Title VII was passed.

So What Happened Next?

Realistically speaking, the issue of sexual harassment did not make much of an impact, or even an appearance, for several years. Lawyers and plaintiffs were focused on bigger concerns—hiring, promotions, pay, and discharge decisions. That Bill Johnson was commenting publicly on the size of Mary's breasts or making a nuisance of himself with his juvenile humor about women wasn't yet considered a meaningful reason for legal concern.

For the most part, sexual harassment was not truly recognized as a serious legal concern until the mid-1970s. It then took some 25 years for the law to develop into something that was relatively certain. Even now, in 2007, there remain numerous uncertainties in the law. In reality, judges are still trying to figure it out, in part because Title VII was never created with sexual harassment issues in mind. The fact is that we're fixing large potholes with silly putty because Congress never even recognized that the potholes existed when the law was passed.

CHAPTER 7

Round Pegs and Square Holes: Using Discrimination Law to Prohibit Harassment

The Civil Rights Act of 1964 in general, and Title VII in particular, is truly an exceptionally important law, and one that has paid immense dividends. While discrimination still exists at various levels of consciousness, the face of America's workforce has changed drastically since 1964. Gone are the concepts of "colored jobs" and "white jobs." Fading away are the ideas of "male jobs" and "female jobs." (Fading away, mind you, but not gone— go into a hardware store or a grocery store and ask yourself where the men and women are—you'll still see meaningful vestiges of the past, such as bakeries dominated by women, and meat and plumbing departments staffed solely by men).

Title VII and Its Applicability to Sexual Harassment

Title VII's effect on sexual harassment is another matter altogether. Given the nature and timing of the law, one can hardly say that Congress was focused on the problem of sexual harassment when it passed Title VII in 1964. In fact, given the accidental manner in which the prohibition against sex discrimination was added to the statute at the very last minute, many of the members of the 1964 Congress would have been amazed to learn that, years later, Title VII was being used to prohibit sexual jokes and comments at work. Nevertheless, that is exactly what has happened.

Unfortunately, however, employing Title VII as an anti-harassment tool is a bit like using a knife to eat peas—you'll get some peas but you'll leave a meaningful number of them behind. Remember that Title VII is expressly worded as an anti-discrimination law. That reality creates a serious problem in dealing with harassment situations because it establishes the requirement that unlawful actions must be "because of sex."

In effect, we can say that if a man "hits on" or "comes on to" a woman at work, he is doing that "because she is a woman." He wouldn't do the same to another man. Consequently, he effectively is involved in a form of sex discrimination. However, because the term fits the situation better, we refer to the man's sexist actions as sexual harassment.

Similarly, if a woman "hits on" or "comes on to" a man at work, she is doing that "because he is a man." She presumably wouldn't do the same thing to a woman. Thus she too is involved in sexual discrimination, which we again refer to as sexual harassment. We even say that if a gay male manager asks a male subordinate for sexual favors, he is doing that "because the subordinate is a man." Again discrimination arises since the gay male presumably wouldn't ask a woman for the same sexual favors. However, we characterize that discrimination as sexual harassment due to its sexual nature.

The Square Peg–Round Hole Problem

This background leads to a very large square peg in a round hole problem. Specifically, the discrimination background of Title VII inadvertently creates something that might fairly be characterized as "the bisexual defense." If a manager is willing to "hit on" or "come on to" members of both sexes equally, he's not doing anything in violation of Title VII because *he's not discriminating*. In fact, he literally is treating each sex equally, although he also is acting like a complete moron.

Lest the reader think the above conclusion is absurd, consider the 2000 case of *Holman v. Indiana Department of Transportation*. There, a married couple, Karen and Steven Holman, worked for the state of Indiana, both reporting to a male supervisor named Gale Uhrich. An apparent equal opportunist, Uhrich allegedly touched Karen, stood too close to her, and ultimately asked her for sex—an offer that she turned down. Around the same time, Uhrich also asked Steven, Karen's husband, to have sex with him. The latter offer was apparently completely and totally independent from the offer Uhrich had made to Karen. In any event, the Holmans ultimately sued over Uhrich's behavior. Amazingly, however, despite the obvious sexual harassment, the Holmans lost. In the words of the United States Court of Appeals for the 7th Circuit: "Title VII does not cover the 'equal opportunity' or 'bisexual' harasser … because such a person is not discriminating on the basis of sex. He is not treating one sex better or worse than the other; he is treating both sexes the same albeit badly."

Bizarre certainly, but an incorrect result? Not under the limitations of Title VII, which prohibits only sex *discrimination*. The law simply wasn't written for

Judicial Analysis …

The Holman case isn't the only one where embarrassed judges reached a result they didn't like. However, give judges like these credit for honest judicial analysis instead of creating law that doesn't exist. Further, realize that some courts are more prone than others to stretch a law to cover situations that don't fit within that particular statute. If you're wondering how your federal court does on this topic, ask a lawyer. And while you're at it, ask that lawyer if the 9th Circuit (the western states) and the 4th Circuit (the southeast) are really reading the same statutes. Sometimes it seems like these and other varying courts reside in different universes rather than different parts of the country.

the kinds of circumstances presented by the Holmans, causing somewhat embarrassed judges to make decisions that they know look silly to the average American. (Whether someone like Uhrich also is embarrassed is less certain, but one can certainly envision an interesting strategic discussion between him and his lawyer—"OK, let me make sure I understand my options correctly: I can either lose the case or I can say that I'm proud to be a bisexual?")

So What Do We Do About This Mess?

So far, we have done virtually nothing through the legislative branch to make this situation any better. The quickest and most effective remedy would be to amend Title VII to add a separate harassment provision, although that would be difficult so long as the law remains focused on the issue of discrimination. The better answer might be to pass a new law that deals only with issues of harassment and hostile work environment. In fact, some efforts have been made in that regard, but only a few states (and not the federal government) have actually enacted such specific legislation.

Alternatively, since the courts of the United States are constitutionally permitted to interpret statutes, they might more broadly craft prohibitions against harassment and hostile work environment. In general, however, the courts have been hesitant to do that, for two primary reasons. First, there is not always common ground among judges as to what is and isn't harassing behavior (as later chapters discuss, the courts look to what is "reasonable," but what is reasonable to Howard Stern presumably differs greatly from what is reasonable to the leaders of NOW).

Second, and perhaps even more importantly, the courts have been loathe to turn Title VII into a "civility law." Doing so would not only create great consternation as to what is and what is not civil, it also would invite a landslide of new cases. In fact, the federal court judges are generally tired of hearing complaints over minor transgressions and political correctness. Consequently they have become reticent to opening the courthouse doors to such matters by attempting to apply Title VII to non-legislative and uncertain definitions of "appropriate behavior."

And How Does All This Affect the Average Employer?

To be candid, the average employer is quite frustrated by the uncertainties of the law. The good news is that progressive employers have taken circumstances into their own hands. As will be discussed in greater detail in the upcoming sections of this book, many employers no longer even try to define what workplace behavior is acceptable and unacceptable by sole reference to "sexual harassment." To do so, after all, brings into play all the uncertainty and misunderstanding that exists in the federal courts, including the bisexual defense.

Instead, smart employers are defining their expectations in nonsexual and nonracial terms. They are simply prohibiting "behavior that the company believes to be inappropriate." As discussed later, this approach offers a very helpful solution to the problem. It eliminates some of the confusion and lifts much of the fog. However, for better or for worse, it also gives employers a tremendous amount of discretion in deciding what is and what is not appropriate. Thus far, courts have permitted the use of such discretion. Whether that will remain the case, however, is yet to be seen.

CHAPTER 8

Reasonable Women, Welcomeness, and Other Early Concepts

Given that the courts are making this stuff up as they go, it might come as no surprise that the law on sexual harassment began with a few mis-starts and some odd early developments. What is unfortunate is that the courts don't usually tend to go back and revise their initial drafts and correct their early mistakes. Consequently, some of the law's early oddities continue to exist in one form or another.

What caused the courts to struggle the most throughout the 1970s and the 1980s is the same problem that continues to cause confusion today: there exists no legislative language or legislative history related to issues of harassment. Most significantly, there exists no universal definition of what actually constitutes legally actionable sexual harassment.

Despite the vagueness and uncertainty of the courts' collective task, a few concepts have remained remarkably consistent. For example, and for quite understandable reasons, the courts are unwilling to define sexual harassment by reference to the entirely subjective feelings of the alleged victim. Some people are simply oversensitive, and permitting the victim to define the crime would create utter chaos. Significantly, a key principle of American law is that everyone should be able to determine in advance if his or her action is going to cross the line. That would not be the case, however, if the definition of unlawful harassment changed according to the subjective feelings of each and every alleged victim.

Well, Everyone Knows What's Reasonable, Don't They?

In a world without guidelines, courts tend to fall back upon the concept of "reasonableness." That's all well and good, except not everyone agrees as to what is reasonable and what is not. Often what is "reasonable" lies in the eye of the beholder—what is entirely reasonable to you may seem utterly ridiculous to me. The good news is that imposing a "rule of reason" at least has the positive effect of eliminating claims by the truly oversensitive claimant. The bad news is that defining "reasonableness" is like defining "obscenity"—leading to the famous observation of Supreme Court Justice Potter Stewart: obscenity may be difficult to define, but "I know it when I see it."

Legitimate concerns of uncertainty aside, the term "reasonableness" does tend to do two helpful things. First, as noted above, it usually eliminates from the mix an allegation that is based entirely upon something like low-level political correctness. Second, virtually everyone can usually agree that certain egregious behavior is inherently unreasonable. Everything in between, however, is subject to the interpretation of whatever judge or jury is analyzing the facts, leading to tremendous uncertainty. In Chapter 9, we will analyze the courts' current standards of "reasonableness" in an effort to inform you about how to protect yourself from liability. In the meantime, it helps to know a little more about how we got where we are today in regard to the concept of reasonableness.

Legislators Being Unreasonable

More and more legislatures seem unwilling to subject their statutory creations to the concept of "reasonableness." Instead, these legislatures try to account for every detail and every situation, thus virtually eliminating the ability of a court to apply common sense to a situation. Such criticisms are often directed to federal sentencing statutes, wage and hour laws, and the training requirements imposed by the state of California (as shown in Chapter 25).

Are Reasonable Men Different from Reasonable Women?

There once was a sexist joke that essentially asserted that the concept of a "reasonable woman" was a complete oxymoron. That might seem like only an outdated joke, but the term "reasonable woman" (instead of "reasonable person") indeed has been used by a number of courts to define sexual harassment. The implicit thinking behind this analysis was that the use of a "reasonable person" definition wouldn't be enough to eliminate sexual harassment. Stated differently, some courts apparently decided that a man, even a "reasonable man," wouldn't recognize sexual harassment if it hit him over the head. Thus they looked instead at inappropriate behavior through the eyes of a "reasonable woman."

To be fair, a "reasonable woman" standard might make sense if all sexual harassment was directed against women, but that clearly isn't the case. Nevertheless, the courts dawdled about with the idea of a "reasonable woman standard" off and on throughout the 1980s and some of the 1990s. At some point, however, most courts seemed to be content to focus on the broader concept of a "reasonable person standard." Perhaps those courts finally real-ized that if one is using a sex discrimination statute as the basis upon which to prohibit sexual harassment, women and men should be treated equally for purposes of defining "reasonableness."

Nevertheless, as late as 2005, the 9th Circuit Court of Appeals, which has federal jurisdiction over the states of California, Oregon, Washington, Idaho, Montana, Nevada, Arizona, and Hawaii, held in the case of *EEOC v. National Education Association* that "reasonable women" could sue if they were allegedly more offended than men by the rantings and ravings of an out-of-control male boss. Amazingly, the court found sexual harassment liability even though the boss in question apparently ranted and raved against men and women in an approximately equal manner. In addition, none of the boss's statements was even sexual in nature. Nevertheless, according to the court, "sexual harassment" existed because "reasonable women" could be offended by the boss's style, even though reasonable men were apparently not as troubled by the situation.

One might legitimately question whether the 9th Circuit's approach was in itself sexist due to its pro-female protective mentality, although the judges on that court would likely be offended by such a suggestion. In any event, the 9th Circuit's decision shows that not only do the courts fail to agree on what is reasonable, they sometimes can't even agree as to whether men and women are equally reasonable. Further, while the idea of applying different definitions of reasonableness to men and women seems dubious in light of the equal rights law that underlies the applicable analysis, the courts have clearly strug-gled in defining sexual harassment in any precise manner.

But Is It Fair to Say I'm Not Guilty Because She Welcomed My Neanderthal Behavior?

Another somewhat dubious early concept involved the idea of "welcomeness." If the concept of the reasonable woman might have created some overly sensi-tized definitions of harassment, the concept of welcomeness seemed to go the precise opposite direction. "Welcomeness" creates a defense to a sexual harass-ment claim that essentially harkens back to the outdated use of "provocation" as a way to defend against a rape claim. In both circumstances, the defense effectively acknowledges that "yes, I acted like a complete pig, but she was begging for me to be that way."

In early rape cases, the defense of provocation might have arisen due to the fact that the victim was dressed in "skimpy clothes" or was acting in a manner that allegedly invited the offender to take advantage of her. "Welcomeness" establishes a similar concept. Here the harasser asserts that he acted unreasonably only because the victim's own bad behavior invited the harassment. In fact, behavior that has periodically been used to support the welcomeness defense has ranged from provocative dress to participation by the victim in "dirty jokes" to behavior that allegedly gave the impression that the victim "wanted" the harasser to be rude and crude.

Interestingly, the defense of welcomeness took the courts in two fundamentally different directions. Some courts effectively excused what was obviously some pretty bad behavior by a number of crude men. In the case of *Reed v. Shepard*, for example, the 7th Circuit rejected a hostile work environment claim because the complainant "welcomed" the crude behaviors of her co-workers. In that case, the male employees put a cattle prod between the plaintiff's legs, handcuffed her, and told lewd jokes as well as made suggestive remarks about oral sex. However, while the court described the males' conduct as "depraved," the court rejected the plaintiff's complaint because she too used offensive conduct, engaged in exhibitionistic behavior, and participated in sexual banter and horseplay.

By comparison, other courts, hesitant to give someone a free pass based upon something as unseemly as the concept of welcomeness, created what was essentially a defense to that defense. These courts essentially concluded that a woman *was allowed* to welcome sexually harassing behavior so long as she felt obliged to do so in order to become "accepted" in the harassing environment in which she worked. Somewhat similarly, other courts have held that a woman could participate in the raunchy behavior and then change her mind and sue for harassment, but she first had to "give some type of notice" that future harassment would now be unwelcome.

This "defense to a defense" and the "change your mind" concepts may have been well intended but, to take them to their logical extreme, they create some very mixed messages regarding appropriate behavior. They also add a layer of complicated legal issues without really focusing on the actual elimination of sexually harassing behavior. Fortunately, then, the courts eventually seemed to come to a loose agreement that these welcomeness-related concepts weren't solving the problem. However, the courts still felt that something should be done about the "victim" of sexual harassment who herself had openly participated in the sexual activities or comments that led to her claim in the first place.

In the case of *Carr v. Allison Gas Turbine*, the court again focused on a situation where the complainant was herself a player in the game of sexual antics at work. The case arose in Indiana, where Allison Gas Turbine (a division of General Motors) had a plant. Mary Carr started working at the plant as a drill operator, but she later became an apprentice in the tinsmith shop. As the court stated (in fact, understated), Mary was the first woman in that shop and "her male coworkers were unhappy about working with a woman." However, instead of reporting the harassment, Mary participated in many of the unseemly activities that occurred at work. In the words of one of the three appellate judges to hear the case:

Actions Speak Louder Than Words

The record, considered as a whole, offers ample support for the conclusion of the experienced trial judge that Mary Carr was a participant in the ribald antics of the tin shop. For years, she actively participated in the vulgarities of life in the tinsmith's shop. She now claims that she was a victim of the uninvited antics but … [her] words and conduct belie her argument.

For a variety of reasons, the court reviewing Mary's case ultimately found in her favor, but Mary's own behavior made their decision a difficult one. In fact, most courts now generally agree that one cannot both "play the game" and sue "because of the game." Rather than phrasing the issue as one of "welcomeness,"

however, courts now usually state that there exist two tests to determine if behavior is legally harassing: (1) the behavior must be inappropriate to a "reasonable person" and (2) the complainant herself must have found the behavior to be offensive. The first of these tests is considered to be an "objective test," while the second is purportedly a "subjective test." In reality, neither test is particularly objective nor easy to apply, but how an employer can protect itself in regard to this issue is a topic for Chapter 13 of this book.

The above developments aside, many courts and lawyers still refer to the "welcomeness defense" instead of discussing the objective "badness" of the behavior and the subjective feelings of the alleged victim. Such continuing references are unfortunate as they create some potentially awkward circumstances. Take the manager who goes for after-work drinks with several of his associates. Further, assume that the best recipe for potential sexual harassment is to "add meaningful alcohol and stir vigorously." At some point, the manager, lost in the swirl of six margaritas, decides he simply has to kiss the most attractive of his female subordinates.

An interesting issue arises from the above situation—was the manager's kiss sexual harassment? Many human resources experts would answer "yes," but that answer would be incorrect under the welcomeness rule. Stated crassly, but legally correctly, how does one know that a kiss is unwelcome until one tries? In fact, the welcomeness test raises the possibility of a "one free kiss rule," a "one free ask out rule," and a "one free dirty joke rule." Of course, that all seems ridiculous. However, the minute one creates a welcomeness defense, these possibilities arise. As a result, while it seems vague and lawyerish to say that harassment doesn't exist unless the victim was subjectively affronted, that test is a definite improvement upon the welcomeness defense.

Consensual As a Concept

Fortunately, as discussed in chapters to come, the term "welcomeness" has to a degree been merged into the more workable term "consensual." If bad conduct is consensual, it's also "welcomed," but the concept of "consent" seems easier to understand and more applicable to real life.

Additional Early Complications Arose As Juries Came Aboard

Not only were the early days of the law on sexual harassment a bit uncertain from a legal standards perspective, the situation became even more complex when a new statute titled the Civil Rights Act of 1991 was passed. That law permitted juries to handle Title VII cases for the first time. (Remember—Title VII was passed in 1964 to stop race discrimination, and no one at that time felt that jury trials were likely to help solve that difficult problem. If you were black, living in Mississippi, and suing to prove discrimination in 1964, did you want a jury to determine the merits of your case?).

In the world of sexual harassment, the advent of jury trials created three interesting problems. First, many jurors are ill-equipped to understand the complicated law in the sexual harassment area. However, they are not the least bit hesitant to apply their own notions of what is and what isn't "appropriate behavior." Second, with juries comes the need for courts to provide jury instructions, and that has proven to be a difficult task—it isn't easy to explain all the nuances that we've discussed so far. And third, with jury trials comes expert witnesses who allegedly "aid" the jury in its analysis of the case.

Numerous cases exist that demonstrate the problem with creating jury instructions that are able to make sense of the complicated law in this area. In general, however, those cases are not discussed in this book. While they make for interesting academic discussion, they don't offer much help to an employer that is trying to understand what it takes to avoid the problem of sexual harassment in the first place.

However, in a development that should worry all employers, the creation of jury trials often leads to the development of "expert witnesses." For better or for worse, this trend continues today, particularly in California, where many sexual harassment cases involve "experts" whose sole role is to opine about what an employer should or should not have done in a particular situation. These experts are potential nightmares for employers because their focus is on second-guessing in a perfect Monday morning quarterbacking environment. The result is additional pressure on every employer "to get it right" when problems arise.

Expert vs. Expert

These experts can be paid hundreds of dollars per hour, and usually there is one employed by the plaintiff and one used by the defendant. This leads to what often are rather silly "battles of the experts." However, once one side brings in an expert, the other side often feels obliged to do the same just to counteract the first expert's opinions.

Finally, the concept of juries leads to an interesting litigation problem. Stated simply, the biggest cad in the workforce can become a self-professed Sunday School teacher in the jury room. In fact, the same idiot who three days ago told his co-worker Sue that she "sure looks good in them tight jeans" may now be prone to tell his cojurors, "I can't believe this poor woman had to put up with those dirty-minded men in her sales office."

In any event, more on what employers can do about this mess in Chapter 13. Let's first talk about what happens when the courts decide that sexual harassment is unlawful only if it is severe or pervasive.

CHAPTER 9

It's Got to Be Severe or Pervasive, Whatever That Means

Title VII is not a "code of civility"—to constitute legally viable sexual harassment, the actions in question must rise to a certain level. As Judge Richard Posner stated in *Baskerville v. Culligan International Co.*, Title VII was designed "to protect working women from the kind of male attentions that can make the workplace hellish for women," but it was "not designed to purge the workplace of vulgarity." In light of the difficulty of finding a proper standard between those positions, the United States Supreme Court decided in *Harris v. Forklift Systems* that the conduct in question must be "sufficiently severe or pervasive to alter the conditions of the victim's employment and create an abusive working environment."

Let's think about the Supreme Court's statement for a minute—"severe or pervasive" is a pretty high standard. The average idiot who "just doesn't get it" could do a lot of stuff before he or she crossed that particular line.

A Few Examples of Actions That Were Found *Not* to Be Either Severe or Pervasive

We'll begin with the term "severe." Can legally actionable sexual harassment arise from one episode of bad behavior? Of course. A sexual assault certainly fits that scenario as might other seriously bad behavior. But "severe" is a strong term. It certainly presents a higher standard than words like "inappropriate," "foolish," or even "bad" behavior. In short, some significantly awful actions have been found by the courts to constitute something less than "severe" misconduct.

The most famous sexual harassment case in the United States is *Paula Jones v. William Jefferson Clinton*. In that case, Paula Jones, then an employee of the state of Arkansas, alleged that then Governor Clinton had her brought to his hotel suite. Purportedly, after some small talk, Governor Clinton then made a number of suggestive comments to her and eventually dropped his pants and his boxers and asked if she was interested. She refused the invitation, after which some further small talk occurred. Bill, of course, denies the allegations, which he claims were politically motivated. Who knows who is telling the truth, but the district court in Arkansas dismissed the case on the basis that the allegations did not establish severity for purposes of a sexual harassment case.

Other cases echo the Clinton case, holding that one action or even multiple actions did not rise to the level of severity required by the law. They included a case where a manager told a female employee to "sit on my face," a case where a female worker was called a "dumb blonde," a "bitter woman," and was subjected to rumors of her having an affair, and a case where a male supervisor told a female subordinate to remove her skirt and stand in front of him in leotards and hose.

The Stupidity Clock

Who are these idiots who say such ridiculous things? Under what rocks have they been hidden? Well, unfortunately, you probably have employed some of them. Be forewarned. Their stupidity is time activated. When the time is right, they will go off.

Well, ok—the term "severe" may not have been a wise choice—but how are we doing with the concept of "pervasive" behavior? Again, the results are mixed, with numerous cases finding the existence of no legally actionable harassment despite some pretty bad facts. Let's look at a couple of examples.

In one case, a co-worker's four requests in four months to have sex with a female employee were found not to be pervasive. In another case, five come-on's by a supervisor over a period of time were also determined to not constitute pervasiveness. Also found not to be pervasive was a case where a supervisor asked the plaintiff out on dates, called her a "dumb blonde," placed his hand on her shoulder several times, put "I love you" signs in her work area, and teased her about her relationship with a co-worker.

Good Lord, Are There Any Bad Actions That *Are* Covered by This Law?

The good news is that for every case in which pretty bad behavior was excused, there is a case where bad behavior was found to violate Title VII. In a 4th Circuit case, a potential claim was found to exist where the supervisor called the plaintiff "honey" and "dear," touched her shoulders, asked what kind of underwear she wore, and inquired as to what birth control she used, then said that it was his turn to have his way with her. The 7th Circuit found five instances of harassment to constitute pervasiveness. In other cases, a district court in Nevada determined that six incidents in three months was enough and a district court in Kansas held that enduring 18 months of periodic comments created pervasiveness. The 2nd Circuit found vulgar comments, lewd gestures, statements about the plaintiff's body, and some grabbing to be severe.

The problem at the end of the day is that judges are people too, and we all seem to have our own personal feelings about what is reasonable and what is not. A thousand factors can influence where a particular person draws the line of reasonableness. Is the judge liberal, conservative, or somewhere in between? Is she a prude or a partier? What kind of mores did her parents have? Those mores aside, who did she hang out with in school—the nerds or the cool kids? And is she an empathetic person or someone who feels that people should be punished for even minor transgressions?

Faced with all these factors (times 12 in a jury trial), it may sometimes seem a bit arbitrary as to what is severe or pervasive and what is not. Cases can be found that reach completely polar opposite conclusions despite virtually similar facts. What a mess, and good luck trying to figure out what's unlawful and what's not. For what it's worth, like many capable lawyers, the author of this book provides sexual harassment advice depending upon the judicial circuit where the employer does business—California, for example, is quite different from Texas (in many, many ways).

So Why Did the Courts Create Such a Vague Standard in the First Place?

Believe it or not, when the Supreme Court created the severe and pervasive test, the justices did not think they were establishing a vague or particularly high (or low, depending upon one's perspective) standard. In fact, the "severe or pervasive" standard is built on something called the "reasonable person" test. Supposedly, according to the legal test, a reasonable person, whoever he or she might be, would not be offended sufficiently by boorish workplace behavior unless that behavior rises to the point of being severe or pervasive.

To many, defining the standard of "reasonableness" by using the terms "severe or pervasive" is too lenient. As noted from the first set of examples above, a lot of pretty awful behavior has been excused under this particular standard of law. One wonders then why this particular definition was judicially created.

Quite frankly, the answer comes down to three key considerations. First, the concept of "reasonableness" is a crucial one in American law, and for good reason. Many of our laws are so lengthy and so complex that they become over-regulated morasses that make common sense an irrelevant part of the analysis. A rule of reason does the opposite—it relies upon common sense as the means of creating a standard, and judges then offer examples of what fits and what doesn't fit within the concept.

The only problem with the rules of reason and common-sense analysis is that they lead to uncertainty in some cases. As discussed above, numerous factors affect the drawing of the judicial line in the sand. However, at the end of the day, most of us can agree most of the time on the "that wasn't a big deal" and "that was really bad behavior" cases. Unfortunately, for the many situations between those extremes, a fair amount of uncertainty exists.

The second key consideration behind the use of the severe or pervasive standard is that the courts are simply loathe to draw too low a line, given that they are doing all this through a law (Title VII) that technically has nothing to do with sexual harassment in the first place. Had Congress provided some detail about harassment concerns, the courts might apply a more specific standard of analysis. But remember, sexual harassment wasn't even considered as a problem or as part of what the law was prohibiting when Title VII was passed.

Third, and finally, the courts have been very concerned that if they set the line too low, they'll open the door to a flood of harassment/hostile work environment cases, some of which may have little to do with discrimination or protected characteristics. Recall that at the beginning of this chapter we highlighted the fact that "Title VII is not a civility code." Perhaps someday Congress will pass a law requiring that people must treat each other to a specific standard of civility. (If passed today, by the way, a good name for that law would be the Lawyer Preservation Act of 2007—the number of cases filed in California alone could require a complete revamping of the state's judicial system). In any event, Title VII is not the law that was created to ensure certain standards of civility, and the courts are not prone toward opening the gates of litigation to an avalanche of "he didn't give me flowers for professional assistant's day" and "she won't smile at me" lawsuits.

Lines of Reason

Don't jump ahead for now, but there is a graph in Chapter 16 that might help you understand where the lines of reason are drawn in sexual harassment cases. As you will see in that chapter, the lines of reason also impact the proper levels of discipline for bad behavior.

Given Where the Courts Are, What Are Employers Supposed to Do to Ensure an Effective Workplace Based on Respect for the Individual?

Chapter 13, as well as the final chapter in this book, discuss the benefits of a workplace based on appropriate behavior, respect for the individual, and the value of supporting diversity. All employers should consider the benefits of such an approach to business. Most employers already act in such a manner.

For employers that simply aren't willing to settle for the level of boorishness created by the terms "severe or pervasive," there exists a better alternative. No employer is bound to the courts' standard for defining harassment. Subject to an important exception discussed below, the employer is free to set a different standard, in the same manner that an employer establishing an alcohol testing program need not create a limit of "drunkenness" represented by a blood alcohol reading of .08 or higher. In fact, most employers find a violation in the case of an employee who reports to work at a much lower standard of alcohol impairment, such as a .02.

So let's assume that "severe or pervasive" equates to a .08 level of drunkenness. What standard do we use to get down to a more workplace-friendly level of .02? Simple—let's eliminate the term "severe or pervasive" from our workplace policies and replace it with the concept of "inappropriate behavior."

Granted, defining what behavior is "inappropriate" isn't always perfectly clear either. However, putting examples into one's policy will help greatly. To help the employer along, a sample appropriate workplace policy is on the accompanying CD. Some of the examples in that policy refer to "touching people inappropriately," "jokes or comments of a sexual or racial nature," "sending inappropriate or sexual e-mails," and "exhibiting sexual pictures, including on your computer."

Fortunately, most workplaces in America are now unlikely to be dens of iniquity, or even places where raunchy talk prevails. However, there continue to be exceptions to progress. Nevertheless, for most employers, using the term "inappropriate behavior" instead of focusing on "sexual harassment" has created the flexibility needed to support an environment of "mutual respect." In short, progress clearly has been made, but employers also should understand that risk exists if they get over-enthusiastic about eliminating all questionable behavior.

The Danger of Defining "Inappropriate Behavior" Too Firmly—the Problems of "Zero Tolerance" and "Protected, Concerted Activity"

Although technically bound by the limitations of the law, e.g., was a decision discriminatory or was it not, judges and juries are nevertheless affected by whether a decision was fair. Therein lies the first problem with an employer taking discipline for an employee's inappropriate behavior too far. Assume, for example, that an employer fires an employee for telling a single sexual joke, or for saying a swear word at work. Depending upon what state he or she is in, the employee may have a difficult time making out a viable claim of law. However, if the case gets in front of a jury, the employee is likely to win because the employer's actions will be perceived as overly aggressive and unfair.

In short, while an employer should base its policy upon inappropriate behavior, to fire a worker for a relatively minor transgression is dangerous. Such was the case with the infamous "Seinfeld" case involving Miller Brewing Company. There a manager with nearly 15 years of experience and very little prior discipline was fired after talking about an episode of the "Seinfeld" show at the office. The episode in question had some sexual moments in it, mostly related to the fact that Jerry Seinfeld had a new girlfriend and he was having serious problems remembering her name. One of the other cast members on the show had a suggestion—the girlfriend's name rhymed with a female body part, which helped Jerry greatly in regard to his memory issue. The girlfriend was "Delores" and the body part was "clitoris," and the manager thought that was remarkably humorous.

Upon coming to work after watching the above episode of the Seinfeld show, the manager told a number of co-workers about the story portrayed by the show. Apparently many of the co-workers enjoyed the manager's commentary but one female employee did not. She reported the manager for sexual harassment and the company fired the manager for violating its sexual harassment policy. The manager then sued and a jury of 12 women in Milwaukee, Wisconsin awarded him $26 million in damages (including $1.6 million against the woman who reported his behavior).

Unfortunately for the manager, his victory was a hollow one—an upper level court reversed the jury's decision, although largely for technical reasons. The point, however, is that Miller Brewing Company overreacted and the jury punished the employer for its overly enthusiastic discharge decision. Other, less notable cases have led to other, less exceptional cases where an employee was fired for using some relatively minor obscenities and won the ensuing lawsuit.

The question that you should be asking yourself is why someone like the manager at Miller was fired for his behavior. Certainly he had violated company policy, but his conduct seemed to deserve a written warning rather than discharge. In many of these cases, however, the wrongdoer is fired because his or her employer has instituted something called the "zero tolerance, sexual harassment policy."

To be blunt, zero tolerance policies can be dangerous. Certainly it makes sense for any employer to say "we don't condone harassment." However, some people get confused by the concept of zero tolerance and end up applying the policy in a way that eliminates any notion of common sense. That apparently is what happened in the Seinfeld case, where someone within the company assumed that any violation of the policy led to discharge (as opposed to an appropriate level of discipline). The same thing happened several years ago in a Georgia public school that had issued a new "zero tolerance policy against weapons in school." That particular policy included a definition of a "weapon," including guns, knives, and chains. However, the school district made some not-so-good nationwide news when it expelled an elementary schoolchild for having a Tweety Bird wallet with a small chain on it. Once again—a good idea gone bad due to the term "zero tolerance."

No More or Less Than Zero

So is there a term that is more useful than "zero tolerance?" Not really, and zero tolerance is not really an inappropriate expression. That said, you can try alternatives like "we don't put up with" or "we prohibit" sexual harassment. More importantly, just remember that whatever term you use to scare the daylights out of people, that term doesn't mandate the discharge of every violator of the underlying policy.

The National Labor Relations Act Poses a Second Problem for a Policy Based on a Low-Level Limit of Inappropriate Behavior

Most every employer is aware of the National Labor Relations Act (NLRA), a law that was passed in the 1930s to create rules related to the union environment. However, most employers naively think the law only applies to employers with unions and to union organizational campaigns. However, a crucial section of that law has nothing to do with unions, and this particular section can impact the kind of respectful behavior a company can require in the workplace.

When Congress passed the NLRA, its primary purposes were to legally authorize unions and to protect workers in regard to union organizing. However, Congress did not choose to permit "union organizing" so much as it decided to protect workers involved in "concerted action." More specifically, even in a non-union environment, the NLRA prohibits discrimination and retaliation against workers involved in "protected, concerted activity" over a term or condition of work.

Under the concept of protected, concerted activity, an employer cannot prohibit workers from discussing salaries or workplace concerns. If three workers are upset over the 1.1% pay raise they just received and they complain vehemently to management, they cannot be fired for being ingrates. More importantly for our purposes, these employees cannot be fired even if they get a little rambunctious about their complaint, including throwing in a few choice obscenities.

Much of the law created under the NLRA was devised in a different era, including the 1950s. In that era, when men ruled the world, we recognized certain language as "shop talk." By so characterizing a lengthy list of obscenities and inappropriate sexual statements, the law essentially approved such language "while at the shop." Presumably, the same employees had to behave better when at home or at their church, but the "shop" was a different place, similar perhaps to another place of apparent male sanctity, "the locker room."

Since the 1950s, time has gone by and the "shop" may now be a much more diverse place than it was before. Further, the law of harassment now applies to the shop. Consequently, many employers have changed their policies and their expectations in regard to crude language at work. However, the NLRA hasn't changed, and the National Labor Relations Board (NLRB) has to a meaningful degree failed to conform its law to the movement toward respect and proper behavior in the workplace.

For example, the NLRB in 2004 decided the case of *Media General Operations*, in which an African-American employee had been informally designated as a spokesperson by other workers concerned about perceived race-based favoritism in the workplace. The employee in question got angry during a work meeting while discussing the issues in question and, in front of a fairly large audience, called the Caucasian manager leading the meeting a "son-of-a-bitch, redneck bastard." In fact, the same employee repeated that slur on several different occasions and ultimately was fired for doing so.

The employee in question filed a claim with the NLRB, asserting that he was fired for exercising his rights under the NLRA. His claim was based on the concept of protected, concerted activity. Somewhat amazingly given that the case was decided in 2004, the NLRB found that the employee's words were not sufficient to be "unprotected" and therefore, he had been fired in violation of the law. Fortunately, the 4th Circuit Court of Appeals disagreed and reversed the decision, but the NLRB's decision certainly raises a conflict between what employers are doing to support a respect-based workplace and what the NLRB is doing to continue to justify certain questionable language at work.

Smart employers need to be cognizant of the problem presented by the NLRA's protected, concerted activity provision. Other NLRB cases have challenged the ability of an employer to even create a policy prohibiting inappropriate language in the workplace, under the theory that such a policy could "chill" the rights of employees to raise workplace concerns. While current law permits such a policy, the policy cannot always be enforced according to its specific terms. There is no question that certain words will be found to be "protected" under the NLRA.

Your Lawyer and Your Policy

Please, please, please have a capable lawyer review your policies. The NLRA can affect everything from your no-solicitation policy to your open-door policy. And few lawyers even recognize such issues. Get some legal help in this area now, and get it from someone who specializes in labor law.

Advice to the Employer in Light of All This

So what's an employer supposed to do in light of this mess among severe and pervasive harassment, zero tolerance policies, concepts of inappropriate behavior, and the dangers of overreactions?

The best advice to an employer sifting through the sands of uncertainty is to be balanced, reasonable, and a bit conservative. However, don't be so conservative as to become over-reactive. Here is a suggested road map, in as summary a fashion as possible:

1. Don't pay too much attention to what the courts are doing—focusing on the severe or pervasive standard isn't going to achieve a workplace where differences among people are respected.
2. Get rid of your 10-page anti-harassment policy that is confusing enough that even your managers don't understand it. Substitute a simpler policy that focuses on inappropriate behavior, uses examples of harassment as

teaching tools, and provides numerous mechanisms for employees to raise legitimate concerns (see Chapter 13 for more on that latter point).

3. Don't use the term "zero tolerance" or, if you do use it, explain what it really means—we don't put up with bad behavior around here, and you will be disciplined for your actions, in whatever manner is appropriate under the relevant facts and circumstances.

4. Don't under-react or over-react. Take a balanced approach that should solve the problem without being unduly aggressive. At the same time, if obviously bad behavior occurs, act immediately and appropriately to stop it. Further, if behavior occurs that could be construed as harassing, treat it as such—it's better to deal with the issue of inappropriate behavior than do nothing. However, discharge may not be appropriate in situations involving low-level problems.

5. Train, train, and train some more in order to teach managers and employees about respect, nonharassment, nondiscrimination, and diversity in the workplace. And see Chapter 25 on effective ways to conduct such training.

CHAPTER 10

The Wonders of E-Mail and the Internet

Speaking of severe and pervasive, can anything be as severe and pervasive as the Internet? And how about all those e-mails that come floating in from SuzySex@iloveu.com? Granted, some of those e-mails are caught by your spam filters, but many are not. And try as you might, you can't screen out all the porn sites either. Remember when www.whitehouse.com (as opposed to www.whitehouse.gov) led one to a porn site? Who would have thought that trying to check out the White House would get you in trouble?

What on Earth Does Porn Have to Do with This Book?

Good question. Porn is absolutely everywhere, including in your workplace. And guess what comes with the porn? Sexual harassment, of course! Yet, good luck in trying to remove the porn from the office. You can write all the 16-page electronic communication policies you want (and, yes, many of them are regrettably that long), but they aren't always going to work.

People are amazingly resourceful when it comes to accessing the Internet and trading sexually oriented e-mails while at work. Even those who seem computer-challenged are somehow able to avoid the firewalls and get into the great electronic world of sex. Don't you wish they could be that creative in their real jobs? Perhaps you have them working in the wrong areas of expertise—sex seems to interest them the most.

What Can You Do About the Internet?

Unless you're Al Gore, the answer seems to be that you have limited control over virtually all aspects of the Internet. Yes, firewalls help and a discussion about Internet and e-mail policies can be found at the end of this chapter. Before discussing firewalls and other protective devices, however, let's talk about reality. One reason why you can't control porn on the Internet is because *no one can control porn on the Internet.*

According to 2007 figures from Fujitso Internet Filter Review, every second that passes finds nearly 30,000 Internet viewers on porn sites. And those of you in Elmhurst, Illinois and Stockton, California are doing more than your share to increase those numbers—those being the top two cities in the U.S. in terms of porn searches done by local inhabitants. Further, there currently exist an estimated 42 million porn web sites, which altogether constitutes 12% of the Internet. To make things worse, the same study suggests that 8% of all e-mails (an approximate 2.5 billion e-mails per day) are porn-related.

Even more problematic, an estimated 20% of male workers and 13% of female workers admit to visiting porn sites while at work. And the problem is not limited to American workers. While an amazing 89% of porn is produced in the United States, the visiting of porn sites seems to be a worldwide problem, with countries as diverse as Finland, South Africa, and Pakistan included among those whose inhabitants apparently visit porn sites regularly.

So are you feeling a little worried yet? Perhaps not; after all, you paid a lot of money for your Internet filters. And that money was probably well worthwhile. However, you still should know that according to a government study done in connection with hearings on the Child Online Protection Act, the strictest filters that were tested blocked only 91% of the available porn. Granted, 91% is a pretty good percentage in most statistical categories, but that means 9% of 42 million porn sites were getting through, which is mathematically a scary proposition.

In any event, filters do make sense. The last thing you want at the office is 13% to 20% of your work force checking out porn sites. In fact, numerous sexual harassment situations have arisen from someone walking into an executive's office and seeing porn on the computer. In short, even if you can't get rid of it all, it makes sense to eliminate at least some of the porn, because obviously some workers just can't help themselves. For whatever reason, they just have to watch, even while at work.

Porn and the ADA

Want to hear about a ridiculous case? There is a lawsuit pending as of the date of publication of this book in which a manager fired for spending hours of work viewing porn is now suing his employer. The ex-manager claims that he suffered post-traumatic stress during the first Gulf War, and that periodically viewing porn calms him down and lets him refocus. He alleges that he is disabled under the Americans with Disabilities Act and that his employer should have to accommodate him by permitting him to watch porn when he gets stressed.

Restricting E-Mail

You also can restrict e-mail, but don't over-react. Spam filters seem to work about as well as Internet filters. That means that some porn will get through. In most workplaces, however, the junk porn is zapped by the filters so at least your employees may not be looking at the worst of the batch. However, sexual jokes and other similar material seem to get through with regularity.

Again, be concerned, but don't over-react. Sexual e-mails are so common that one needs to think carefully before doing anything too drastic. Please realize that most of the time, receiving an e-mail that contains some sexual content isn't a violation of the company's policies. However, a violation does exist when an employee reads that e-mail, chuckles to himself, thinks "gee, all the guys would probably like this," and then forwards the e-mail to 12 co-workers. Now you can do something. He has violated your policies and he has been involved in inappropriate behavior.

Should you fire that worker? Probably not for one occurrence. In this situation, discipline should be progressive in nature. Ultimately, however, if the employee doesn't get it, he most likely will eventually lose his job.

Practical Ways to Deal with These Issues

First and foremost, you want to act to protect yourself electronically, but turning your IT folks into the secret porn police may not be the best use of your scarce IT resources. Certainly you need to prohibit porn and inappropriate e-mails while at work, but to constantly audit for violations may not be worth it. Most people are smart enough not to share their sexual passion with co-workers. Nevertheless, if you know of certain use, it's time to at least start coaching. Further, if the use is such that people seem to be watching porn as much as they're working, greater discipline (including discharge) seems appropriate. IT professionals love to tell stories about the guy who watched porn for six hours a day while at work. If that story is true at your workplace, that is certainly a dischargeable offense.

One way to cut down on the porn at work is to let your workers know that your system tracks their use of the Internet. That alone will slow down most of the porn users. Occasional reminders of your policy also would be smart. Reissuing the policy on a yearly basis makes sense as it keeps the fear of use present in the workplace.

IT Doesn't Get Calls

Some of the better firewall systems create a bit of an impact on porn-snooping employees. In these systems, the employee who types in www.sextoys.com is immediately hit with a screen that says "You are not authorized to access this web site. However, if you need to access this web site for legitimate business purposes, please contact Information Technology." Not surprisingly, IT doesn't get many calls for access.

Otherwise, keep your ears and eyes open and ask your managers to do the same. If allegations arise of Internet or e-mail misuse, go ahead and investigate like you would any situation. Realize, technologically, that there exist numerous tracking methods on virtually all computer systems and laptops. Abuse may be easier to investigate that you thought.

My IT Guy Gave Me a 16-Page Electronics Policy, So I Think I'm Covered

In all likelihood, the lengthiest policy you have in your policy manual is your computer use and electronic communications policy. Also, in all likelihood, that policy is overblown, unrealistic, and out of date. Most current computer use and electronic communication policies were written in the late 1990s or early 2000s. They are lengthy and they seek to cover every situation that could ever arise, addressing everything from confidentiality of company property, to accessing porn, to prohibiting streaming videos that use up system memory.

This isn't to say that your policy is unimportant. Particularly crucial is the protection of company assets and, as noted above, it makes sense to try to keep people off porn sites while on the company computer system. Many of the current electronic communication policies, however, limit common sense by creating a rule for everything imaginable (thus the overblown length of the average policy). Take a look at your policy and ask if there is any flexibility there for dealing with "space in-between" problems. If not, it's time for a revision, and a 16-page policy can be reduced to about four to five pages without losing much impact. Further, that streamlined policy will allow you to apply common sense when needed.

You also should consider whether several of the restrictions in your policy still make sense. Most computer use policies prohibit personal e-mails and forbid the use of the company's computer system for personal reasons. Perhaps those restrictions made sense in 1999. In many circumstances, they don't work very well today. With the rise of Blackberries, PDAs, iphones, and many other helpful contraptions, many white collar workers have inadvertently managed to merge their personal lives and their business lives. Very capable workers in highly placed positions may be on the Internet at 3:30 in the afternoon checking on their high school student's whereabouts, be back to work at 3:45, then make a personal airplane reservation at 5:45 before heading home at 6:00. That evening, however, the same individual connects in to the system from her home computer and works from 8:00 to 9:30 and checks her e-mails via Blackberry five more times that evening.

Given this reality, what's personal use and what's work use? For people who travel for the company, should they be required to carry a company laptop and a personal laptop, then switch back and forth depending on what they are doing in the evening in the hotel room? At some point, policies need to be based in both principle and reality. In limiting the use of a company laptop, consider whether a sales manager who logs onto the Internet service provided by the hotel is really misusing your computer, especially since he wouldn't be at that hotel except to assist you. At some point, one should ask "what's my business interest here?" If such an interest truly exists, great. If not, you might want to re-evaluate your lengthy policy. As it is, many policies are simply being overlooked so as to permit some very effective workers to lead their very hectic lives.

On the CD accompanying this book there are two sample policies. One takes the long road and one takes the short road. Your road may be one or the other, or something in-between. You should think through any particular policy, however, to determine whether it fits your needs, it is realistic, and it is based on business need.

CHAPTER 11

Stupid Manager Tricks: The Disaster of Quid Pro Quo Harassment and the Problem with Hostile Work Environments

If one were to categorize sexual harassment from least concerning to most problematic, the list would look something like this: political incorrectness, dumb jokes, mild teasing, sexual banter, serious teasing, crude sexual language, inappropriate touching, incessant sexually charged statements, quid pro quo actions, and sexual assault. Wait, you say, there was a Latin term in there, and you know how real people feel about that Latin stuff that you lawyers like to toss around the playing field.

OK, OK, the Latin isn't fair, but neither is quid pro quo sexual harassment. Let's provide some background to make things clear.

God, I Hate Latin, but Go Ahead and Tell Me What Quid Pro Quo Is

Quid pro quo—it's bad. It's very, very bad. And it can only be done by someone who has authority over someone else, such as an executive, a manager or, on occasion, an hourly lead person. Quid pro quo happens when a manager is dumb enough to turn to a subordinate and say "I'll get you a really big raise this year, but you have to do one thing for me—have sex with me." Quid pro quo also arises when the same stupid manager gets turned down on his offer, then ups the ante by saying "OK, you obviously didn't want the raise—now if you don't have sex with me, you're fired."

Sounds outrageous, doesn't it? Well, it is. And it used to happen all the time. In the 1970s and the 1980s, some managers apparently thought that their power was absolute. In particular, they decided that they could demand sexual favors from female subordinates, and they could hold back raises, promotions, and other workplace advantages until the favors were provided. The more egregious managers even fired subordinates for refusing to have sex with them.

For the most part, male managers were the ones who thought they could get away with conditioning workplace decisions on sex. However, they weren't alone—does anybody remember the Demi Moore/Michael Douglas movie "Disclosure," where the female boss was demanding sex from her male underling? Yes, men and women are both capable of losing their brains and jumping off the quid pro quo cliff.

Women Harassers

Statistics vary, but somewhere between 10 and 15% of sexual harassment cases are brought against women. Only some of those cases are brought by men. Others are raised by women under a "same sex" harassment theory, which is discussed in Chapter 22.

For those who are saying "C'mon, does this kind of stuff really happen?," the answer is "yes." Fortunately, the sheer numbers of quid pro quo cases have dropped dramatically since the late 1980s. However, these situations continue to arise. That said, most managers now have come to realize that asking a subordinate for sex in connection with a workplace benefit or detriment is really dangerous to the manager's immediate employment. And few, if any, companies now put up with a manager who is foolish enough to go the quid pro quo route. Nevertheless, some managers apparently just can't help themselves.

In one notable case from not that long ago, a male shift manager had ultimate authority over the hiring for a vacancy on his crew. A number of temp employees present at the workplace sought the entry-level job, and the manager decided that he would offer the position to a female temp who apparently had caught his eye. Three times in private, he told her that he would pick her for the job if she first had sex with him. Three times she turned him down. However, the temp did not report the situation to management, apparently because she decided no one would believe her (remember, the invitations were all made in private).

After the third offer, the female temp decided that she had to do something. Later that same day, she asked to leave early because she wasn't feeling well. After arriving at her home, she called the manager and inquired as to whether he was alone in the office. When he answered in the affirmative, she then told him that she really wanted the job, but she needed to know exactly what it was that he wanted from her. The manager hesitated, saying "I can't tell you that over the phone, you might be taping this call." The temp's response to that question was short and simple, but effective. She answered "Oh, come on, would I do that?" The manager then walked right into the trap. He responded "You're right, you wouldn't do that—let me tell you what I want from you."

Not surprisingly, the temp was, in fact, taping the call. Amazingly, she didn't even have to lie about that. The manager still fell into the trap. The call was over 30 minutes long and descriptive enough that specific sexual positions were discussed. The temp then took the tape to her temp service, which presented it to the manager's employer, which then fired the manager. A classic case of stupid manager tricks, and a justified discharge if ever there was one.

What was most amazing about the above scenario is that the temp did not end up suing the employer. Rather, the fired manager, who happened to be an African-American, brought suit. His claim was that if he had been white, he wouldn't have been fired for his behavior. What a joke—if this particular manager had been a one-eyed, one-horned flying purple people eater, he would have been fired. This was a case of complete race-neutral stupidity, and the former manager's claim of discrimination was properly dismissed by the court.

How Much Quid and What Kind of Quo Does There Have to Be?

Historically, there has been a fair amount of uncertainty regarding what constitutes both a quid and a quo. Obviously if an employee turns down an offer of benefits in exchange for sexual favors, pay or benefits have been lost. Consequently, the courts have found that situation in and of itself to constitute unlawful harassment. If the employer acted quickly to rectify the situation, however, the victim's damages were usually limited. By contrast, quid pro quo of the ugliest variety—discharging someone for refusing to have sex with a manager, constitutes an obvious and very serious legal violation. Damages in those circumstances can be substantial.

Beyond the obvious cases, plaintiffs' lawyers have sought to establish quid pro quo claims in numerous other situations. Some argued quid pro quo in some fairly petty circumstances, such as a subordinate turning down an offer for sex and then getting an "exceeds expectations" rather than an "outstanding" performance rating (when no monetary difference resulted), or someone not being given a specific office down the hall from one's current office. The courts have largely not been impressed by such claims, but they still sometimes have found liability if the manager truly pushed the subordinate for sex.

In short, the parameters for evaluating quids and quos have always been somewhat uncertain except in the obvious cases. As discussed later in this chapter, however, the Supreme Court decided two cases in 1998 that made this uncertainty largely irrelevant. Before evaluating such legal issues, though, let's jump to today, where quid pro quo cases often arise from romance and misunderstandings rather than power.

Quids and Quos Aren't Always About Power, They Also Can Be About Desperation

As stated previously, most managers these days understand that they can't be stupid enough to employ quid pro quo as a basic management strategy. As a result, comparatively few cases now arise where a manager engages in traditional quid pro quo, that is, offers up a promotion in response for sexual favors or fires someone for failing to agree to sex. That doesn't mean, however, that the concept of quid pro quo is dead. In fact, it is very much alive, although most often in a different format than previously has been the case.

Picture a high-level male executive, age 55, who has a less than satisfactory marriage. And then consider a 35-year-old male sales manager who is recently divorced. Then add in two attractive young women working, respectively, in a clerical job and a sales position. The clerical employee, a former exotic dancer, needs money due to the after-effects of her own divorce. The female salesperson apparently is just enjoying what she somewhat naively perceives to be extra mentoring from her boss.

In the case of the 55-year-old executive and the clerical employee/former exotic dancer, a sexual liaison begins that at first fills mutual but different needs. The executive buys the former dancer new furniture and toys for her kids and even provides $10,000 for a down payment on her home. According to the executive, the sex "is the best he's ever had." According to the clerical worker, the sex is "not unpleasurable."

As for our second couple, the sales manager begins asking his female protégé to accompany him for after-work drinks. At first the female sales worker enjoys the extra attention, but then she begins to think that maybe this is a bad idea. Still, a few kisses are exchanged, some more than "just friends" hugs occur, and at some point the manager decides he is unequivocally in love with his associate.

Ultimately both relationships end awkwardly. Not long after buying her house, the clerical worker starts dating someone her own age and calls off the relationship with the older executive. As for the female salesperson, she tells her boss that she can't date him and then quits her job. Both men are deeply hurt and both try desperately to continue the relationships, in part through e-mails they send. The executive tells the former dancer that their sex was the best ever, then offers to pay her more money if they can just have sex 15 more times (not 14, not 16, but 15, and no, I'm not making any of this up). The female salesperson, in the meantime, ignores the flurry of romantic e-mails from her former boss and won't return his calls.

Ultimately, both women report the above situations to their current and former employers, respectively (remember—the sales worker had already quit). They demand money in settlement for the quid pro quo harassment that has occurred. They seek to prove their cases through the e-mails that they, of course, saved. The 55-year-old executive is fired immediately from his job. The sales manager, by contrast, is retained, but his entire yearly bonus is forfeited and he is required to attend one-on-one sensitivity training. The case brought by the female salesperson is settled for approximately $100,000. The case involving the clerical worker is still continuing as of the date of publication of this book.

Men behaving badly? In all sincerity, probably not. More like people being people—after all, relationships fail all the time and often one of the parties to the relationship goes to great lengths to try to keep the romance alive. In the case of a manager dealing with a subordinate, however, what really occurred in these two cases was very bad judgment. Anyone can empathize with someone who is desperately in love in the wrong situation, but almost everyone would question why a manager would have put himself into that position in the first place.

As for the law, it is neither judgmental nor empathetic. However, it is quite clear. The above behavior by the 55-year-old executive constitutes good, old-fashioned quid pro quo sexual harassment. The affair he enjoyed with his underling was quite consensual, that is, welcome, and therefore not against the law. But when she called the affair off and he offered money for her to continue it, the manager stepped over the legal line as well as the line of good judgment.

As for the sales manager, it isn't entirely clear that he is guilty of quid pro quo harassment. At a minimum, we seem to have a quid—the mentoring and additional sales advantages he gave his female subordinate are probably enough to show an offer of employee benefits. However, this situation may be missing a quo—from an employment perspective, nothing bad happened to the salesperson when she turned away the manager. Granted, a forced quit, or constructive discharge, can constitute an adverse action, but the courts have usually required more to happen than pressure being placed on the plaintiff to have a relationship. In any event, legal niceties aside, the awkwardness and public relations problems that could arise from these facts was enough to convince the company in question to settle the case for meaningful dollars.

Training Makes a Difference

Can training prevent these kinds of human train wrecks? In all honesty, perhaps not. However, that isn't to say that you should give up. If there is one thing underscored throughout this book, it's that training does make a difference.

Since 1998, Quid Pro Quo Is Probably a Misnomer, but It's Still Useful As a Training Concept

In 1998, the U.S. Supreme Court decided two cases that significantly changed the landscape of sexual harassment law. For purposes of this book, we'll evaluate a case called *Faragher v. City of Boca Raton*, but an important companion case (*Burlington Industries v. Ellerth*) was decided with *Faragher*.

The facts in *Faragher* are, in a word, outrageous. The key individuals in the case all worked as lifeguards for the city of Boca Raton, Florida. Here, in a nutshell, is what happened during several hot summers between 1985 and 1990.

Beth Faragher, a college student, was groped, was asked about sex, and was made the subject of numerous comments regarding sex and her body. A supervisor once told her to date him or "clean the toilets for a year." Another manager tackled Faragher and said that while he didn't find her attractive, he would have sex with her. Numerous comments were made about other women as well, and at least one female recruit was told that the female lifeguards were expected to have sex with their male counterparts. The problems and bad behavior went on almost continuously.

Faragher eventually sued and the case slowly worked its way up the judicial ladder. When the Supreme Court decided to review the *Faragher* and

Ellerth cases, lawyers had the sense that changes in the law would result. That, however, was an understatement. In a very complex and lengthy decision, the Supreme Court essentially held as follows:

1. In cases involving quid pro quo, the employer is automatically liable for the wrongdoing of its manager, largely because the employer vested the manager with the power to act. However, in order for a situation to actually constitute a quid pro quo scenario, an economic harm must result. If no harm occurs, the case is evaluated instead from the perspective of a hostile work environment situation (i.e., was there sex-based inappropriate behavior that rose to the level of being severe or pervasive?).

2. Where a manager is responsible for sexual harassment based on a hostile work environment, the employer again is automatically liable. However, and this is a big however that will be discussed in detail in Chapter 13, an affirmative defense is available to the employer in certain circumstances. Specifically, if the employer has a well-written policy against sexual harassment, trains employees regarding that policy, and responds quickly and effectively if problems arise, the complaining employee has an obligation to mitigate the problem by allowing the employer to address the concern rather than simply filing a claim in court.

3. Finally, if a co-worker or co-workers are responsible for the hostile work environment sexual harassment, the employer is not automatically responsible or liable, because the co-workers are not vested with management authority. Instead, the employer is liable only if "negligence" exists, that is, the employer was aware or should have been aware of the harassment and the employer failed to take effective steps to stop or prevent the harassment.

Points 2 and 3 above create significant issues for employers and are addressed in their own chapters (Chapter 13 and Chapter 12). Point 1, which now defines what is quid pro quo and what is not, is deserving of additional analysis in the context of the present chapter.

Due to the decision in *Faragher*, we now know that "quid pro quo" liability exists only if something bad happens. In fact, quid pro quo itself is now something of a misnomer—the issue really is whether an adverse economic

The Negligence Standard

Prior to *Faragher* and *Ellerth*, most courts treated manager and co-worker harassment by employing the negligence standard, or even something less. Some courts seemed to ignore the prevention side of the negligence issue and looked only at how effective the employer's response to the harassment had been.

consequence follows from the manager's misbehavior. If it does, liability to the employer automatically results. If not, liability exists only if a hostile work environment can be proven.

In short, for employers, the *Faragher* case both giveth and taketh away. No quid pro quo exists unless something bad happens. However, if economic harm does occur, the employer is guilty as a matter of law, even if it takes immediate remedial steps to lessen the harm. In a sense, the employer can act to mitigate its liability but it can't avoid that liability if economic harm has occurred.

As for managers involved in non-quid pro quo sexual harassment, the issue arises as to whether the misbehavior was severe or pervasive. That same standard applies to non-manager sexual harassment as well. The question is—how bad was the behavior? It's not enough that someone says something stupid. In hostile work environment cases, the behavior must be (1) nonconsensual or unwelcome, (2) severe or pervasive and (3) based on sex. These standards will be evaluated in the next chapter in the context of co-worker harassment, while manager hostile work environment will be considered again in Chapter 13.

CHAPTER 12

Co-Worker
Harassment:
Party All the Time

America is a strange and interesting place on all sorts of levels. One of those levels is the contrast between the expectations of law and the implications of reality. To explain, let's consider two examples of reality.

It's Sunday night at 9:00 p.m. Television sets all over America are tuned to one of the hot and popular (at least as of the date of this book) shows on the tube—"Desperate Housewives." In this particular episode, one of the housewives is ticked at her significant other. As a consequence, she decides to make it with both the maid and the gardener. The scene is sexy and funny, and Joan Morgan, one of your employees, is just dying to talk about what happened.

Joan, however, has a problem. "Desperate Housewives" is over at 10:00 on Sunday night. Who is she going to talk to at that hour on a Sunday—her spouse? Good grief, that's not going to happen. Not about "Desperate Housewives." So instead Joan waits until the next morning when, conveniently enough, she'll see a bunch of her friends at your workplace. In fact, a fascinating 20-minute discussion, heavy on the sex scene, occurs in the office hallway first thing in the morning. Beyond the fact that no work is getting done, this 20-minute discussion creates a serious problem for the American employer.

So does the scenario involving Rich Wilson, one of your warehouse workers. Rich has satellite radio and every morning on the way to work he tunes into the Howard Stern Show. On this particular morning, rowdiness is oozing from the radio. As Rich drives to work, Howard is interviewing Mysty the Stripper, and the interview is intensely X-rated. To complicate things further, the interview ends just as Rich pulls into the company parking lot. Rich laughs all the way into the warehouse, where he then tells everyone who will listen about what transpired between Howard and Mysty.

The Prurient: Always with Us

Employers hoping that society will change sufficiently to eliminate the issues created by "Desperate Housewives" and Howard Stern might as well quit hoping. Remember, "Peyton Place" begat "Dallas," which begat "Melrose Place," which begat "Desperate Housewives." And this chain doesn't even consider non-network cable. America isn't going to lose its infatuation with sex any time soon.

Is This Sexual Harassment?

Do the above scenarios constitute sexual harassment? The emphatic legal answer is "it depends." Technically speaking, if everyone who hears from Joan about "Desperate Housewives" and everyone who listens to Rich go on about Howard and Mysty "consents" to those discussions, no harassment occurs. However, if someone is offended, we have a problem, even if no one complains about the "harassment."

When the Supreme Court decided the *Faragher* case, it made a clear distinction between sexual harassment by a manager and sexual harassment by an hourly co-worker. In general, companies have automatic liability for the sexual exploits of their managers, whether the harassment is quid pro quo or of the hostile work environment variety. However, companies are not automatically liable for the actions of their hourly employees.

What the Supreme Court did in the case of hourly employees was to establish a "negligence" standard. The employer is guilty if it knew or should have known of the harassing behavior and failed to take timely or adequate steps to stop the harassment. The good news about this test is that there is no automatic liability. The bad news is that liability can arise under this co-worker negligence standard in a surprisingly easy manner, and most managers are oblivious to that risk.

So What's the Danger? Don't Most Companies React Pretty Strongly to Harassment?

If you said that most companies react pretty strongly to harassment, you would be woefully and completely wrong. On the other hand, if you said that most companies react pretty strongly to *complaints of harassment*, you would be absolutely correct. That distinction, however, makes a huge difference in the reality of the workforce, for several reasons.

First, employees are not required by law to report harassment by co-workers (by contrast, as discussed in Chapter 13, they may effectively be required to do so in regard to manager hostile work environment, or risk losing their case in court). What that means is that some employees will put up with a lot of sexual commentary, including some pretty bad harassment, from their co-workers without complaining. In many ways, that's their choice, but an employee who delays reporting harassment to his or her employer inadvertently increases the chances of employer liability.

Second, most managers don't think that they have any duty to do anything about sexual discussion and sexual antics unless someone complains about such behavior. The reality is that they may well have overheard Joan's description of the threesome scene in Desperate Housewives or Rich's reiteration of Howard and Mysty's interview. However, absent a complaint from another worker, most managers write off such discussion as "people being people." That, for better or worse, is a serious mistake if one remembers the standard for co-worker liability established in *Faragher*.

Under *Faragher*, co-worker liability arises if the employer knew or should have known of the liability yet does not take sufficient steps to stop the harassment. Nowhere in that standard does the question arise "and did someone complain of the behavior?" As a result, managers who know of the banter but fail to act absent a specific complaint may well inadvertently have created sexual harassment liability.

Finally, managers and co-workers alike fail to understand that an employee's failure to voice a complaint about sexual banter is not the same as consent. Simply put, silence is not acquiescence. Remember again the law—one is not required to complain, but liability arises if the company knew or should have known of the harassment but failed to take appropriate steps to stop the problem.

An Example

You want a real story. Ok, here's one that proves that truth is, indeed, stranger than fiction. A manufacturing company has an hourly crew that sometimes work days and sometimes works nights on a rotating shift schedule. During the day, there is considerable management around and the crew behaves accordingly. At night, however, under limited management oversight (and no HR presence), the crew in question transforms itself. The crew members magically become "the party people."

It's difficult to describe the crew's actions without being vulgar—these folks were custom made for the "Jerry Springer Show." They enjoy telling stories about sex, they compare sexual techniques, they share sexual pictures, and they even read pornography to each other. The antics are led by an attractive woman in her mid-30s. She isn't your typical worker—among other things, she likes to flash her breasts at her co-workers. She also likes to talk, and talk, and talk some more about sex. At one point, she even gives her co-workers a seminar on how to properly satisfy a man orally, using a hammer as a visual aid.

Later, this same woman is made the hourly crew leader, meaning that she must provide orientation to new workers. If the new employee is a man, part of the orientation (apparently done in sight of the rest of crew) involves her sneaking up behind the man, taking her bra off and then jumping on his lap and pulling her t-shirt over his head. Try finding that one in your standard orientation manual.

To make a long story short, this circus goes on for approximately two years and no one ever complains. In fact, the reality is that everyone on the crew can fairly be said to have consented to (and, in fact, very much enjoyed) the behavior in question—with one unfortunate exception.

One co-worker, a male who is religious, is put off by the crew's behaviors, but he never complains. Certainly the co-workers do not see him as a game player, as he does not typically participate in the crew's fun and games. However, he also does not challenge the behavior. One night, though, the good times come to an end, at the regrettable expense of the religious co-worker.

Late into the night shift, the co-worker, whom we'll call Bill, and the game-playing female, whom we'll refer to as Christie, have an encounter. They are working together sorting out materials as those materials flow down a flume. Bill is using what looks like a wooden paddle to help perform the sorting. At some point in that process, Christie says something sexual to Bill and the proverbial straw breaks the proverbial camel's back. Bill tells Christie—"I've had enough of your little adolescent ways. I've had it with your little potty mouth." Christie replies, "Well then, why don't you shut me up?" Bill responds, "I know better than that. There's nothing I could ever do to shut you up."

At that point, Christie offers up an interesting challenge. She states, "If that's the way you feel, why don't you punish me for what I've done?" She then adds: "After all, look what you're holding in your hands," that is, the wooden paddle. She then turns and offers up her rear end as a target. Unfortunately, Bill takes the bait—hook, line, and sinker. He swats Christie on the rump. The next morning, Christie reports to Human Resources that Bill has physically assaulted her.

When asked by HR, "Good Lord, what were you thinking?," Bill responds that he hadn't been thinking. However, he then adds, "But can I tell you about Christie?" Bill, who is fired for his behavior, tells HR about everything, from the orientation to the pornography readings. His exit interview lasts for over two hours. Following that interview, HR immediately asks the night managers if they have been aware of all that had gone on over the course of the last two years. The answer was "well, yes." When asked why they had done nothing to stop the problem, they responded, "but no one ever complained."

The aftermath of this situation was substantial. The two night managers were fired as were Bill and Christie. Bill threatened to sue, and he had a very good sexual harassment case until he hit Christie. At that point, however, he blew it. Christie, on the other hand, did sue, effectively claiming that if she had been a man, the company would not have fired her. She justifiably lost her case, but the company spent tens of thousands in attorneys' fees before the case was dismissed. All because the managers waited for someone to complain.

Interestingly, none of the other co-workers in this circus had any right to complain of sexual harassment. They all had joined in with the fun, and thus they had legally "consented" to the inappropriate behavior.

No Longer Than 15 Minutes

By the way, don't conduct a discharge by asking, "Good Lord, what were you thinking?" The above case was obviously not "normal." In most discharge meetings, the goal is to respectfully and professionally end the employment relationship in as reasonably quick a fashion as possible. Be polite, get to the bad news without shooting the breeze about small talk for 15 minutes, then discuss forward-looking issues like benefits and COBRA information. If a discharge meeting lasts longer than 15 meetings, it's usually lasting too long.

Good Grief, This Is All Quite Mad

Indeed, co-worker sexual harassment can be quite maddening. But people are people, and people talk about sex. What makes all this so difficult is that Americans see sex on TV, at the movies, and in advertisements. They hear

about sex on the radio. They are, in fact, barraged about sex. But when they come to work, they're supposed to forget about all that and act appropriately to each other. Unfortunately, some people simply can't make that transition.

Worse yet, the courts have not clearly defined what is and what is not sexually harassing behavior. In fact, as we discussed in Chapter 9, to define what constitutes a "hostile work environment" under the law is a very difficult task. And the courts don't often agree as to what is unlawful harassment and what is not.

Defining a Hostile Work Environment Is Not an Easy Thing to Do

As previously stated, judges have consistently held that Title VII is not "a civility code." Rather, to establish sexual harassment, the inappropriate actions must rise to a certain level. As discussed in detail in Chapter 9, the level is supposed to be established by reference to a "reasonable person standard." Most commonly stated, that reference is framed by asking if the sexual behavior was "severe or pervasive."

There is no use repeating the analysis in Chapter 9, where several case examples are used to define what might be severe or pervasive behavior. In the context of the current chapter, let's instead continue to discuss the need to manage inappropriate behaviors. If managers are tuned into the issues and if they realize they have to act *before someone complains*, the chances of legal liability arising go down significantly.

Be Alert, Coach, Counsel, Discipline, and Where Appropriate, Discharge

Think once more about the co-worker negligence standard—the employer is liable if it knew or should have known of the sexual harassment but failed to act to stop the behavior in question. That makes it sound like the managers of America's employers have to become the secret morals police. In short, are the country's employers now faced with a search and destroy mission in order to avoid sexual harassment liability?

The answer fortunately is "no," although the law technically would encourage that level of prevention. However, any employer that treats people as always suspect and spends too much time dictating the social mores of its workers is going to demoralize its workforce. The key concept here is balance—stop the behavior before it gets too problematic, but do that in a reasonable and evenhanded manner.

A number of prevention systems are discussed later in this book. Those include focusing on "inappropriate behavior" instead of sexual harassment, teaching employees about respect for the individual, and getting on board the diversity train. Otherwise, the secret is in coaching the low-level problem, disciplining the more problematic harasser, and firing the person who just doesn't get it.

"Coaching" in this context is something of an art form. Most managers haven't a clue as to how to do it. They are awkward or embarrassed about even starting the conversation. Sometimes HR professionals can help, and sometimes they can't. In the interest of providing assistance, here is what an adept manager should have said to our old friends Joan Morgan (the "Desperate Housewives" fan) and Rich Wilson (the Howard Stern devotee):

I overheard you talking to all your friends about ["Desperate Housewives"/ Howard and Mysty]. Pretty good show, was it? Well, let's talk for a minute. Look, I'm not a prude, but you need to be more careful at work. I realize that most of that discussion is just good fun among the folks who are involved. However, there is often someone who is offended. Look, neither you nor I want to get into legal trouble. I have zero problem with you discussing anything you want after work, but if you could stay away from those discussions here in the office, I'd be appreciative. Otherwise, we might have to have a different discussion. Thanks, [Rich/Joan] for understanding. I know this might seem silly to you, but it isn't silly to some others and I'd like to keep us both out of trouble.

Of course, if coaching doesn't seem to be doing the trick, discipline might have to follow. More often than not, that doesn't mean discharge for the lower levels of inappropriate behavior. However, those who don't get it are often fired, and those who act with higher levels of stupidity may lose their jobs without the opportunity for a coaching session.

Write It Down

Managers would do well to write down what they want to say more often. When left to wing it in a coaching discussion, many managers struggle, leave out important points, and end up not saying very much. Script it out and, if asked, even show the employee the script. It probably uses the right words while the verbal discussion often doesn't.

Chapter 16 of this book discusses the expectations of the law in regard to how companies should remedy sexual harassment. The options are many, and remedies don't focus solely on discipline. Before dealing with remedies, however, let's touch on one more aspect of the *Faragher* case as well as how sexual harassment allegations are properly investigated.

CHAPTER 13

Building a Prevention System: Manager Harassment and the *Faragher* Defense

By now, you're probably tired of hearing about the Supreme Court's decision in *Faragher*. However, we can't leave that case until we discuss one more crucial part of the Court's decision. Once again, we're going to focus on the issue of employer liability for manager sexual harassment.

Manager Hostile Work Environment vs. Quid Pro Quo

We discussed the problem with quid pro quo sexual harassment in Chapter 11. If you're having trouble remembering, "quid pro quo" is an alternative term for extreme stupidity. It arises when a manager says, for example, "if you have sex with me, you'll get promoted" or, more appropriately after *Faragher*, "you're fired if you won't have sex with me."

As we discussed in Chapter 11, the employer is automatically liable for a manager's quid pro quo harassment. In fact, liability is automatic even if the manager was told *not to get involved in quid pro quo actions.* So why the absolute liability? Because the employer vested the manager with management authority.

Also noted in Chapter 11, but not focused on there, is the fact that employers have automatic liability for a manager's hostile work environment harassment, even though what we're talking about is sexual banter or touching rather than a quid pro quo. The good news, however, is that the Supreme Court viewed manager hostile work environment cases in a more forgiving light than it did quid pro quo cases. The reason for that varying perspective is that true quid pro quo cases involve an adverse employment action and therefore cause economic harm to the harassed worker. By comparison, hostile work environment sexual harassment is problematic stuff, but it usually doesn't involve an economic loss.

How Much Trouble Am I in If My Manager Creates a Hostile Work Environment?

Unfortunately, the fact that the Supreme Court viewed manager hostile work environment as less significant than quid pro quo is only somewhat helpful. As stated in *Faragher*, automatic liability still arises. In realistic terms, that means damages for pain and suffering as well as potential punitive damages, since there is usually no actual economic harm that accompanies a hostile work environment case. In short, however, the company is still potentially in deep doo-doo.

The good news is that the *Faragher* case offered employers a serious carrot to create systems that seek to do the right thing. Specifically, the Court stated that if the employer creates an adequate system for preventing and effectively dealing with concerns of sexual harassment, it can escape automatic liability even if the hostile work environment is created by a manager.

Power Requires Care

These manager liability discussions should show you how important hiring and promotion decisions really are. Treat them as such. You are bestowing power on these managers. Choose carefully.

An Adequate System for Preventing and Effectively Dealing with Concerns of Sexual Harassment

The reality is that the Supreme Court's decision in *Faragher* provides, at least on its face, a practical and helpful solution to employers who want to get things done the right way. While holding that manager hostile work environment harassment creates automatic liability, the Court reached out to employers and offered up what it referred to as an affirmative defense. The availability of that defense depends on the efforts of the employer to prevent and/or deal effectively with harassment.

Think of the Faragher defense as essentially consisting of four steps. First, the employer should create an anti-harassment policy that is well put together and understandable to the average employee. Second, the employer needs to train *every* employee, including new hires, on the policy and its operation. Third, if manager hostile work environment sexual harassment arises, the employer must respond in a timely and effective manner. Finally, the employer should be able to show a consistent history of such timely and effective responses.

Assuming that an employer satisfies all the elements of the Faragher affirmative defense, something magical should happen if manager harassment nevertheless occurs. Specifically, assume the stereotypical case, that is, that a female subordinate has been harassed by her male boss. However, rather than reporting such harassment to her employer, the harassed employee brings a charge or a lawsuit against that employer. According to *Faragher*, the female subordinate will lose that case, even if she was sexually harassed. The Court's theory is that the woman in question failed to mitigate her problem, as presumably the qualifying employer would have solved the problem had she just managed to bring that problem to the employer's attention.

Good stuff indeed, at least for the employer willing to spend sufficient time and resources on establishing a prevention and response system that meets the *Faragher* standard. And, yes, the standard can be met, but only with care and some meaningful focus. All employers should strive to fit within that category of company.

Beware—the *Faragher* Defense Has Some Holes in It

Strive, yes. But can an employer guarantee that it will satisfy the *Faragher* requirements? Not always.

Many courts by now have evaluated a particular employer's effort to achieve the defense. In some instances, the employer was granted an escape from liability. In other situations, the employer wasn't quite so fortunate. Let's discuss the reasons for such inconsistent results.

First, the good news is that most employers have by now established a legitimate harassment avoidance policy. An employer without such a policy should consider the sample policies included on the accompanying CD ROM. The two samples on the CD take quite different approaches to the same problem. However, differing approaches are fine so long as the policy sufficiently addresses the need to stop unlawful harassment and creates a system through which concerned persons can raise complaints.

Review Your Policies

Employers generally don't review their policies often enough. Law changes as do problems and court precedents. Policies become outdated pretty quickly. They should be reviewed every two to three years.

As for training, most employers by now have conducted such training for their managers. Regrettably, many have neglected sexual harassment avoidance training for non-management workers, especially with respect to teaching persons how to raise issues and concerns. Some courts have refused to apply the *Faragher* defense where the complaining employee had not been trained or had not been sufficiently trained as to what to do if harassment occurred.

Where employers have most often failed to create facts sufficient to obtain *Faragher* relief, however, is not with loose policies or insufficient training, but with inadequate response to harassment that occurs. Too many employers fail to do one or more of the following:

a. react to a concern on a timely basis
b. respond effectively to solve the problem that has occurred
c. follow up to ensure that no further problems have arisen
d. act consistently over the course of time to show that they really do intend to stop unlawful harassment
e. create an environment that consistently is based on nonharassment, respect for the individual, and the importance of appropriate behavior.

Meeting the *Faragher* Standard—the Steps and the Requirements

It shouldn't be that hard to meet the standard set forth in *Faragher*, yet companies fail far too often in asserting the affirmative defense. The reality is that the defense should be raised and should be effective every time a manager gets involved in hostile work environment harassment. The problem is that employers often don't focus on the *Faragher* defense *in advance of* a problem arising.

In short, some employers *aren't listening*. Well, not on my watch. AHEM—NOW HEAR THIS, EMPLOYERS—WAKE UP AND LISTEN: *HERE'S WHAT YOU HAVE TO DO TO AVAIL YOURSELF OF THE FARAGHER DEFENSE*:

1. Create a Simple Policy Focusing on a Few Straightforward Items

As previously stated, the policy should be the easy part. However, some employers don't even have an anti-harassment policy. More commonly, employers create a seven-page policy that can hardly be read by a practicing lawyer. Keep it simple and focus on the key components.

First, the policy should be understandable to the common person. No legal terms—employees don't really need to know what "quid pro quo" means and they certainly don't care to hear about "vicarious liability" and "prima facie cases." Keep it simple—your 10-year old should be able to understand this policy.

Second, don't focus on the term "sexual harassment." As discussed in several chapters above and to follow, that term is full of legal nuance. Instead, build your policy around the concept of "inappropriate behavior" and "bad judgment." Those terms aren't restricted by legal definitions and court interpretation, yet they really are the essence of what an employer should be prohibiting. A good policy should essentially shout out this warning: **"Hey, don't be stupid—inappropriate behaviors and bad judgment in the area of personal interactions violate our culture and they could get you fired."**

Third, use "sexual harassment," "racial harassment," and the like as examples of inappropriate behavior. Examples are good for any common-sense policy, for example, "don't use sexual language, don't call people inappropriate names, don't send sexual or other inappropriate e-mails, don't spend time on sexual Internet sites, and don't tease people just because they are different from you."

Fourth, your policy should tell managers and everyone else not to involve themselves in inappropriate behavior and bad judgment. Everyone, and that means everyone, needs to hear that simple message.

Fifth, the policy needs to expressly state that action will be taken if inappropriate behavior occurs. How much discipline depends on the circumstances, as discussed in Chapter 16. Additional remedies also vary by the case, as noted in Chapter 16. However, the policy needs to explain that if inappropriate behavior occurs, action will be taken to remedy the problem.

Sixth, and this one is absolutely crucial to the *Faragher* defense—the policy should inform an employee who has been subjected to inappropriate behavior exactly what to do to solve the problem. That employee should know precisely where to turn, who to get help from, and what kind of help is available.

Seventh, as a direct corollary to the sixth point above—don't make an employee go to just one place to get help, and for certain don't make an employee stick to the "chain of command." Urge the employee to go to Human Resources for assistance, but also permit him or her to report concerns to other members of management at a certain level and above. You also can consider an 800 number, but remember that anonymous claims of harassment are exceptionally difficult to investigate.

Eighth, discuss the fact that an investigation normally will occur and that the complaint will be kept confidential, to the degree that is reasonably possible. If you want to briefly describe what "investigation" means, go ahead, but that probably isn't necessary. However, don't make the mistake of saying in your policy that complaints "will be kept confidential." That isn't likely to happen, through no fault of the employer. In short, once you start the investigation of a claim, people will chat even if you tell them not to chat. More about this issue in Chapter 14.

Ninth, use terms like "respect toward the individual" and/or "an appropriate workplace in which differences are respected." While these terms sound soft and a little new age to some, the intent of these terms is to stop inappropriate behavior (which, of course, is your true goal).

Tenth, don't use the term "zero tolerance." Granted, you want harassing behavior to never appear in your workplace, but "zero tolerance" confuses people. Some employees who have done very low-level inappropriate things have been fired due a manager's misunderstanding that "zero tolerance" means everyone must get discharged for a violation, no matter how insignificant a violation it is.

2. Train Workers Regarding the Policy and Your Expectations

Training is absolutely one of the essential components of a *Faragher*-compliant system. In fact, as of the date of publication of this book, three states

(California, Connecticut, and Maine) have passed laws requiring specific anti-harassment training. For now, understand that training *must* include telling managers *not* to harass anyone and must inform victims of harassment what to do to address their concerns. Some training is more effective than others in accomplishing these goals. Other training is of more use in creating a defense system. Unfortunately, the most effective training is not necessarily the best training for establishing a legal compliance defense. In any event, the topic of training, from state law requirements to choices, warrants its own chapter in this book, that is, Chapter 25.

3. If a Problem Arises, Respond on a Timely and Effective Basis

To utilize the *Faragher* defense, an employer must demonstrate that when a problem arises, it will respond on a timely basis and it will take action to solve the problem. The most common problems relate to focus and failure on a manager's part to understand the importance of a complaint about inappropriate behavior.

As for focus, a timely investigation of a harassment claim is crucial. Too often an investigation takes weeks, and that simply isn't justifiable in most cases. It's the rare situation that can't be investigated in two to three days. Focus on the concern and make it a priority. Otherwise, you'll see the *Faragher* defense slipping away. To make things easier for you, investigations and how to do them are addressed in their own part of this book, Chapter 14.

With respect to the failure of a particular manager to address harassment concerns on a timely basis, the deficiency sometimes isn't their fault. Victims of harassment often approach a manager with great trepidation. They are afraid to come forward although they very much want to do so. Consequently, they often begin their speech by saying "I don't really want to be here and I don't really want you to do anything, but I'm being picked on due to my sex." Unfortunately, some managers take that statement literally and don't do anything with the complaint. Such an approach leaves the employer in a hopeless position with respect to the *Faragher* defense (and the negligence standard

that applies to co-worker harassment). The reality is that 95% of the time, this complaining employee really does want something to be done, as soon as possible, but she is afraid of retaliation and concerned about her personal reputation. Managers need to help the employee get over such concerns, involve Human Resources, and deal with the issues on a timely basis.

4. Be Consistent

Through consistency, put yourself into a position where workers know what to do, know what *not* to do, know where to go to raise a concern, and know your expectations regarding behaviors at work.

For better or for worse, stuff happens in our world of sexual innuendo and sex-based marketing and entertainment. Even the best employers have to deal with inappropriate behavior issues. Further, as noted above, they have to deal with such issues quickly and effectively.

What often differentiates a good employer from one that is not so good is the culture that is created at the workplace. If an employer stresses a respect-based workplace, harassment is less likely to occur. Similarly, if an employer responds effectively to concerns that arise, employees will be less afraid to raise issues and potential harassers will be less likely to harass.

Employees should know the employer's expectations. Through training and effective response to concerns, workers should be aware of the rules and abide by them. That isn't to say that an effective employer has to be a tyrannical employer. Quite the contrary—the employer that is likely to best insulate itself from liability under *Faragher* is the progressive employer that creates a pleasant work culture while still maintaining a certain line against inappropriate behavior. You should work to be that employer. For further ways to help you do so, check out Chapter 28.

Private Eyes: Investigating Allegations of Harassment

There are few events as disruptive to the workplace as an internal investigation into a complaint of harassment. These investigations inevitably extend beyond the accuser and accused, and they usually cause quite a stir within a group of co-workers, a department, and sometimes the entire company. There really is nothing a company can do to keep onlookers completely oblivious to an ongoing investigation, but there are several steps that can be taken to minimize the "grapevine effect" and limit potential legal liabilities. This chapter will help companies conduct investigations, quite literally, by the book and avoid the common pitfalls that often lead to expensive settlements or unfavorable judgments. You will learn how to schedule and conduct investigations, select an investigator, identify and organize witness interviews, maintain the appropriate degree of confidentiality, and effectively summarize the results of the investigation.

What Is a "Complaint of Harassment" Anyway?

A "complaint" is any allegation that someone has treated someone else in an unwanted or inappropriate manner with respect to one of the protected categories identified in the other chapters (sex, race, age, religion, . . .). Further, by "someone" we don't just mean current employees. It really doesn't matter if the person complaining is a former employee, a customer, a supplier, or a vendor (as discussed in greater detail in Chapter 23). Likewise, the alleged harasser can be a former employee, a customer, a vendor, and so on. As long as the company has the ability to prevent the alleged harassment, the company could be held liable for failing to do so.

Do We Really Need to Investigate Every Complaint?

If someone makes a complaint of unlawful harassment, either directly or indirectly, the company has a duty to investigate. Sometimes we see an error made where a company doesn't investigate legitimate complaints based on the circumstances under which they arose. For example, an employee notifies the human resources director during her exit interview that her former supervisor asked her out on several occasions and generally made inappropriate comments that made her uncomfortable. No problem since the employee is leaving anyway, right? Wrong. The problem is that if any other employee has a similar problem with this supervisor in the future, the company may be directly liable because it failed to conduct a proper investigation the first time.

This scenario is a little trickier: the same terminated employee complains about the same supervisor, only this time the company conducts an investigation and finds no supporting evidence that any harassment occurred. A few months later, the former employee files an EEOC charge accusing the same supervisor *and* another co-worker of harassment. What are the company's obligations now? Even though it already conducted an investigation into the conduct of the accused supervisor, the employee has now provided new information that gives rise to an independent duty to investigate. The company should look into these new allegations and make another determination about their legitimacy. The results of the prior investigation can and should be considered, but do not allow the company to forego the second investigation.

Another mistake employers sometimes make is failing to take complaints seriously based on a preformulated opinion about the complaining party. Susie is always complaining about *everything* and, of course, she is in your office again. Whether humanly possible or not, the investigator should clear her head of any preconceptions—prior complaints are relevant but cannot form the basis for conclusions. Likewise, even problem children employees sometimes raise legitimate complaints. Always remember—even if it appears a complainant is acting in bad faith, the failure to conduct a thorough investigation could not only prevent the company from uncovering the bad faith but may actually strengthen the case of the disingenuous accuser.

Why Is It So Important to Investigate Every Complaint?

An organized, thorough, and professional investigation can often protect a company from liability risks, limit future wrongdoing, foster an atmosphere in which employees feel free to raise concerns, and promote an open and respectful company culture. Employees will understand that the company takes its nonharassment policy seriously and will take the remedial action necessary to maintain a work environment free from unlawful harassment. In addition, in many cases, an employer that engages in a prompt, appropriate investigation can avoid punitive damages and preserve certain affirmative defenses that it will be able to assert if the complaint is later litigated.

In a case called *Kolstad v. American Dental Association*, the Supreme Court explained that if an employer takes "good faith efforts" to comply with the law, it often can demonstrate that it "never acted in reckless disregard of federally protected rights." So what, you say? Well, that is the standard a plaintiff has to meet to establish punitive damages, and you should do all you can to avoid punitive damages.

The employer can go a long way to satisfying its good faith efforts and avoiding punitive damages by conducting a thorough investigation and taking any necessary action. Two key questions to ask internally when responding to a complaint are: "Was there anything we could have done to prevent the alleged harassment? And how can we keep it from happening again?" The company will be in a great position to eliminate punitive damages if there was no way for it to have known that the harassment was occurring and steps were quickly taken to stop the harassment once it was discovered. Carving out punitive damages is kind of like taking away a snake's fangs. You may still get bit but it is going to hurt a whole lot less. Punitive damages can total $300,000 under many federal discrimination statutes and are completely unlimited under certain race and state law discrimination claims.

As discussed in greater detail in Chapter 13, companies that conduct well-planned investigations also may be able to eliminate damages altogether in some situations. Typically, in the absence of a well-disseminated nonharassment policy and an effective procedure for reporting complaints, a company will be held directly or vicariously liable for the unlawful actions of its supervisors. In other words, if a supervisor sexually harasses an employee, that harassment will be automatically imputed to the company. However, in *Faragher* and *Ellerth*, the Supreme Court created an "affirmative defense" for certain types of harassment claims made against supervisors. The defense is available for "hostile work environment" claims where the alleged harassment does not result in a "tangible employment action" such as discharge, demotion, or undesirable reassignment. The theory is that the employer will not be bound by the harassment of a supervisor if it can show (1) that it exercised reasonable care to prevent and correct promptly any harassing behavior; and (2) that the plaintiff unreasonably failed to take advantage of the corrective opportunities provided by the employer. Employers can help preserve this defense by consistently and thoroughly investigating complaints of harassment.

Two recent cases illustrate the importance of conducting proper investigations. In *Scarberry v. ExxonMobil Oil Corp.*, a female employee filed a lawsuit alleging sexual harassment based on "demeaning graffiti" she found in her work area on two separate occasions. Within days after the employee complained about the graffiti, Exxon removed it, interviewed potential witnesses, and held several meetings to review the company's anti-harassment policy.

After the second incident of graffiti, Exxon heightened security by adding more guards, lights, and surveillance cameras. The Court dismissed the case and concluded that the company "demonstrated that it promptly investigated and took progressively more serious remedial action that not only ended the harassment by specific employees, but was also reasonably calculated to demonstrate to all employees that its policy against sexual harassment would be enforced." In contrast, the Court awarded punitive damages to the plaintiff in *EEOC v. Harbert-Yeargin, Inc.*, where the investigators of a complaint failed to seek out all potential witnesses, several employees and supervisors were unaware of the contents of the company's antidiscrimination policy, and the company "failed to exact any discipline for the offending conduct."

Who Should the Investigator Be?

Selecting the appropriate person to conduct an investigation into a harassment complaint is one of the most important decisions a company faces. The investigator should be neutral, experienced, open-minded, and detail-oriented. The person selected should be someone the company would feel comfortable putting on the witness stand. Thought must also be given as to who would be the most appropriate person given the particular aspects of the complaint. For example, if a female employee has complained of sexual harassment, she may be more willing to share the specifics of the complaint with a female investigator. Trained human resources personnel may be better investigators than operational managers who are unaccustomed to conducting investigations.

Train Your Investigators

Amazingly, a lot of people who investigate harassment cases have never been trained to do so. Even more amazingly, a lot of untrained investigators are decent investigators. However, train them anyway, using an interactive role-playing course. Plaintiffs' lawyers always ask investigators of harassment situations, "have you been trained to investigate these cases?" The answer must be "yes."

Harassment and Discrimination

In contrast to HR professionals, operational types are often results-oriented rather than process-oriented. Asking a manager to conduct an investigation is like having Dale Earnhardt, Jr. take you on a leisurely Sunday drive. Using managers as investigators may also open the company up to future retaliation claims, because management employees are often more involved with work-related decisions than human resources personnel. What if, for example, a district manager conducts an investigation and, six months down the line, is involved in the decision to transfer the complaining employee to a less favorable sales territory? The complaining employee may argue that the manager transferred him in retaliation for making the complaint. These types of claims are much easier to defend against if the manager is kept out of the loop during the investigation.

Another investigator option is your security or loss prevention manager. Such persons may have been police officers in a past life, and they can be effective in investigations. However, they aren't likely to know the law regarding sexual harassment. Worse yet, they aren't likely to be tactful, and even an inadvertent lack of sensitivity can make this type of situation worse instead of better. In general, go with the human resources option if you have one. If not, or if the situation is messy enough, consider bringing in a lawyer or a consultant to investigate. The cost is worthwhile in the right case.

If a complaint of harassment is litigated at a later point in time, the company's investigation file will almost always take center stage. This also means that the company's investigator will be a key witness. The results of an investigation and the investigators' conclusions are generally not privileged, because the company relied on them to make a decision regarding the validity of the complaint. That means that the complaining employee's lawyer will get to see how the company conducted its investigation, second-guess the investigator's decisions, and generally try to poke holes in the investigation process. With this landscape in mind, when feasible, the investigator should be accompanied by another person when conducting the interviews of the complainant, the accused, and any other key witness. This individual will take copious notes but usually should not ask questions so that the witness does not feel "double teamed." Just as with the interviewer, the accompanying per-

son should be a neutral personality who is outside of the witness's chain of command.

A final point on the role of the investigator. He or she should not make the ultimate decision with regard to whether any inappropriate conduct took place and, if so, what actions should be taken. Rather, the investigator should objectively and systematically gather and report the facts to whoever the decision maker will be. This is because the investigator could ultimately be a witness. It will be more difficult for the employee's lawyer to establish a bias if the investigator's only role was to report the facts. Likewise, the ultimate decision maker cannot be accused of manipulating the investigation in order to reach a particular result since he was simply relying on a factual summary provided by someone else. That said, for a smaller organization, these lines might cross, but try to maintain as much objectivity as possible in the investigation process.

What Steps Should Be Taken Before Conducting Interviews?

One of the most important factors courts consider when deciding if a company can rely on the defenses discussed above is whether the complaint was investigated on a timely basis. That said, you should come up with an investigation plan before taking any action. Consult with your employment lawyers to develop a thorough investigation plan that will withstand scrutiny from potential challenges by either the accuser or the accused in future litigation. When identifying preinvestigation steps that must be taken, the company's first action is to determine whether any risk exists that the complainant could continue to suffer from the alleged harassment. If so, the company must immediately take steps to cut off this possibility.

If the allegation is harassment by a supervisor, the company could place the supervisor on a paid leave of absence pending the outcome of the investigation, temporarily transfer the supervisor to a different department or assign him to a different shift, or take some other action that would eliminate the possibility that the supervisor and the complaining employee would come into contact. The action taken should focus on the accused rather than the complainant to avoid an additional claim of retaliation. If feasible, the best option is usually to put the supervisor on a paid leave to reduce chatter and prevent future interaction with the accuser. Under this scenario, notify the supervisor that the company received a complaint and will be conducting a full investigation, no decisions have been made at this juncture, he will have the opportunity to explain his side, and under no circumstances is he to contact any witness or the complaining party about the allegations or the investigation.

The accused, as with all witnesses, should be told that any communication with others will be deemed interference with an ongoing investigation that may result in independent grounds for termination. It is appropriate to provide the accused with general information about the nature of the complaint at this stage with the caveat that the company is still gathering information about the specific allegations. The company should also consider requesting that the accuser provide a detailed account of her complaint in writing. Unlike with other witnesses, it is very helpful to have the accuser put her complaint in her own words. That way, the accuracy and description of the complaint cannot be challenged in the future. The investigator should request the complainant to provide locations, names of witnesses, dates, times, and a detailed description of every action or event that she contends was inappropriate or unwanted. She should also identify the names of any other witnesses likely to have helpful information.

Once the written complaint is received, the investigator should follow up with the accuser and confirm that there are no additional facts, witnesses, or allegations that the company should consider. If any additional information does come to light, it should also be submitted in writing and added to the original complaint.

Some of the other preinvestigation steps an investigator should take are: (1) select the individual who will sit in interviews with the investigator; (2) identify and review the relevant policies and procedures; (3) pull and review the personnel files of the accuser and the accused (look for dates of employment, any prior discipline, handbook and anti-harassment policy acknowledgment forms, etc.); (4) identify any possible motive for the accused to make a bad faith complaint (i.e., recent discipline or poor performance); (5) identify any prior complaints levied against the accused or made by the accuser; (6) pull any previous investigation files for similar complaints and review the company's prior course of action; (7) identify all relevant witnesses and prepare a preliminary interview schedule; (8) identify a private office or other location where the interviews can take place; and (9) prepare a list of questions for each witness.

Electronic Evidence

If appropriate under the circumstances, pull and review e-mails and the Internet history of the complainant and the accused. Ensure that the employee handbook contains a disclosure and acknowledgement of the company's right to view an employee's e-mails and Internet usage.

Smart employers should keep a master log of all the steps taken to prepare for and conduct the investigation, as the company may need to rely on this log later to establish that the investigation was complete. In any event, once the investigator has an investigation plan in place, it will be time to start conducting interviews.

Who Should You Interview First and How Should the Interviews Be Conducted?

The investigator should generally explain to any witness what allegations are being investigated and why the witness is involved. Review the importance of providing truthful information, go over the company's anti-harassment policy with the witness, notify the witness that there will be no retaliation for participating in the investigation, and caution the witness that their discussion should not be shared with anyone else. Witnesses often ask the investigator not to tell anyone about what they have said for fear of getting someone else in trouble or causing problems with others. Explain that, while absolute confidentiality is not possible, information obtained during the interview will be reported only to those who have a business need to know.

During the interview, the interviewer or, better yet, the person accompanying her, should take detailed and thorough notes, indicating the name of the witness, date, time and location of the interview, who was present, the length of the interview, and the identity of the interviewer. Start with open-ended questions and eventually move to narrower, more focused questions. Always end with a catch-all question such as, "Is there anything else that could potentially relate to these allegations that you would like to share with me?"

The investigation notes can include a general assessment of the demeanor and general credibility of the witness. If the witness provides you with relevant information, ask if he or she is willing to provide a statement. If such a statement is appropriate, the interviewer or the note-taker should prepare the statement and review it with the witness. Some companies have witnesses write their own statements. That can work, but often the 45-minute interview that just occurred will be reduced by the employee to two short paragraphs.

The first person interviewed should normally be the complaining employee. If everything has gone according to the plan, the investigator will already have the accuser's statement as a guide for the interview. The purpose of the interview is to obtain any further information needed to flesh out the allegations and identify any additional witnesses who may shed light on the complaint. The alleged offender usually should be interviewed next to get the other side of the story, although there are times when third-party witnesses may best precede the interview of the alleged offender. When you get to the alleged offender, ask him first what happened in broad terms. However, don't hide the allegations from him. When appropriate, provide him with the full details of the complaint so you can get both his reaction and his full side of the story. In some cases, the interviewer should review the complainant's statement with the accused and ask him to respond to each factual allegation by way of an admission, a denial, or an explanation.

To the extent the accused denies the truthfulness of the complaint or a particular incident, ask him to identify possible motives or alternative explanations for the inconsistencies. Also request the identities of all witnesses who support the accused person's version of the events. Also ask the accused to submit a written statement responding to the complaint, summarizing his position, and identifying all witnesses who could corroborate his version of events. Finally, remind the accused that no decisions have been made and that you may need to speak with him again in the future. Instruct him not to contact the complainant, the witnesses, or anyone else in the workplace about the allegations.

Now that the investigator has heard both sides, it is time to frame the issues. Review the accusations of the complainant and responses of the accused and identify points of agreement and disagreement. It may be necessary to re-interview the complainant to discuss the accused person's version of events and obtain more clarity on the facts in dispute. Identify the names of any witnesses who may be able to help resolve the discrepancies for every fact that remains in dispute. In most cases, those are the interviews to conduct next. When conducting third-party interviews, identify the complainant and the accused, and state those facts alleged to be within the witness's knowledge. At the conclusion of the interview, the investigator should prepare a statement for the witness to review and sign. Understand that investigations often require the investigator to adjust and be willing to explore avenues that may not have been known during the planning stages. Feel free to revise or add to the investigation plan if necessitated by additional facts.

How Do You Conclude an Investigation?

Now that the investigator has reviewed all the background materials, familiarized herself with the company's previous treatment of others in similar situations, conducted all interviews, and gathered all witness statements, it is time to communicate the results of the investigation to the decision maker. Prepare a written, dated, and signed investigation report summarizing the allegations, factual findings, witness statements, and credibility determinations. The report is not likely to be privileged. In fact, it is probably the most important evidence created in the investigation. Among other things, the report should not contain legal conclusions such as "David sexually harassed Maggie." Instead, the report should identify the facts, "David admits to asking Maggie out on several occasions in violation of the company's fraternization policy."

You should usually have legal counsel review a draft of the investigation report prior to finalizing and signing.

Once the report is finalized, the investigator should meet with the decision maker and review the report. It is perfectly acceptable for the investigator to make a recommendation regarding the facts and the meaning of the facts to the decision maker if requested. However, the decision maker should make the ultimate determination as to the whether the accused engaged in any conduct in violation of company policy, and, if so, what level of discipline is appropriate. Remember, whatever action is taken must be reasonably calculated to end the harassment.

Once a decision is made, the investigation results should be communicated to the complainant and the accused, either by the investigator or the decision maker. Prepare a script for these meetings and have it reviewed with your lawyers to ensure that all statements are factually supportable and that no admissions are made that could injure the company's legal position. If disciplinary action is to be taken against the accused, meet with the accused first and communicate the results and the disciplinary action to be taken. Regardless of the action taken, stress that the accused must avoid any conduct that could be perceived as retaliatory. It is usually best to tell the complainant only that the investigation confirmed that the accused violated company policy and the company has taken appropriate disciplinary steps. Also tell the complainant to immediately report any efforts by the accused or anyone else to retaliate.

If no harassment is found, explain to the complainant that her allegations could not be corroborated, but that the company's policies have been reviewed with the accused. Encourage the complainant to immediately notify

---

Deal with Disappointment

Recognize that no matter what you decide as a result of your investigation, someone is going to be disappointed. Be prepared to deal with that disappointment. Don't just dismiss someone from your office if he or she needs to talk. Don't refuse to give someone feedback about why you decided what you did. Be tactful, however, especially if credibility determinations caused you to land in one place rather than another.

the company of any future conduct believed to be discriminatory or retaliatory so that it may be investigated. The investigator should also follow up with the complainant and the accused after the investigation to ensure no future harassment or retaliation occurs. "Building bridges" after the investigation is a topic discussed in detail in Chapter 18.

CHAPTER 15

Dealing with Witnesses, Credibility Issues, and Clarence, Anita, Bill, and Paula (the "He Said, She Said" Problem)

Asking a decision maker how much fun it is to make credibility determinations after an investigation is kind of like asking Mrs. Lincoln how she enjoyed the play. No one likes to be the one deciding who is telling the truth. The important thing to understand is that the courts give employers a great deal of latitude in making credibility assessments and expect them to do so. This chapter identifies helpful techniques that will help decision makers judge witness veracity in an objective way that satisfies the requirements of the law.

The Business Judgment Rule: You Don't Have to Be Right

Courts typically obey the "Business Judgment Rule" when reviewing the employment decisions of employers. The Business Judgment Rule is a fancy way of saying we will keep our nose out of your business decisions as long as they appear reasonable. Some judges have explained that the court will not act as a "super-personnel department" that re-examines the business decisions of employers. Other judges have explained that they would not substitute their "business judgment for that of the employer."

In an investigation context, the application of this rule provides decision makers with the flexibility to actually make decisions. Employers are not required to prove that the alleged harassment occurred in order to act. Rather, employers must simply present enough evidence to establish a good faith belief that the conclusions reached after an investigation were accurate. A California case called *Coltran* explains this standard.

In *Coltran*, the Supreme Court of California reversed the trial court's holding that the employer had to prove to the jury that the alleged acts of sexual harassment actually occurred in order to lawfully terminate the accused. The Court explained that the termination decision need only be a reasoned conclusion supported by the evidence gathered through an adequate investigation that included an opportunity for the accused employee to respond. In other words, the employer's burden is to establish that its decision was objectively reasonable. Since *Coltran*, many other courts have confirmed that an employer who fires an employee under the mistaken but honest impression that the employee violated a company policy is not liable for discriminatory conduct. Of course, the reverse is true as well. Employers are equally free to conclude that no unlawful discrimination occurred after an investigation and take no action against the accused. In these situations, it is essential that the accused and accuser be closely monitored to protect against any future harassment or retaliation.

What Is a Good Faith Belief?

Now that we know the general standard, how is it satisfied? Basically, courts will look at whether the actions taken at the conclusion of an investigation are objectively reasonable in light of the results of that investigation. As explained in the last chapter, part of this test is the sufficiency and thoroughness of the investigation. Another important factor is whether the employer's actions are consistent with past practice. This area is where we most often see employers get into some trouble.

Karen complains that her supervisor Jim has asked her out on multiple occasions, made inappropriate comments to her, and tried to kiss her a week ago at the holiday party. The company has a well-written policy regarding unlawful harassment and has consistently terminated other managers for similar misconduct. The investigation reveals that Jim likely did treat Karen inappropriately. The problem is that Jim is a great guy, loved by all, *and* one of the top salespersons in the company. The decision maker, deciding that Jim is simply too valuable to lose, gives him a verbal warning and tells him he "needs to knock off the stupid behavior." Can the company justify its decision as a reasonable one based on Jim's value in other areas?

Usually not. The courts do not like to factor an employee's relative worth into the reasonableness equation, although some companies have been successful arguing the contrary. Preferably, the inquiry is more narrow and does not include factors like those used to describe Jim. The key question is whether the employer's investigation established that it was reasonably likely that the alleged discrimination or harassment actually happened. If so, the Court will expect the employer to take whatever actions are necessary to ensure the misconduct will never happen again. In making the determination as to whether the employer's remedial actions were sufficient, consideration will be given to the company's treatment of similarly situated employees. If past remedial measures effectively stopped the misconduct, the company will typically be expected to act in a similar fashion.

This does not suggest that employers must treat the accused in the same manner each time it verifies the legitimacy of a complaint. An employee found to have used inappropriate language around a co-worker after his computer ate his year-end report is not similarly situated to an employee who groped his co-worker. Likewise, an employee with 20 years of service is not similarly situated to someone with the company for 6 months. Although the accused individual's value to the company should not be the key factor in crafting appropriate remedial measures, past contributions may be considered and the punishment should fit the crime.

Termination Alternatives

As we discuss in Chapter 16, the correct response to misconduct is not always to fire the employee. The severity of the misconduct and the factual circumstances must be considered. Employers walk the razor's edge and can be held liable for being too heavy-handed just as easily as for not acting at all. If other effective means exist to prevent future harassment short of termination, those options should be carefully considered.

You Can't Assess Credibility If You Aren't There

Some employers prefer to save time and money by conducting witness interviews over the phone or via e-mailed questionnaires. While sometimes that approach cannot be avoided, remote investigations are far less effective than those conducted in person. It is difficult to imagine a more effective means of assessing witness credibility than to have the opportunity to sit down face to face with them and look them in the eye when asking questions. Behavioral scientists have created an entire body of work regarding the common mannerisms and physical gesticulations demonstrated by those who lie. We are all generally familiar these tendencies: (1) the inability or unwillingness to maintain eye contact, (2) unjustified defensiveness and anger when asked innocuous questions, (3) shiftiness and discomfort, and (4) excessive sweating and fidgeting. It is not necessary to be an expert to pick up on these signs.

Indeed, lawyers often videotape witness depositions to capture the tell-tale characteristics of an untruthful witness for the eyes of the jury. Just as Jack Bauer would not interrogate a suspected terrorist over the phone, we understand that it is often more important for the jury to see the actions of a witness than to hear his words.

Another good reason to conduct in-person interviews is the message it sends to the company's other employees and, if the issue is litigated, to the court. By conducting an in-person investigation, the company establishes its commitment to its policy for preventing unlawful harassment and its desire to eradicate any form of that harassment. A complaining employee would be hard pressed to argue that a company is not serious about compliance when it requires an investigator to drop everything and get on a plane to conduct interviews mere days after receiving the complaint.

Corroborate When Possible

Witness credibility should be independently assessed through objective evidence whenever possible. There are usually opportunities to corroborate or controvert the stories told by the complaining employee and the accused. Were there any witnesses who observed the misconduct? Are there any documents that would tend to prove or disprove the allegations? One good example of an actual company investigation that effectively ferreted out the truth involved an attractive young woman who complained that her supervisor had come on to her at a company appreciation party held at a large bar. Specifically, the employee complained that, while she was dancing, her supervisor approached her and started to "dirty dance" with her on the dance floor. She claimed to feel uncomfortable but admitted to dancing with him because he was her boss. However, she explained that after a few minutes of dancing, the supervisor became increasingly aggressive and began to grope her in a manner that made her extremely uncomfortable. At this point, she pushed away from him and returned to the bar area.

No interviewed employee witnessed the alleged dancing. However, several witnesses confirmed that the accused supervisor was playing pool most of the evening and was always with at least one other person. Other witnesses saw the complaining employee taking several shots of alcohol, stumbling, and appearing generally inebriated. The investigator also noted that the receipt submitted by the complainant for reimbursement had over $100 of purchased alcoholic drinks. The investigator concluded that, while someone may have been dancing with the complaining employee, it was apparently not her supervisor.

While the above corroborating evidence was fairly easy to discover, there are often other less obvious ways to fact-check someone's story. For example, if Karen says Jim was calling her but Jim says Karen initiated the calls, ask to look at their cell phone bills. Also, if the harasser denies being at a certain place at a certain time, see if there is anyone who can vouch for his whereabouts. Standing alone, none of these steps establish whether any misconduct actually occurred, but they will prove helpful in making and defending a decision.

Consider Motives

Another important factor to consider when assessing the credibility of a witness is motive. Does the witness have any reason to make something up? Does the complaining party have any performance issues? Does the alleged harasser have any history of misconduct? The investigator should also explore possible motives of third-party witnesses. Are any of the witnesses friendly with the complaining party or the accused? Does any witness have something to gain if either party's employment is terminated? Sometimes employees band together and exaggerate or mischaracterize the actions of a boss they just don't like. On other occasions, an employee may lie to protect a friend. These possibilities and interrelationships must be considered and addressed to objectively measure the results of an investigation.

Recording Credibility Observations

Just as with other investigation notes, documentation of a witness's credibility should be described objectively and carefully considered. Credibility assessments are best recorded at the end of the section of the investigative report addressing that particular witness. Instead of simply concluding that a witness lied, however, the investigator should identify the conduct observed to support such a conclusion. For example, an effective credibility transcription may state, "Randy appeared nervous during his interview. He frequently shifted in his chair and repeatedly asked if he was 'done yet.' Randy became defensive when asked about whether he had stopped by Ginger's house and stated 'it's none of your business.' Randy also contradicted himself on several occasions. These facts cause me to question Randy's credibility."

In the Case of a Draw

What if the investigator has conducted all interviews and reviewed all relevant documents and still cannot assess what actually happened? This is the "he said, she said" scenario in its truest sense. The potential liability for allowing misconduct to go unaddressed places extreme pressure on companies to discipline or terminate the accused even in the absence of evidence. However, taking an adverse action against the accused employee without any evidence to support the alleged wrongdoing can be just as dangerous. It is not wise to take action against an accused employee when discipline is not warranted by the facts. Instead, the investigator should review the company's policies with the accused and the accuser and follow up frequently with both to confirm the problems have been resolved.

If, however, the accused and the complaining employee's positions are so diametrically opposed that it does not make sense for the two to continue to work together, other alternatives should be considered. Look for alternative arrangements that would not constitute discipline and that would be acceptable to the parties. For example, the accuser may feel more comfortable reporting to a different manager. Likewise, the manager may be willing to transfer to a different office. These types of arrangements, discussed more in the next chapter, help to prevent future problems when the investigation does not resolve the underlying complaint.

Discovering Other Misconduct

Oftentimes, even when the actual complaint is not verified, some form of misconduct or violation of company policy is uncovered in an investigation. For example, assume the investigator found no evidence of sex discrimination but did conclude that the accused used inappropriate language in the workplace. In these circumstances, the accused may be subject to a disciplinary action short of termination for "the lesser offense."

Disciplining Witnesses Who Provided False Information

Investigations sometimes uncover evidence establishing one or more of the witnesses provided false information or otherwise interfered with the investigation. Also, during interviews, each witness should be told not to discuss the details of their interviews or the ongoing investigation with anyone. The complaining party and the accused should also be warned not to contact any witnesses about the investigation. Nonetheless, sometimes the accuser or accused will contact witnesses to "poison the well" or get updates on the investigation. This type of misconduct constitutes independent grounds for discipline and should not be tolerated. Likewise, any employee demonstrably providing false information should be seriously disciplined. Such discipline will preserve the integrity of the investigation process and establish its importance to all employees.

CHAPTER 16

After the Investigation: Do We Fire All the Harassers?

OK, we have now conducted an investigation and we have managed to work our way through various misstatements, complications, exaggerations, denials, and maybe even a lie or two. We also made whatever credible determinations we had to make. We've even written all that down in a nice document that discusses the investigation, our findings, and our determination that inappropriate behavior did or did not occur. Are we done?

Of course not. In fact, everything you have done so far is just a preliminary to the big event. It's time now to figure out how to remedy this whole mess.

Here's Your Legal Obligation—and Don't Forget It

The law on sexual and other forms of harassment is simple in one way—if something bad occurs, you have to fix it. Stated differently, whatever action you take must make the problem go away. Anything less is not enough—the remedy *must end the problem that has occurred.*

So does that mean you have to fire all the harassers? No, of course not. In fact, the law does not establish any kind of specific remedy. What to do is left up to you. You're free to fire people where appropriate, to do less where legitimate, and to craft some extremely creative remedies if they will solve the problem. Theoretically, you could make a harasser sit in a corner wearing a dunce cap under a sign that says "I am a foolish man," if that prevents the occurrence of further sexual harassment. However, while such an approach might be effective, it also will get you time on the Internet and that would likely be a bad thing.

Some Obvious Watch-Outs and Some That Aren't

Let's discuss the obvious watch-outs first. If the sexual harassment is pretty bad, a "coaching session" isn't likely to make much of an impact. Similarly, if the sexual harassment was relatively minor, you don't need to go overboard on the remedy. In Chapter 9, we discussed the infamous Miller Brewing Company "Seinfeld" case. As you may recall, the company was hit with a $24.4 million verdict for firing a manager with 15 years experience and virtually no record of discipline who had been involved in fairly minor sexual harassment. The jury was incensed with the over-reaction (or they were big fans of the Seinfeld show).

In short, the law is: don't go too far or fail to go far enough. Remember that.

Tying the Remedy to the Level of Inappropriateness of the Behavior

As we also discussed in Chapter 9, no one is really all that clear on what severe or pervasive means. We can agree, however, that there are gradations of inappropriate behavior. Use those gradations as well as repeat violation standards to gauge the level of discipline that is appropriate to whatever situation you're facing.

"Zero Tolerance"

The term "zero tolerance" has found its way into the employment arena in areas other than harassment. Additional popular contexts are drugs, violence, and even rudeness (e.g., the recently popular "no assholes" rule). The use of the "zero tolerance" term in these contexts might send an effective message to abusers of various company expectations, but it also tends to confuse not just managers, but judges and juries as well. Don't set yourself up—you may say you have zero tolerance for rude supervisors, but there is no way that you'll be able to enforce such an expectation.

Here's an illustration that may or may not help you. It evaluates the level of inappropriateness and uses that to both consider potential liability and the correct discipline to be taken. The illustration is explained immediately following its depiction.

Discharge is usually appropriate for conduct above the line used by the law to define unlawful sexual harassment.

This is the line of Severe and Pervasive Conduct

As employee behavior gets closer to the line of severe or pervasiveness, discharge becomes more likely.

Between the lines of political correctness and pervasiveness are various types of inappropriate behavior that need to be addressed through counseling and warnings.

This is the line of Political Correctness

Low-level behaviors = coaching opportunities

Let's discuss what the above illustration is intended to show. The key line is "the line of severe and pervasive conduct." That's the line where the courts differentiate between what is and what is not "unlawful" harassment. Much of what occurs below that line may be boorish, but the behavior hasn't risen to the level of illegality.

The reason the severe and pervasive line is so crucial is that the employer wants to ensure that its employees and managers never cross that line. To keep such a disaster from happening, the employer needs to define its own limits of acceptable behavior as less than what the courts define as harassment (which, again, is why your policy should use the term "inappropriate behavior" rather than "sexual harassment" as the fundamental concern being addressed). In addition, the employer needs to discipline those who are guilty of inappropriate behavior before they cross the line of unlawful harassment, so that behaviors at the workplace don't rise to the level of unlawful activity.

As can be seen in the chart, discipline also certainly occurs below the line of severe and pervasive behavior. Such discipline can take many forms, but the most common is a mixture of a firm written warning (perhaps framed as a "final warning") followed by training. However, the closer the bad behavior gets to the legal line, the more likely discharge will occur. That is in part because "severe or pervasive" behavior really is completely unjustified in the workplace, and behavior that rises to anything close to that level may constitute a terminable offense. In addition, because the legal line of severe and pervasiveness is uncertain and may change from court to court, the employer may best read the line to be a little lower than it is simply to avoid the risk of liability.

Certainly behavior that is above the legal line of harassment leads to discharge in virtually all cases. In most instances, in fact, employers don't allow pervasive behavior to go on long enough to even get above the line. However, a one- or two-shot situation that is severe could immediately cross the line before the employer ever knew what happened. This could be, for instance, a sexual assault or a quid pro quo situation. Fortunately, discharge usually follows such stupidity.

To the converse, some "inappropriate behavior" is of a very low level. That is why the line of political correctness is included at the bottom of the illustration. Let's discuss a few examples, after defining the term "political correctness." What does political correctness mean? As generally understood, it means never saying anything insensitive to anybody about anything. Good luck on that. That line is a pretty low one and people can cross it inadvertently without really meaning to do anything bad.

Do you know Cathy Jones? Cathy is a sweetheart of an employee from Alabama. All her life she has called everyone she meets "honey." One day, a co-worker reports Cathy to human resources for using the term "honey" in addressing him. Good Lord, is that sexual harassment? No, it's instead an overly sensitive co-worker complaining about Cathy's lack of political correctness.

Other forms of political correctness arise through a single joke being told, a loose comment about the opposite sex, or a relatively inconsequential statement that is inappropriate but not directed at the individual who reports it. So what do you do about such low-level behavior? As the graph says, coaching is appropriate for that level of problem.

When it comes to political correctness, most people, with appropriate coaching, still may not agree with the complaint made against them. Cathy, for example, will never get why she shouldn't call people "honey," especially since she's been saying that to men and women alike all her life. Just picture her response to your coaching: "But, honey, what's wrong with calling people honey?" However, people like Cathy are likely to acquiesce in the coaching just to avoid a future problem.

By the way, it is the line of political correctness that makes the concept of "zero tolerance" so awkward, as discussed in Chapter 9. If everyone gets fired

---

"Watch It, Honey"

So does that mean it's ok to call everyone "honey?" If you truly call everyone "honey," it's ok (it also probably means you're a woman, not a man). If you limit your use of "honey" to the opposite sex, things get a little more complicated. If you use that term for only some members of the opposite sex and those folks are co-workers, you're heading down the wrong road. If you insist on pawing those co-workers as you call them "honey," you're an idiot. On the other hand, if the "honey" in question is your spouse, go for it.

under the terms of a zero tolerance policy, poor Cathy gets fired too. How fair is that? So remember the Seinfeld case and don't overreact. If you insist on using the term "zero tolerance," realize what it is you're really saying, i.e., "we don't put up with inappropriate behavior around here." But also remember that's different from saying "we fire everyone who says or does something inappropriate."

Make Sure the Remedy Is Both Disciplinary and Proactive

Hopefully at this point you understand why the remedy must be disciplinary in nature and how extensive the discipline should be relative to the behavior. Unfortunately, that doesn't end the analysis. To truly ensure that one "has taken reasonable steps" to end the harassment, one must think about proactive remedies as well. Otherwise, the job is only half finished.

The proactive side of the remedy analysis has nothing to do with discipline. Instead, its focus is on taking steps to ensure that what occurred is less likely to reoccur even if the discipline doesn't automatically sink into what can sometimes be some fairly hard heads. Possibilities include additional training, separating the individuals involved in the situation, and facilitating a proactive discussion if the alleged harassment was caused by a legitimate misunderstanding.

Here are some possible proactive remedies. They won't all be used in a particular set of circumstances. Sometimes one such remedy is enough. This set of remedies, by the way, is hardly inclusive. Creative approaches make a lot of sense in some circumstances.

1. Training

The concept of training to avoid harassment and discrimination is important enough to warrant its own chapter in this book. However, Chapter 25 is oriented more to compliance with legal requirements and the effectiveness of various training options. The purpose of also addressing training in this remedy chapter is to underscore the fact that if something bad happened, more

training may be required. Again, however, don't over-react. If a massive new anti-harassment training initiative is implemented within five days after Jenny reported Barney for harassment, everyone will know that the training is really about Barney and Jenny.

That aside, at some point after a harassment situation is remedied, some type of training may make sense. In some cases, the training may be limited to a one-on-one discussion with the person who acted inappropriately. That can be true particularly for managers and executives, as further discussed in Chapter 17. In other cases, the training might be done informally or formally in a department or a work group, particularly if the behavior involved a meaningful number of people. Finally, if a harassment situation suggests that the company's policy and procedures simply aren't clear enough or well enough known, the training may have to be employer-wide in order to avoid further issues.

2. Separation of the Individuals Involved

Chapter 18 of this book addresses the after-remedy, clean-up, and building of bridges process. It includes a discussion of why separating a harassing manager from an employee victim may make a lot of sense. Separation can occur in co-worker situations as well. Sometimes the best thing to do is to move the involved individuals away from each other. That move may limit the possibility of further sparks going off.

Be cautious, however, that you don't always transfer the victim. Look at that scenario from her eyes—"Wait, I had to put up with this harassment, I had to come to HR for help, and now you're moving me to a different job? Why the heck don't you move the jackass who did it instead?" Indeed, she may have a point. On the other hand, sometimes the victim wants a new start and would welcome a move. Talk with her (or him) and then evaluate your options. Also, realize that a transfer is not legally required, but it may make sense in a number of cases.

3. Facilitation of a Discussion to Resolve a Misunderstanding

Some sexual harassment situations have nothing to do with bad behavior. The problem may arise from the break-up of a dating relationship or a misinterpretation of a friendship. Occasionally what one person thinks is consensual flirting, the other party feels is one step over the line. Firing someone in these circumstances can easily be seen as unfair or over-reactive. Occasionally even formal discipline may be a bit strong, although it would be a mistake on the employer's part not to take some action even in a misinterpretation situation. Taking no action could later be alleged to constitute a failure to remedy the issue.

In appropriate circumstances, a memo reminding the accused employee of the company's policy may be enough discipline. In the lightest of circumstances, some employers put that memo in an investigative file rather than the employee's personnel file, so as to keep the employee from being branded a sexual harasser for the remainder of his or her career. In addition, an employer might consider bringing the two individuals together to facilitate a discussion intended to settle down the situation. Granted, this kind of facilitation would be considered by some employers as too touchy-feely, and in some circumstances the employer is indeed better off *not* playing amateur counselor. In other circumstances, however, a soft touch might facilitate a solution to a co-employee friendship gone wrong due to the most innocent of circumstances.

4. Re-Establishing the Rules and the Policy

In some instances, the inappropriate behavior can be pervasive but not intentionally harassing, such as where an entire work crew is discussing sex and playing flirty games. When management finally becomes aware of such circumstances, it must do something even if all the behavior truly was consensual. In these circumstances, the employer is highly unlikely to fire everyone in the department. In fact, it might even seem odd to give every employee a formal written warning. However, the employer has to do something to protect itself legally.

On occasion, the best remedy is to more or less start over by reestablishing the rules. Perhaps a new policy is published, with everyone signing off that they will comply. In addition, the retraining discussed above may be appropriate in these circumstances. Employees should specifically be told that if their behavior does not change, formal discipline will follow (assuming no discipline or only a policy reminder has been issued so far). Again, do not "do nothing."

However, a proactive approach may be healthier than formally warning everyone, thereby throwing the entire department into a morale funk.

5. Giving Someone a "Decision Day"

Too often employers discipline someone but they fail to get the individual to realize why there is a problem. Sometimes the best action in sexual harassment cases (or, indeed, in other situations involving performance and conduct issues) is to make the individual be part of the solution. Some employers use something called a "decision day" to move the issue forward. The employee is given a paid day off with only one task to accomplish—prepare a reasonable-length memo that discusses what the employee is going to do to change the situation.

In the best of cases, the employee is forced to address the issue. In the worst of cases, the employee refuses to prepare a memo, which typically leads to discharge, since it is now obvious that the employee is unwilling to accept that there is a problem (and therefore he or she is very unlikely to change his or her behavior). In most instances, the employee writes a memo that acknowledges some responsibility but also includes a statement that the situation is not entirely the employee's fault. That response isn't ideal, but it may be a starting point for an additional discussion. At a minimum, it brings the employee into the picture as something more than just the recipient of a formal written warning.

Part of the Solution

Perhaps the name "decision day" isn't the best terminology for what is a sincere and serious step in the discipline process. Among other things, employees will end up calling these scenarios "D-days." If you want to go with alternative names, that's fine. You may not even need a name for the concept. Just say that "we really want you to help be part of the solution here, and this is how we want to start that process."

---

6. Setting Up a Personalized Way to Raise Further Concerns

One final thought, for use in difficult cases where ramifications are likely to last a while after the investigation. Counsel the victim very specifically on what he or she is going to do if anything else happens. Give that person a particular point of contact or two (and take a look at the follow-up 1-3-5-3 rule discussed near the end of Chapter 18.

Cases where this approach is effective could involve a harassment claim against a group of co-workers, a rough environment (say, a mine or a steel mill), or even a claim made against a high-level and fairly powerful executive. Hopefully your remedy is such that nothing further is going to occur. However, knowing that these matters take time to go away, giving the victim a special way to seek assistance could be helpful.

Don't Be Afraid to Be Creative in Your Remedies

The above ideas for proactive remedies should help, but don't be afraid to craft your own solutions. Remember you do have latitude under the law, but the remedy has to be reasonably calculated to stop the harassment. Remember as well that if you get too cute, you might negatively affect morale or get your company on the Internet.

Creativity is even more significant as the behavioral problems affect higher-level employees. For that reason, those persons have been given their own section in this book—the next chapter, Chapter 17.

Be Results-Oriented in Your Thinking—Sometimes Discharge Is Appropriate Even If the Behavior Wasn't Over the Top

Finally, you should realize that some situations are so difficult to remedy that it may not be worth trying. Let's take an example. It involves Juanita and Carlton, supervisor and subordinate respectively, who for six months have been involved in a secret but very heavy-duty relationship. Carlton, however, has tired of hiding their involvement and has now started dating someone from outside the workplace. Juanita is furious and has started sticking Carlton with the worst assignments and has threatened to fire him if he doesn't "get his act together."

Carlton finally comes to management to seek help. After investigating, it becomes clear that Juanita is punishing Carlton not for bad performance but for the break-up of the relationship. Juanita and Carlton have both been good performers and Juanita is incredibly apologetic and says she now understands and nothing bad will happen again. The problem, however, is that Juanita and Carlton are IT workers in a five-person group and there is nowhere to transfer either of them. So, given these bad facts, what is the proper remedy?

In all likelihood, someone has to go. That may not be fair, but given the small work group and no other options, the safer bet for the employer is a discharge. However, to add some creativity, the employer in question decides to offer Juanita a three-month severance package, which fortunately she accepts. Is this a gutless employer paying its way out of a problem? No, in fact, it's a pragmatic employer that realizes that the chances of this five-person group getting back to normal is unlikely any time soon. Better yet, the employer used the severance option to resolve the problem. But what if Juanita had turned down the package? The employer then would have to make a harder decision, but if it fired Juanita, it would be doing that for a legitimate business reason and it should prevail in any case that follows.

Sometimes being results-oriented is smart, but don't be too Machiavellian either. There often are ways to work things out, but sometimes there are not. Look at all the circumstances and don't be afraid to think outside the box. And get help if you need it—good employment lawyers are good business people too—call one of them if things get sticky and you need some creative ideas.

"Sensitivity School" for Those Who "Don't Get It"

A common conception is that sexual harassment is caused primarily by the thick-headed Neanderthal male who is a factory worker or perhaps a salesman. Certainly sexual harassment occurs in many environments, including manufacturing and sales. However, some of the messiest and most complicated harassment cases arise from the actions of high-level managers, many of whom simply seem not to "get it."

Why Is This So—Aren't These Smart People?

High-level managers are, in fact, intelligent human beings. The operative words in this last sentence, however, may be "human beings" rather than "intelligent." As we have said on a number of occasions, sex issues often arise simply from people being people. Was Evangelist Jim Baker really having an affair because he wanted to undermine his own religious position, or was he just a person making a sexually oriented human mistake? Did Bill Clinton intend to discredit the presidency through his fling with Monica Lewinsky, or was he just a person making a human error?

When religious and governmental leaders fall prey to sexual encounters and sexually oriented mistakes, your managers may end up doing the same. Stuff happens, and there may not be much you can do about it. Remember that according to a recent poll, 12% of managers have had sexual trysts with subordinates. Are these renegade supervisors, or did hormones just overcome logic?

Renegades

If you truly have a renegade supervisor who will never get it, you might be able to skip this chapter. True renegades are rare, but if they exist, you need to find a way to get rid of them. Cases involving serial sexual harassers are very risky.

In What Ways Don't Highly Placed People Get It?

Sexual harassment situations of all kinds can occur in regard to high-level leaders and executives. Most often, however, the problem is either a sexual affair with an underling (often five or six levels lower in the organization) or the manager has a dirty mouth and is a bully. Sexual affairs may occur because of the allure of the high-level leader—some people seem attracted to such an executive. As for bullying and inappropriate language, there are particular industries that seem more likely to create such a persona.

In the past, manufacturing might be the place for someone with a dirty mouth. Concerns are now more likely to arise, however, in other areas. Prime examples are financial companies, law firms, doctors, and elected officials. In some cases, egos appear to be part of the problem. Some high-level executives, including lawyers, seem to think that they're above the law. Fortunately, it would be absolutely incorrect to say that the average lawyer, doctor, or stockbroker is a bully or can't control his or her mouth. However, things happen in these industries and others.

So Let's Fire the Idiots and Be Done with It

As time moves on and employers become more sensitive to sexual harassment problems, organizations seem more willing to fire higher-level leaders for their sexual exploits and bullying. However, that doesn't always happen, and sometimes for understandable reasons. Some of the leaders who are guilty of errors in sexual judgment can be very difficult to replace. In the case of a law partner or a financial analyst, such persons may be responsible for bringing in millions of dollars per year into their businesses. Firing them could create a financial disaster.

Given these difficult circumstances, firing most often occurs if the employer has taken a hard position on harassment problems or simply feels that the leader can no longer be effective in his or her position. Discharge also may occur if the news of the sexual situation hits the press. Once public pressure or bad press builds, a discharge may be the only appropriate response, even if that does mean a loss of leadership or income. Surprisingly, however, many of these situations don't get out in the public. They are dealt with quietly instead.

No Comment

If a sexual harassment case involving a high-level person gets into the press, you need to be responsive. "No comment" is a really bad response, because everyone assumes it means you're guilty. Also, don't present the alleged wrongdoer in a public interview unless there are no alternatives. If you do and he says something stupid, your case just got worse. Instead, offer someone to the press who is friendly, effective, sincere, and knows when to quit talking.

Dealing with These Things Quietly Sounds Suspicious and Even a Little Slimy

Is it wrong to try to keep these types of problems quiet? Not really. No employer wants bad publicity, particularly among senior leadership. Further, there is no law requiring that people be fired for making mistakes that relate to sexual harassment. Remember the test—the employer must take reasonable steps to stop the harassment. Such steps can include discharge in appropriate cases, but discharge is not required if there are other means to stop the harassment.

Expensive Settlements

To be candid, cases involving high-level people usually settle, and often at a cost that is greater than the case's worth. Publicity can outweigh the merits or lack of merits in a case.

Given these circumstances and the employer's possible goal of retaining the manager/executive/lawyer/stockbroker who overstepped his bounds, what is the best course of action? Certainly some type of discipline is appropriate. For persons at this level, financial implications often work better than formal discipline. In many cases, the employer may decide to withhold a bonus or not grant a stock option. Such a penalty in some instances can be in the six figures. To be frank, this usually wakes up the manager who doesn't get it. At a minimum, even if the manager still doesn't "get it," a financial penalty might make him not do anything bad in the future whether he agrees with the situation or not.

How to Make Someone "Get It"

Perhaps some high-level executives have such a large ego that they can't accept that the world isn't solely about them. In most instances, however, education has an impact. But that education can't simply be about appropriate behavior. What works best for higher-level managers is a discussion of business risk and business interests.

In many cases, high-level managers who have chosen to have an affair with the receptionist or who insist on bullying their subordinates are best sent to "sensitivity school." Obviously, however, there is no such institute of higher learning. Instead, there are lawyers and consultants who are capable of making a difference in terms of convincing these managers to change their behaviors.

"Sensitivity Training" Can Take Many Forms and It Can Be Effective

With respect to what sensitivity training is the most effective, the answer may well depend on the executive. In general, and at the risk of sounding a bit sexist, men seem to deal better with male trainers and women appear to relate better to female trainers. However, for some executives, an encounter with a trainer of the opposite sex can turn on some light bulbs.

As to the particular background of the trainer, strategies again vary greatly. Lawyers can be effective because they describe the risk to the business, the potential cost to the executive, and the nature of litigation. Human resources consultants can do similar things, but business executives are more likely to respect lawyers than consultants. The same may not be true, however, for governmental leaders and politicians. Some employers have instead chosen psychologists for sensitivity training. That approach can be effective for the right person, but, in general, the psychological approach tends to be more inward-looking than focused on risk.

Pick Your Lawyer Carefully

If you use a lawyer as your outside counselor, pick carefully. Hard-core litigators may not be your best bet. Employment lawyers are usually more personable, used to training, and knowledgeable about the specific law in question.

As to what is said to a problem-child leader, executive, or heavy hitter, the straightforward business approach seems to work well. That approach focuses on the law, the risk to the business, and the cost to the associate. Here is an example of the message to be presented to the executive or leader:

Look you idiot [by the way, the two preceding words are to be thought rather than said], it doesn't take much for someone to sue an employer—the average filing in the United States is about $250. And plaintiffs' lawyers love suing a high-level person like you. They believe you'll settle for meaningful dollars just to avoid the publicity. Worse yet, if you're found guilty of sexual harassment, the company is pretty much automatically guilty as well. To make matters worse, in many instances, you can be sued personally. Imagine telling your spouse that you just got sued for sexual harassment and you need to put your homeowners' insurance company on notice. Also, picture the publicity. If this gets in the news, no one really cares if you're guilty or innocent. All they'll remember is that you got named in a sexual harassment case.

Think of it this way—you're a good looking guy who makes good money. In some ways, you may even have a target on your back. I'm not saying that someone is out to get you. But if you hit on the wrong person, or if you get sexually involved with someone at work and it falls apart, you're unbelievably vulnerable to litigation. Be smart. Don't open yourself up to the risk just because you said the wrong thing to the wrong worker or because you felt compelled to have sex with the receptionist.

Does this speech work on most executives and leaders who have stepped over the line? Yes, at least to a degree. Further, even if it doesn't work, the employer gets credit for taking steps to stop any further harassment. Beyond the financial penalty discussed above, sensitivity school in and of itself is a "reasonable step" to prevent further sexual harassment. In that regard, the trainer should write a report about the training and the executive or leader should sign a statement that he or she attended the training, had the chance to ask questions, and understood what he or she was told.

Can Higher-Level Executives Be Targets for Sexual Harassment Situations?

In the speech above, there is a comment about the executive or leader being a target. Is that true? Well, at least in a sense, the answer is "yes."

In general, there have been a very small percentage of cases where allegations were totally fabricated simply to extort money or seek liability against a high-level executive or leader. However, when that executive or leader does something questionable, the chances of litigation go up dramatically, even if the questionable behavior was not exceptionally bad. At that point, the executive or leader has opened the door to allegations of harassment, and there definitely are some people who would jump through that door. That includes situations of the affair gone bad (does anyone remember *Fatal Attraction*?) and the sexual offer rejected but then reframed in court as an alleged statement of quid pro quo harassment.

There's Always a Way

Also remember what was said earlier in this book. Not all states permit individuals to be sued for sexual harassment, but there is always some claim that can be made to get someone into court.

More awkwardly, a top-level executive or leader can be attractive to well-intended members of the opposite sex. Psychologists say that power can be sexy, and that seems to sometimes be the case. But if the attraction leads to a broken affair, a claim of harassment is highly likely to follow. Worse yet, plaintiffs' lawyers will tell you that they love these types of cases—the allegations are juicy, the executive always looks like he took advantage of the subordinate, and the avoidance of publicity in and of itself carries a price.

Fortunately, most executives and leaders are good people who would not step into these traps. However, once again, high-level leaders are people too, and they make mistakes. If so, and if the leader needs to be retained by the employer, monetary discipline and sensitivity school are both good ideas. But if the same leader makes the same or a similar mistake a second time, there is probably no alternative other than discharge. A "serial sexual harasser" case is nearly impossible to defend, as the law firm Baker Hostettler learned in light of a jury verdict of $7.5 million in such a case a number of years ago.

CHAPTER 18

Dealing with the After-Effects: Building Bridges, Appropriate Documentation, and Closing the Loop

Assume for a minute the following set of circumstances: Sandra, an hourly production worker, has come to the company's human resources professional and raised a concern of sexual and racial harassment. The alleged bad guys are three hourly co-workers. There was no reason for the company to have been aware of the alleged harassment, so this is the first notice that the company has of the problem.

Based on what we know so far, the company isn't guilty of anything. It had no knowledge of the harassment and the facts weren't such that the company "should have known" of the problem. When Sandra reports the problem, however, a legal duty arises. The company must undertake a timely investigation of the allegations. In addition, if a problem occurs, it has to take reasonable steps intended to remedy the harassment.

Ok, so back to the facts. What the three co-workers were alleged to have done was to make sexual and racial remarks to Sandra. The statements are crass and stupid, but not dramatic. They are mostly inappropriate jokes. In all, the harassment is a 2 or a 3 on a scale of 1 to 10, with 10 being the worst possible harassment. However, as a result of its timely investigation, the company does conclude that the inappropriate comments were made and it correctly decides that it must take action to resolve the problem.

Since the harassment was not dramatically bad, the company decides to retain the three male workers. That decision is based largely on the above facts and the lack of prior discipline in the three employees' files, and in small part on Sandra's specific statement to the company that she did not want the three workers to be fired. To remedy the problem, however, the company places each employee on "final warning," expressly explaining that any further inappropriate behavior will lead to discharge. In addition, in response to Sandra's request that she not have to continue to work directly with the three co-workers, the company offers her a transfer to an equivalent job. Sandra accepts the transfer.

Now how are we doing legally? Pretty well, it seems. The company investigated on a timely basis. It took reasonable steps intended to stop the harassment. It also involved Sandra in that process and, at her request, transferred her to a different position. Remember—the legal test for remedying harassment is whether the steps were reasonable and whether they did what they were intended to do. In fact, the company checked back with Sandra several times after the employees were disciplined, and she confirmed that no further harassment had occurred.

If All Is Well, What's the Point?

In the above scenario, all certainly seemed well. However, a bubble was about to burst, and it's a bubble of which every employer should be aware. Understand we're dealing with people here, and that means that the legal duties requiring certain actions may not be enough to truly resolve a particular harassment situation. Assuming that the employer acts in the manner that the courts have set forth—human nature often creates a problem that most courts don't consider. Specifically, what are the after-effects of a harassment situation and how should they be handled?

And thus let's go back to Sandra's situation. Less than two weeks after the company has disciplined the hourly workers and transferred Sandra, she reappears in human resources and says she is quitting. When asked why, Sandra refers to the sexual harassment situation. The human resources professional is perplexed. He asks if further harassment has occurred. Sandra answers in the negative. He then asks if the new job is ok. Sandra says yes. Now even more confused, the human resources professional asks, in light of everything being ok, why Sandra wants to quit? She responds, "Well, those three guys were my friends, and now they won't talk with me. I feel like I'm getting the cold shoulder from them and I've had enough."

The human resources professional spends over an hour trying to talk Sandra out of quitting. He is unsuccessful. However, he hasn't heard the last from Sandra. A short time later, she sues the company, the three co-workers, the human resources professional, and two managers. Her complaint is for sexual harassment and she claims that her quitting amounted to a "constructive discharge," that is, the circumstances were such that she essentially was forced to quit.

Before dealing with the law, let's start with what might be an obvious point: why did the three disciplined workers stop being friends with Sandra? *Because they didn't want to get fired.* After all, they had just been told that if they said anything else that was inappropriate, their employment would end. If you were in the same situation, you might stay away from Sandra for a while too, especially if she was no longer on your work crew because she had transferred away.

> ## There's Always Baggage
>
> Be forewarned—almost all cases involving post-remedied harassment carry baggage for a while. Don't think that the situation described above is unusual. It's not.

The Cold Shoulder Sandra Got Was Not Sexual Harassment

Sandra's claim of sexual harassment seems misplaced. After all, she acknowledged to the company that the sexual harassment had stopped. In reality, what she was now complaining about were the after-effects of sexual harassment. She was getting the cold shoulder from her three former friends and she didn't like it.

Responses to Sandra's predicament are highly varied, even among human resources experts and the courts. Some say that, in fact, Sandra was harassed or retaliated against, even though no new sexual misbehavior had occurred and even though the employer (as opposed to the co-workers) had not done anything retaliatory. Others say that she should understand the situation better—having complained about her friends' behavior, she shouldn't also complain that they were now not talking with her. Additional commentators opine that Sandra's expectations put the employer in an impossible situation. Having threatened the three co-workers with discharge, how can the employer also be expected to rebuild the friendships that apparently had been broken?

What the Courts Are Doing with This Type of Issue

In a word, what the courts are doing with this situation is struggling. Sandra's case eventually went to the Tennessee Supreme Court. That court held that there was a duty on the employer's part to take steps to deal with the fact that Sandra's co-workers had "ostracized" her. That decision seems questionable given Sandra's admission that no further "sexual harassment" had occurred. In some ways, what the court appears to be requiring is that employers must try to get their workers to like each other, at least in post-harassment situations. That obviously is not only naive, but it's an impossible standard to meet.

Other courts also have struggled with the issue of post-remedy problems and tensions. Some decisions state that the employer has no duty in that arena absent further harassment or management retaliation. Others disagree, stating that the employer must take further follow-up steps to deal with the "ostracization" concern.

Before leaving the law and discussing practical alternatives for addressing the issue, one additional aspect of the Tennessee Supreme Court's decision bears comment. While finding a duty to deal with the after-effects of sexual harassment, the court determined that the company in question satisfied that duty and, in fact, was essentially a role model for handling such matters. In the case, both the human resources professional and the first line manager had gone out of their way to build bridges among the workers. Those efforts included having lunch with various workers, seeking to get people to communicate with each other, and otherwise trying to tear down the walls that had been built. Both managers deserve great credit for their efforts, but the legal requirements the court related to such actions still seem questionable.

The Right Mender

To make matters worse, many of your managers are going to struggle to deal with the concept of mending fences in these circumstances. First, they don't have time. Second, they may not have the soft skills needed for the job. As a result, consider appointing someone to the task rather than just turning to the direct supervisor of the harassed person.

Faced with These Problems, What Should You Do?

Here is a "how-to" guide for dealing with the after-effects of any type of harassment or discrimination problem. This guide also can be used to deal with virtually any kind of workplace problem where issues arise among various workers.

1. You Can't Deal with a Problem Unless You Know Why It Has Occurred

Let's go back to one of the basic assumptions of this book. People are people. They have emotions, they are sometimes irrational, and they require considerable care and feeding. And why does ostracization occur? Because emotions, friendships, and human reactions are involved in the sexual harassment remedy.

In most situations, one or more male employees harass a female worker. However, the majority of harassment isn't evil—many situations involve joking taken too far or simple ignorance. Take a situation where a number of workers are fairly regularly involved in consensual sexual banter, but one day Jim steps over the line and offends Jane. When Jane reports Jim to management, an investigation occurs. The resulting turmoil is predictable—people are embarrassed, someone is disciplined, and feelings are hurt. Some of the co-workers support Jane, and others are upset that she reported Jim instead of dealing with the situation privately.

Lines get drawn and sides are chosen in many of these scenarios. Time often heals the problem but, if the Tennessee Supreme Court is right, the employer cannot simply let time go by. Instead, it must seek to affirmatively clean up the after-effects. In doing so, however, the employer must understand why these situations are so humanly complex. Otherwise, trying to solve the problem becomes even more difficult.

2. You Can't Solve the Problem If You Aren't Sensitive to Human Issues

Further, understanding the problem isn't enough. You may have to be empathetic to both sides. And you have to do that without undercutting the discipline you gave to the offender.

Talking to the harassed worker requires empathy, but it also demands the skill of a counselor. The employee has to figure out where to go from here. And she needs to be realistic. Post-remedy, the world is a different place than it was before. No one can reasonably expect that things will suddenly magically be better. Tension will be in the air and you should help the employee realize that. You also should offer a place to talk if needed. In some situations, an employee assistance program also might be helpful, but for goodness sake don't suggest to the employee that "she needs" to go to EAP "because she has a problem."

Also, when talking to the harasser, get a gauge on his or her sense of guilt. If the harasser thinks he has done nothing wrong, you have a problem. He needs to understand the issue, and if he doesn't, you need to find a way to get through to him.

On the other hand, if the harasser gets it, and is sorry for what occurred, you need to help him or her get back to normal too. That can occur through suggestions on how to act, discussing an appropriate apology, and even facilitating a session between harasser and harassee to discuss what happens next (see more about this option below).

Remember that human feelings are all over the place in these circumstances. In some occasions, conversations need to occur with co-workers as well. Such co-workers are usually on one person's side or the other, and they may need your assistance to find a middle ground.

3. You Must Be Proactive Rather Than Reactive

Having read the above, some of you may understandably be saying, "So why is this my problem?" The answer is that you're doing all this as the best means to keep yourself out of court and out of trouble. We understand that you'd prefer to be an employer instead of leading the singing of Kumbaya at summer camp. However, being an employer means dealing with employees, and doing that effectively and with some compassion can save you serious liability.

In addition to knowing that remedies lead to human reactions, you should plan ahead to deal with the situation. Don't wait for a complaint. Sometimes waiting a few days to see how things go can be effective. However, you need to at least talk to the harassee and the harasser about what to expect and you should tell them that they can come talk to you if issues arise. If you send them out unprepared, problems are more likely to occur.

4. Communicate with People Individually, Make Suggestions, and Push Buttons

As stated above, don't be afraid to talk with people about realism. We're not asking you to add to the drama, but we are suggesting that you not hide your head in the sand. Making proactive suggestions is ok. Pushing buttons such as telling a harasser that an apology might help also can be effective. Knowing which managers can influence which employees is important as well, and getting those managers to help clean up the mess may be a very good move.

5. Where Appropriate, Put People Together and Facilitate Solutions

In some circumstances (or, on occasion, if you just want some good entertainment), facilitating a discussion between harasser and harassee may be effective. Be cautious—this approach is not a simple one. In addition, there is no need for a three-way discussion if the harasser is being fired.

In fact, absent exceptional circumstances, do not try to facilitate a three-way discussion in cases where someone is clearly going to be fired. Inevitably, the discussion will make the situation worse instead of better, and it serves no real purpose.

If you do a three-way discussion, be ready to lead people through the awkward parts. Also, let the involved parties know what is going to happen in this meeting so that there is a known purpose and agenda. Further, do not let someone take over the meeting in furtherance of his or her own objective as opposed to trying to resolve the problem. Make suggestions as needed, and help the individuals express their concerns. But remember, you are not a psychiatrist—"Why, Jenny, do you feel this way?" may be appropriate in some circumstances, but not in a work meeting. The better question in the workplace could be "Jenny, can you and Doug still work together, and what does he need to do to help in that regard?"

6. Use the 1-3-5-3 Rule

As part of the post-remedy stage, employers need to remember that the situation isn't likely to be actually finished even though discipline has been handed out and the file has been closed. One way to force follow-up is to abide by the 1-3-5-3 rule.

One day after the remedy has been implemented, the employer should touch base with each of the involved parties to see how things are going. If all is fine, the employer should touch base again on day three. If things are still good, reconnect again on day five and again at the beginning of week three.

If during these reconnections, concerns are expressed, further contacts are needed. In some cases, the bridges are rebuilt very slowly. Further, even if all seems fine on each of these 1-3-5-3 contacts, continually tell the affected employees to come to you if any further concerns arise, from additional harassment to retaliation to simply needing someone with whom to talk.

7. Document Your Actions

Documentation is not only your friend in court, there's nothing wrong with creating evidence that is a little bit self-serving. If you work hard to deal with the post-harassment situation, take some written credit for that. Write a memo that sets forth what you did, why you did it, and that no problems have been reported to you. In addition, if further issues do arise, note them and state your plan for resolving the problem. Then write another memo when the issue is resolved.

Document Well

Remember—almost all documents are discoverable. That, however, shouldn't keep you from documenting, although it should force you to document well. By the way, drafts of documents (paper and electronic) are discoverable too. Discard them as soon as you no longer need them.

---

8. Make Sure People Know What to Do to Get Help

As stated in point 6 above, make sure that everyone involved knows that they can come to you to talk. In addition, there may be someone else whom the workers can turn to, such as an EAP counselor or a human resources professional. For the employer, the key is to ensure that the employees have somewhere in management to direct their concerns (rather than, say, to a union, or to Felipe, the office gossip).

9. Realize That Some Things Take Time

Sometimes hurt feelings take a long time to overcome. As the poets say, time does heal most problems, but the average employer always wants that time to go by in a hurry so that everyone can finally get back to making widgets. Patience can be a virtue and some things can't be hurried.

10. Understand That Building Bridges Doesn't Always Work, and Some Problems Can't Be Resolved

Despite the employer's best efforts, there is no magic dust to be sprinkled on the participants in our sexual harassment recovery project. Remember Sandra? That employer thought everything was going swimmingly until Sandra quit and a lawsuit quickly followed. Given everything the managers were doing to make things better, it was hard to understand why she quit except that she had by then talked with a lawyer and decided to sue.

If it is obvious or seems unlikely that all is going to work itself out, go to plan B. On some occasions, that might mean firing a harasser simply because there is no feasible alternative. In other situations, for a larger organization, it could help to require a transfer of enough significance that little future interaction will occur among harasser and harassee. Some remedies need to be infused with realism, as not all harassment situations can be resolved successfully with both the harasser and the harassee remaining together in the workplace.

CHAPTER 19

Special Situations: Dating and Other Relationships— Consensual Behavior Isn't Sexual Harassment

Have you ever told your 9th-grade daughter that she can't date that 12th-grade boy who keeps asking her out? That strategy probably worked pretty well, didn't it? After you tell her that she can't date him, guess what? That's now the only boy that she wants to date. So, who cares? This is a book about workplace issues. Well, think of it this way—some of your employees are a lot like your teenage daughter and her 12th-grade suitor.

You Might As Well Face the Reality

The reality is that co-workers date, from two hourly workers on the same shift to a boss and his administrative assistant. In fact, your sales manager and the new guy in marketing got together just yesterday. According to a dating poll conducted by Lovespring International, here's what may well be happening at your workplace:

> You'll have better luck finding your next date at the office rather than at the corner pub. 17% met the man they last dated at work, 16% met him while hanging out at a bar or club and 12% via online dating services. A whopping 57% say they've dated someone with whom they worked.

> Of those dating where they work, 39% say it's with someone in the same department. In most cases (67%), the work love-interest is a peer, but for 12% the office tryst is with a subordinate and 11% have dated a boss. For most (67%), the office affair isn't widely held knowledge at work: 25% say it was a secret and 43% say only a handful of colleagues knew.

To make things really scary to the average employer, the Lovespring analysis concludes by stating as follows: "A bit of discouraging news: Workplace romances are fleeting—only 17% of those who dated at the office report they are still together with their workplace squeeze." And that is bad because? As discussed below, most date-related harassment cases revolve around the breakup of the relationship rather than the relationship itself.

The Love Contract

This may speak the obvious, but dating relationships are complicated enough without throwing in the concept of working together (or, worse yet, one working for the other). Chapter 20 discusses some ways to deal with that problem, including something called the "love contract."

To make things worse, the Lovespring poll may seriously underestimate the office dating scene. According to a study done by CyberCollege, more than 60% of singles (in a poll of 30,000 female subjects) have had at least one office affair. Based on the CyberCollege poll:

The majority of females (single and married) have had sex or an affair with their supervisor. But it's not just supervisors that are involved. A high percentage of women (single and married) admit to dating or having sex with clients. One woman said, "Sure I've dated some of them, and if they've been cute I've spent the night with them. If we both want to do it, why not?"

Well, why not indeed? It's just people being people. Good clean, all-American kind of fun, and it sure beats just working together.

This Must Mean Sexual Harassment Is All Over the Place

You should be worried, but despite the statistics above, you may not have sexual harassment at all. Remember what we've said all along—consensual behavior is *not* sexual harassment. Thus, as long as dating relationships are consensual, you don't actually have sexual harassment. Instead what you have is the perfect breeding ground for later claims of sexual harassment.

Consensual Is Legal

By the way, when we say that dating is not sexual harassment, we're talking about the legal definition of sexual harassment. Consensual behavior changes everything under the law. Your policy could be more restrictive, but again, telling people they can't date isn't very realistic.

OK, so dating among co-workers, or even between a superior and a subordinate, do not automatically constitute sexual harassment. In a real sense, no one in the dating relationship is actually harassing anyone else (although beware the "favoritism" problem that is discussed in Chapter 24). As described below, however, some dating relationships do create a series of potential problems for nonharassment reasons. Nevertheless, all is fine from the harassment perspective so long as the relationship remains stable.

Indeed, even flings or one-night stands don't count as automatic sexual harassment. Take the situation where two co-workers end up in the same bar on a Saturday night by complete coincidence. Neither was evenly vaguely aware of the other being there until they bumped into each other at about 1:00 a.m. By then, however, the alcohol had kicked in and serious hormones were on the loose. By 2:00 a.m., our two co-workers were off to a condo to spend the night together. Harassment? No. The potential for a big problem come Monday? Absolutely.

As noted by the Lovespring poll, office affairs can indeed be fleeting. Further, as the singer said, "Breaking up is hard to do." In fact, the end of the dating relationship (short or long) can lead to sexual harassment claims.

Why Is a Dating Break Up My Problem? I'm Their Employer, Not Their Mother

To understand the relationship between office dating and potential sexual harassment, ask yourself the following question: when was the last time that both partners in a dating relationship decided to end that relationship at the same time? The answer, of course, is almost never. And thus the scene is set for claims of harassment.

Take two scenarios—the office love affair that has dominated break room talk for three months, and our co-worker couple that met at the bar and decided to have some alcohol-laden sex.

Ginnie and Antonio are married and dating. Unfortunately, however, the person they're dating is someone other than the person to whom they're married. Ginnie and Antonio, who are co-workers in Information Technology, have been carrying on a sexual relationship for about three months. The heat of their passion is the number one topic of discussion among the entire IT crew. Yesterday, however, Ronald, Ginnie's husband, accused Ginnie of having an affair because when he called her on "those nights she was working late," he could never find her. Ginnie, in a panic, tells Antonio that they have to stop seeing each other.

Unfortunately, Antonio's marriage is pretty much on the rocks anyway, so he tells Ginnie that rather than stopping their affair, they should legitimize it by both leaving their spouses. Ginnie says no way, and tension immediately develops. Ginnie tries to stay away from Antonio and won't talk with him now away from work. Thus he is left with only work time to try to talk her into continuing the affair.

In an alternative universe within the same company, something similar happens to our sex-starved barflies. Calvin and Pam had a great time that Saturday night. The sex was terrific, the pancakes at breakfast were delicious, and the "see you at work tomorrows" seemed perfectly unforced. However, on Monday morning, Calvin approached Pam at break and said, "Pam, you're awesome and I had a great time this weekend, but we're co-workers and we've done something stupid. You're not to blame and neither am I, but we need to go back to being just regular friends." Unfortunately, Pam looks at Calvin and says "What are you talking about? You can't do what you did Saturday night and then just cut it off. We had a great time and I want to do it again." When Calvin explains that he "just can't do that," Pam says, "Well don't pretend I'm your friend then. Screw you. If you're calling it off, I will never talk with you again."

What a mess for all four people wrapped up in these inter-office situations. Further, what a great time to be a human resources professional! Both Ginnie and Calvin decide on the same day to come to Human Resources to raise concerns.

According to Ginnie, Antonio is sexually harassing her and "spreading rumors" that the two of them had an affair. Ginnie denies any part in an affair, but tells the HR professional that Antonio had better stop talking or she'll sue. Ginnie also wants Antonio fired if he "doesn't quit making up these stories." Ginnie obviously isn't being particularly honest, but the company doesn't know that (at least yet).

As for Calvin, he is totally honest, telling the HR professional exactly what happened both at the bar and on Monday morning. He doesn't want Pam to be fired. In fact, he doesn't want the company "to do anything." However, he wants you to know what happened, "just in case this turns into a problem."

What a mess. Just because two well-meaning people had an affair, and two other people got drunk and had a fling. And why again, you ask, is this the employer's problem? Because it's impacting the workplace and the problem is "based on sex." Consequently, it's now up to you to solve the personal issues of these folks, whether you want to or not. Otherwise, you risk liability for not taking "timely and effective steps" to prevent and/or remedy alleged sexual harassment.

Let HR Do It

As we discussed in the previous chapter, managers aren't good as a whole in dealing with problems that affect the workplace due to the break up of a relationship. If you have one, an HR person may be your better choice for picking up the pieces.

Handling the Relationship Gone Bad

Fortunately, most people involved in relationships gone bad are mature enough and able enough to solve their own problems. As the Lovespring poll suggests, many workplace flings don't become known to co-workers, much less management. However, when one or both of the participants in these flings raise concerns to their employer about the after-effects of the break up, the employer should act. But what does "act" mean in these circumstances?

Initially, the employer should realize that the affair gone bad situation is quite different from a quid pro quo or even an unwelcome sexual banter case. In the affair, the parties were voluntarily involved in a sexual relationship. The problem now is to address how to move from the break up to everyone getting back to normal.

Quid Pro Problem

Although, as we discussed in Chapter 11, an affair gone bad can lead to quid pro quo, such as asking the other person for additional sex in return for a raise. Be alert that human desperation due to the loss of love (or lust) leads to some problematic behavior, including at work.

In these post-affair situations, some empathy can go a long way. While discipline may eventually be required, the behavior is very different from that of a Neanderthal who thinks he can say whatever he wants, no matter how crude. In addition, the manager dealing with the post-relationship situation needs to know that he or she is interfacing with at least one hurt person, and that some hurt persons can quickly turn into angry persons.

The investigation in these circumstances needs to be handled with some softness. Over-the-top directness is likely to make things worse instead of better. Further, the sensitivity may need to carry over to interviews of co-workers (assuming the appropriateness of such interviews in the first place), as some co-workers may take sides as to who is the guilty and who is the innocent person harmed in the affair.

Remedies also may differ in these circumstances. Certainly if disappointment turns into vengeance, substantial discipline, including discharge, may occur. Warnings also are appropriate. However, the best remedy in affairs gone bad may be moving the individuals apart. When that isn't possible, the employer probably has to facilitate a three-way discussion into how to preserve the working relationship while closing the door on the personal relationship.

But beware—people being people, an affair can end, harassment can be alleged, remedies can be created and applied, yet three weeks later the happy couple can be right back to having sex. At some point in such circumstances, can the employer say "Take this relationship elsewhere?" Probably, but certainly that will be awkward. A better approach might be to push back and direct the couple to "give the company a plan through which this relationship will not affect work." If no plan or a half-baked plan is forthcoming, discharge is easier. To the contrary, the employees' plan may be that one of them will quit upon finding new employment. The employer may welcome such a plan and may even request such a decision in appropriate circumstances.

Also be aware that everything gets worse if one of the persons involved in the affair/fling is a manager. And things get far worse if the other person in the relationship is a subordinate of that manager. In those circumstances, the two individuals cannot remain in a reporting relationship. Somebody has to move, quit, or be fired. Further, if the relationship is an extramarital affair between a manager and a subordinate, the involved persons are likely to deny the affair and state that they are "just good friends." If so, the employer should respond as follows: "I don't know whether you're having an affair or you're not. That really doesn't matter to me. The problem is that you've created the appearance of an affair, and that alone creates a serious problem. As a result, one of you needs to change positions so that you're not in a reporting relationship."

As for other aspects of a manager's relationship with another employee, see Chapter 21, which deals with issues concerning managerial bad judgment.

What Should Happen with Calvin, Pam, Ginnie, and Antonio?

What should be done with Ginnie and Antonio as well as Calvin and Pam? Well, of course, the answer is "it depends." Lord knows what you'll actually get out of the investigation. Assuming, however, that you actually learn the truth (or something close to the truth), here are two suggested outcomes.

As for Ginnie and Antonio, empathy is great but Ginnie is lying her tail end off. She needs to be told to stop doing that and to refocus on work. A firm written warning related to her lack of honesty is appropriate. As for Antonio, a warning (probably written) to leave Ginnie alone is appropriate, since he is using the workplace to try to get her to continue the affair. Then the employer should seek a proactive solution that hopefully will move these folks away from each other. After implementing that plan, the employer should check in on each person from time to time to make sure that all is ok. If Antonio continues to push Ginnie to resume the affair, he may have to be fired. Similarly, if Ginnie continues to spread false rumors about Antonio, she may have to be discharged.

Calvin and Pam's situation should be easier. Discipline may not be needed at all since the problem seems to focus on a mistake and a related misunderstanding. A facilitated discussion could solve the whole issue. Further, if that discussion suggests that a transfer would be best, that should be considered. In addition, if problems do continue between these workers, discipline may then be needed.

Can I Just Prohibit My Employees from Dating?

Sure, you can always say "No one here can date anyone else at the company." You also can say that "None of my good employees are ever allowed to quit," or even "I would like to add an hour or two to my normal 24-hour day." Stated differently, it really doesn't matter what you say—people are likely to date. Most of us don't fall in love with a particular person on purpose. Stuff happens.

If you fire people who date, you may be eliminating "break up harassment." However, you're also jettisoning good workers. There are better approaches, some of which are described in Chapter 20.

Fraternization Policies: "Love Contracts" and Breaking Up Is Hard to Do

Employers might as well face it—we're addicted to love. Let's add some more statistics to the last chapter. According to a 2006 survey conducted by the Society for Human Resource Management, as many as 40% of American workers have had an office romance. As American workers increasingly spend more and more time in the office, it has become a place for people of like-minded interests and attitudes to get to know each other. It's only natural for interpersonal relationships to develop in such an environment. In fact, according to another study performed by Vault.com, an online job web site, 40% of those responding said they met their spouse either at work or through work.

The problem often arises when "flirting" is misinterpreted, or when a relationship between employees (or even worse, a superior and a subordinate) goes sour. These sorts of situations inevitably stir office gossip, cause tension, impact productivity, and can even result in sexual harassment claims or lawsuits.

You Can't Stop It

If you think dating is hard to prohibit, try telling people that they can't flirt. First, you'll be henceforth called the "big ogre," and second, people will flirt no matter what you say. It's an American pastime.

Unfortunately, there's nothing employers can do to suspend the laws of attraction at the office door. However, it is possible for employers to manage a universe governed both by sexual interest and laws against sexual harassment by taking proactive steps to control their liability.

Efforts of Employers to Regulate Employee Relationships in the Workplace

In the past, some employers have attempted to impose a complete ban on dating among employees. More recently, employers have lifted these strict policies due to legal restrictions, enforceability problems, and the realization that sometimes what is meant to be, will be. The trend now is to try to restrict the dating activities of employees that might be harmful to the employer.

Before an employer can identify what policies and procedures on dating it wants to adopt, it must assess exactly what risks it is willing to take and what liability it wants to avoid. Depending on the type of business an employer engages in, dating and/or spousal relationships among its employees might be more helpful than harmful. For example, think about James and Kate, who are both employed as pilots with an airline. With two children at home and busy travel schedules, both the company and the couple benefit from working for the same employer. The airline always knows never to schedule James and Kate to be flying at the same time, so one of them is always available to be at home with the children. James and Kate never have to haggle with their supervisors over work schedules or call in to work if a babysitter falls through. By working for the same employer, James and Kate can make their relationship work for the airline as well as their family.

Married Employees Are OK, If ...

We understand that saying you should consider employing married couples sounds a little odd. However, some companies have truly made it work. There are law firms and accounting firms, for example, that don't hesitate to hire married students who both meet their hiring standards. That said, it's best to put these folks in different parts of the firm or organization.

On the other hand, dating or spousal relationships could hamper work productivity in a business where partners must work together in a close environment, or where one partner supervises the other. Imagine that Tom is a lawyer who runs his own firm and his girlfriend, Tina, is his secretary. Even in a small office environment, this situation might work well if Tom and Tina have a good relationship. But throw in volatile personalities, frequent arguments over both work and personal matters, along with another secretary who is resentful of the preferential treatment Tina receives, and you have a recipe for trouble.

Risks Posed to the Employer by Employee Relationships

The above examples illustrate that before an employer can decide on a solution to the problems employee relationships can cause, it must go through a risk-benefit analysis. The benefits of allowing dating or spousal relationships among employees will be unique to every company. However, as discussed below, there are some general risks posed by employee dating that will be applicable to a majority of employers and that should be considered carefully when deciding on a proactive policy regulating employee relationships.

1. Hardships in the Workplace

Office romances can be distracting for the participants but are sometimes even more entertaining for the observers, especially for the "office gossip." Almost every office has one employee who thrives on gossiping about her co-workers. It doesn't matter who is dating whom, who is sleeping with whom, who is cheating on their spouse, who is about to get fired—the office gossip knows it all. Not only does she know it all, but she tells it all to anyone, any chance she gets. It doesn't matter if she should be typing up that report for the boss that needs to go out at the end of the day. Sharing the latest dish with a co-worker is much more important to her than any pressing deadline.

Imagine what a blossoming office romance would do for the conversation topics of the office gossip. With a subject constantly changing and evolving before her eyes, she would feel that it was her duty to keep everyone (repeat: everyone) in the office informed of the latest updates. Envision then the level of the office gossip's productivity, as well as the productivity of each one of her co-workers who takes time out of their day to talk to her. It doesn't take long to realize the impact that just one office relationship can have on an employer's operations. The lovebirds are distracted, other workers are distracted by talking about the romance, and productivity dwindles.

2. Sexual Harassment Claims

As discussed in the prior chapter, sexual harassment claims are one of the biggest risks posed to employers by employee relationships. Attempts at flirting, asking a co-worker out, or even consensual workplace romances that end badly have increasingly become the basis of sexual harassment lawsuits.

"Quid Pro Quo" Sexual Harassment. A claim of quid pro quo sexual harassment can arise in a number of ways when employees are involved in workplace flirting or relationships. Again, quid pro quo types of sexual harassment claims arise when a job benefit or detriment is tied to an employee's submission to unwelcome sexual advances. A couple of examples will help to illustrate the point.

Suppose that Tiffany, a young and pretty woman, joins a small-town police force. She draws the attention of Bobby, a fellow officer, who begins to tease her about her petite frame. Bobby gives her the nickname "Itty Bitty Tiffy," and after using her nickname in flirtatious conversations at work for several weeks, finally asks her out one night after patrol. Tiffany accepts, and goes on a date with Bobby.

Noticing that Bobby's nickname seemed to work on Tiffany, a lieutenant, Judy, decides to use the same tactics on Chris, a dispatch radio operator. Judy begins referring to Chris as "Hot Stuff" or "Honey Bun" on the dispatch radio, which other officers can hear. Unlike Tiffany, Chris does not appreciate the new nicknames and tells Judy to stop using them. Judy is confused as to why the nicknames aren't helping her get into Chris's good graces. Judy then tries a more aggressive tactic, coming up behind Chris at the dispatch station, putting her hand on his shoulder and whispering in his ear "If you go out with me tonight, I'll make it worth your while. And that shot at a patrol position? It's yours if you spend the night."

On the surface, both examples appear like flirting. However, there is a key difference between the scenarios. Tiffany welcomed Bobby's attention, while Chris clearly disliked the advances of Judy, his superior, and communicated his displeasure to her. Despite the knowledge that Chris just wasn't that into her, Judy continued her "flirting," escalating the situation through physical contact and offering him a promotion in exchange for his intimate attention. Because Judy has placed Chris's chances at promotion on his acceptance of an unwelcome sexual advance, Chris may have a valid claim for quid pro quo sexual harassment or hostile work environment sexual harassment, as we will discuss next.

Hostile Work Environment Sexual Harassment. Employee relationships on the job site are especially prone to generating hostile work environment claims, because parties that aren't involved in the relationship are nevertheless eligible to bring this type of sexual harassment claim. Again, to bring a hostile work environment sexual harassment claim, an employee only has to show that a reasonable person would find the work environment hostile and that the victim actually perceived the environment as abusive.

To illustrate how easily work flirtation or casual dating can lead to a hostile work environment claim, let's consider again our dating co-workers Bobby and Tiffany. Their relationship is going quite well until Judy, spurned by Chris's rejections, sets her eyes on Bobby. Judy begins to spread a rumor among the officers that Tiffany has been seeing Chris on the side. Bobby hears the rumor and breaks off his relationship with Tiffany.

Tiffany begins to make negative comments about Bobby to other female officers and tells them Bobby was a horrible boyfriend. Tiffany also begins following Bobby around at the station and begging him to take her back. When Bobby refuses, Tiffany breaks into his locker and vandalizes his personal belongings.

Surprisingly enough, both Bobby and Tiffany probably have claims of hostile work environment arising from the demise of their dating relationship. Bobby's claim is much more obvious than Tiffany's—most reasonable people would consider harassing behavior from a scorned lover to create a hostile work environment. However, Tiffany may also have a hostile work environment claim based on the conduct of her supervisor, Judy. Judy, the trouble-maker that she is, spread the unfounded rumors of another workplace romance between Tiffany and Chris that caused Bobby to end his relationship with Tiffany. This may be enough for Tiffany to show that her work environment also was hostile and that she found Judy's conduct abusive.

Sexual Favoritism. A complaint of sexual favoritism based on a relationship between other employees is probably the type of claim most employers don't typically think of when assessing risks associated with employee relationships. However, an employer can be liable if (1) the employee involved in the workplace relationship received favorable treatment over another employee because of his or her participation in that relationship; or (2) an employee not involved in the workplace relationship was adversely affected because of his or her noninvolvement.

As discussed in Chapter 24, preferential treatment arising out of a consensual romantic relationship is not prohibited by law. While this sort of sexual favoritism may be unfair, it is only actionable by other co-workers if the unequal treatment is based on the granting of sexual favors.

For example, consider Haley and Rachel, both of whom are assistant managers at a local ice cream store chain. Haley has aspired to the management position of their store for several years, and has been steadily promoted since joining the company three years ago. Rachel, however, who has no experience in management, was hired on as an assistant manager about six months ago. Lee, the current division manager, has had a crush on Rachel from the moment she applied to work at the ice cream shop. Lee asks Rachel on a date, and she willingly accepts. The date goes well and, a few months into their relationship, Lee promotes Rachel to store manager despite the fact that she's never successfully mastered dipping a double scoop cone.

It's easy to understand Haley's frustration in this situation. Haley has worked hard to earn her promotions, while it appears that Rachel is sailing by because of her relationship with Lee. Regardless of the apparent injustice that has been worked upon Haley, she doesn't have a claim for unlawful sexual harassment here. Lee's preferential treatment of Rachel over Haley is not based on Haley's gender, but rather his feelings for Rachel.

However, this example is easily changed into an actionable sexual harassment claim based on sexual favoritism by altering the nature of the relationship between Lee and Rachel. Suppose that, instead of dating Rachel, Lee dates several women that work for the ice cream store chain. Lee develops a reputation for giving good performance reviews to female employees with whom he has been intimately involved. Lee drops the hint that he is going to have a hard time deciding whether Rachel or Haley will be promoted to store manager after their performance evaluations are completed. Lee eventually propositions both Rachel and Haley for sex. Haley declines, but Rachel accepts. After the performance evaluations are completed, Haley receives a higher rating, but Rachel is promoted to store manager.

Again, Haley has a right to be angered by the situation, but this time she may also have a claim for sexual harassment. Here, Lee's preferential treatment of Rachel is based on the fact that she granted him the sexual favor that he requested in return for a direct job benefit—a promotion over Haley to store manager. Haley will have a much better chance of proving she has been discriminated against because she was unwilling to provide sexual favors, and she suffered adverse treatment while others who participated were treated more favorably.

3. Retaliation

Retaliation claims are also a huge risk to employers but are often overshadowed by the focus on the principal claim of sexual harassment. Employers need to recognize the significance of retaliation claims for several reasons:

1. Retaliation claims are on the rise.
2. A recent Supreme Court decision (discussed in Chapter 27) just made it easier for employees to prove their employer retaliated against them for complaining about discrimination or harassment.
3. Even if the discrimination or harassment claim is true, if the employer takes timely action, a retaliation claim can be prevented.

Paid Leave and Investigation Time

In the Supreme Court case in question, the employer put an employee on unpaid leave while investigating a problem. The problem was that the investigation took 37 days. That leads to two suggestions: (1) consider paid leave in appropriate circumstances and (2) don't let an investigation take 37 days to complete.

If a supervisor terminates her former lover after he ends their two-year relationship, most people would recognize that action as retaliatory. However, an employee may have a retaliation claim after a relationship has ended if *any* negative employment action occurs at work. This is because the law of retaliation focuses in large part on whether a reasonable person perceives a connection between the alleged sexual harassment and the negative employment action. This is not to say an employee who has filed a complaint can't be fired. However, if there is a suggestion that the claim and termination are related, there is a big risk the employer will face liability for retaliating against the employee.

Bye-Bye Love? Policy Choices for Regulating Dating and Other Intimate Relationships in the Workplace

So, now that you are feeling quite risk-averse, what are your options as an employer to regulate dating and other intimate relationships among your employees? As we've already discussed, just saying "no" hasn't worked all that well for most employers. In addition, depending on what type of business you run, allowing relationships among your employees may not completely be a bad thing. More than likely, your company will fall somewhere between the extremes of "complete abstention" and a "dating free-for-all." Therefore, the following types of proactive employee relationship regulation may be beneficial for controlling any liability your company may face in light of an employee relationship gone bad.

1. The Fraternization Policy

Fraternization policies are designed to limit or prohibit employees from personally associating outside of their professional duties, specifically in the area of romantic associations. These sorts of policies come in a variety of forms. A company may choose to prohibit relationships only between supervisors and subordinates, between supervisors and employees over which they exercise direct authority, or among all employees in general. Of these, the last option is probably unrealistic, but the prior limitations are sensible and they should be considered.

Explanation of the Policy and the Reasons behind It. Your employees need to understand exactly what a fraternization policy is and the reasons why the company is choosing to impose it. Intimate relationships are personal, and employees may be resistant to what they perceive as an imposition on a private area of their lives. Indeed, some states have privacy laws that protect employees from intrusive regulations by employers. Before implementing a fraternization policy, check local laws to ensure they are allowed in your area. If they are, be sure to include a reasonable explanation of the company's purpose in the policy. Employees may be more open to accepting the implementation of a fraternization policy if they understand their employer's reasons for instituting it.

> ## Tell Them Why
>
> As discussed more in Chapter 28, education is always a good thing. Don't be afraid to explain the reasons behind a policy. If something is important enough to put into policy form, it's important enough to explain to your workers.

Define What Employees Are Restricted from Engaging in Relationships with Co-Workers. Your company's fraternization policy should clearly outline what employees are restricted from engaging in relationships with co-workers. If your company is going to prohibit relationships between supervisors and subordinates, specify what creates a supervisor/subordinate relationship. Does a supervisor/subordinate relationship apply to a supervisor who has direct authority over a subordinate? Or would a supervisor be permitted to date a subordinate over whom he or she has no day-to-day authority? The policy should try to leave no significant questions unanswered. No matter how specific the policy is, however, employees will probably still have questions, or think that they should be entitled to an exemption under the policy. Be sure to include a contact person so employees will know whom to contact with questions about the policy.

Workplace Discussions of Employee Relationships. This section falls back to our problem with the office gossip. A provision that prohibits gossiping about nonwork matters may be appropriate. Be cautious, however, as a prohibition against discussing terms and conditions of work would violate the National Labor Relations Act.

What to Do If an Employee Becomes Involved in a Relationship with a Co-Worker. If your company's fraternization policy is going to allow office relationships, it may be a good idea to give your employees guidelines on how to conduct themselves properly in the workplace. While most employees understand that intimate behavior should not take place at work, others may construe permission to date their co-workers as permission to bring all aspects of their relationship to the workplace. Again, a straightforward understanding of what is expected of employees who are engaged in relationships with their co-

workers will help the company to keep the distractions and risks of office romances to a minimum.

Consequences of Failure to Adhere to Rules of the Policy. Disciplinary consequences for failure to adhere to the fraternization policy should be clearly outlined. Employees must be on notice that their participation in or behavior associated with an office romance could result in employment-related consequences, up to and including termination if your company so desires.

2. Consensual Relationship Agreements, or "Love Contracts"

Consensual relationship agreements, or "love contracts," are another option employers can use either alone or in conjunction with a fraternization policy to limit the risk associated with employee relationships. A love contract is essentially a type of fraternization policy that requires employees who are in a relationship to disclose the relationship to their employer. The employees and the employer then sign an agreement, or love contract, which contains agreed-upon provisions regulating the employees' behavior in the workplace and the responsibility of the employees if the relationship comes to an end.

A typical love contract may contain the following provisions:

1. Confirmation that the relationship between the employees is consensual
2. Recognition of and agreement to abide by employer's discrimination and harassment policies
3. An agreement to regulate office behavior and act professionally at all times
4. An agreement that, upon dissolution of the relationship by one or both parties, there will be no work-related retaliation
5. An arbitration clause
6. Advice to both parties to consult an attorney before signing
7. A provision waiving the right to pursue a claim of sexual harassment for any events prior to the signing of the contract

Your company's policy on love contracts can be included in the employee handbook and explained along with the company's fraternization policy. An employee's obligation to inform management of an office relationship, as well as consequences for failing to do so, should be clearly explained. As some office relationships may be adulterous or same-sex oriented, the company should also advise employees that all office relationships disclosed to the company will remain confidential.

What to Do When Evidence Suggests Employees Are Involved in a Relationship

If management in your company has become aware of evidence suggesting employees are dating, don't ignore the situation. If you have a fraternization or love contract policy in place, your employees have a duty to abide by company regulations. Remember, those regulations are not in place for the purpose of burdening employees' personal lives, but to protect your company from the risks employee relationships can cause!

If there is evidence employees are dating in violation of your company's policies, meet separately with both employees involved. Remind each employee of the company's policy on office relationships and commitment to preventing sexual harassment. Tell each employee that you have reason to believe he or she may be involved in a relationship with a co-worker, and allow the employee to explain the situation. Depending on what information is learned from these meetings, impose the appropriate discipline according to company policy.

Your company should apply its fraternization policy or love contract policy consistently. If employees are not treated consistently under your company's policies regulating office relationships, you risk Title VII disparate treatment liability.

CHAPTER 21

Dealing with Managers with Bad Judgment and the Implications of Having Alcohol at Company Functions

Both of the issues addressed in this chapter have been touched on elsewhere. However, these issues are significant enough to warrant some additional detail and a chapter of their own. Let's start with managers who exercise bad judgment and then we'll deal with the implications of popping open a few kegs at the company picnic.

Everybody Shows Bad Judgment Sometimes, So Why Pick on the Managers?

Granted, everyone does exhibit bad judgment from time to time. However, the answer to the question "Why then pick on managers?" is an easy one. Because they're managers. For better or for worse, they should know better.

Held to a Higher Standard

But should managers really be held to a higher standard? Yes. If they can't accept that, they won't be effective leaders. The term "leading by example" is a legitimate way to denote the importance of the issue.

The reality is that all humans suffer from moments of human weakness. Jim Bakker, Bill Clinton, numerous Roman Catholic priests, and far too many Congressmen to list by name have screwed up royally. Yet we have every right to expect managers to do better than those they manage. If managers can't be shining examples, then the employees they manage aren't likely to act properly either.

In addition, the law unequivocally holds managers to a higher standard. Remember—quid pro quo involving an adverse employment action leads to automatic liability. Even manager hostile work environment harassment creates automatic liability unless the employer is in position to use the *Faragher* defense. Consequently, if the law requires managers to straighten up and play right, you should require that too.

But, Expectations Aside, Managers Do Mess Up, Don't They?

Regrettably, unfortunately, embarrassingly, and sometimes inevitably, managers will indeed mess up. Often the problem really does come down to the manager simply being human. If a manager falls in love with a subordinate, maybe he or she just couldn't help it. Granted, such a move shows really bad judgment but, as singer Joan Osborne once said "Love comes down anyway it wants to, it doesn't ask for your permission."

To make matters worse, we sometimes inadvertently increase the chances of a manager exercising bad judgment. Alcohol being served at business events is just one possibility. At other times the problem could be work overload, being understaffed for too long, or simply having a frustratingly difficult day. Even good bosses can turn into difficult people from time to time, and that alone can cause an over-sensitive employee to claim harassment.

To make matters even worse, employers can bring the manager problem on themselves. Often the issue is as simple as hiring the wrong person to be a manager. If a person with a controlling personality is asked to manage a process that is inherently not controllable, the employer just raised the chances of a lawsuit by making a bad choice. Often the company could have made a better decision.

You Really Can Make Better Hiring and Promotion Decisions

Many employers believe that hiring and promotion decisions come down to the luck of the draw. Sometimes we get them right and sometimes we just get them wrong. Perhaps, but there are things you can do to increase your chances of success. First, look at your hiring and promotion processes and, as discussed in Chapter 5, do something to make them better. Whether that is utilizing a pre-employment test that evaluates leadership traits, or whether it's a question of conducting better interviews, improving the process increases the chances of getting better outcomes.

In addition, many employers do little or nothing to train managers to be better managers. Leadership training programs are available on the market. So is interactive training that will increase critical reasoning skills in the management environment. Contact those who have a good reputation for conducting impactful training. Oddly, companies sometimes have budgets for litigation but little or no budget to conduct training that might eliminate some of those lawsuits. That's called misprioritizing.

Finally, if you have made an error and placed the wrong person into a management position, do something about that. If the manager in question isn't doing you much good, make a move. Granted, everyone deserves a fair chance to prove himself or herself, but if you wait too long, your credibility will disappear as quickly as the problem manager's has. You simply can't let that happen.

> ## Play Ball by the Rules
> Managers and higher leaders alike start their careers with a "ball of credibility." They are figuratively handed that ball with the position. The ball starts at the size of a basketball. It then gets bigger or smaller over time. If you have a manager who now is holding a medicine ball, promote him. If another manager is playing ping-pong with her ball, work her out of the company.

OK, You've Convinced Me, but What About This Alcohol Thing?

Let's talk about the impact of alcohol on most people. For the average employee, one drink and they start to feel a little better about life. Two drinks and the world's a better place than it used to be. Three drinks and the mind starts to wander. Somewhere around four drinks in, love is suddenly in the air. And when it is, often the only people available to experience it within a particular setting are co-workers.

It seems that every organization has its own tales of employee bad behavior fueled by alcohol. Some of those stories are funny, some are sad, and a few are simply amazing. Here are three of those stories, one from each category.

The Sorry Tale of the Alcoholic Manager

Brian was a very good manager who had been hired to be the director of accounting. Unbeknownst to his employer, Brain was an alcoholic. With all due credit to Brian, he was fully aware of his problem and 99% of the time, he avoided alcohol. That was a wise decision because when Brian started to drink, he always had a very difficult time stopping.

At one point, Brian's employer decided to have a retreat for its higher-level managers. Planning meetings occurred during the day followed by wining and dining in the evenings. The first night, Brian avoided drinking. The second night, however, he decided to have one glass of wine, which apparently became two, seven, and then ten glasses of wine. A happy drunk, Brian told stories to the CFO's wife about his sexual liaison with another executive's spouse at his prior firm, he complimented a female manager on the size of her breasts, and he led the singing of "For he's a jolly good fellow" in honor of the CEO.

The evening's activities wouldn't have gotten Brian fired. The other managers pretty much realized that Brian had too much to drink and, with a little concern and a little bemusement, decided at breakfast that an appropriate coaching session was needed. The coaching session, however, never occurred because Brain failed to show up for the second day of the planning meetings, even though his was the key presentation of the day. After finding and drinking another bottle of wine at the end of the prior evening's festivities, Brian passed out and did not wake up until 4:30 in the afternoon.

Brian ultimately was quite honest about his alcohol problem. And the company was impressively understanding. Rather than firing Brian, they agreed to let him attend a substance rehab program and gave him a last chance agreement. Two months later, however, at a client dinner, Brian fell off the wagon again and he was fired.

Alcoholism is an awful disease. The recidivism rate is extremely high and Brian apparently could not fully stay clean. Unfortunately, that cost him his job, and it is hard to blame the company for its decision. The employer did give Brian a severance package, including yet another rehab program. However, the company didn't feel that it could continue to risk Brian's behavior given that he was the second-highest-level financial person in the entire organization.

The Tale of the Happy Nude Water Skier

Stories are always told about the company picnic and the company holiday party. Why these two particular events? One word: alcohol. Once the beer starts flowing, amazing things happen. Who knew that Brianna in accounting always yearned to be a pole dancer? It turns out that she had simply been too shy to try until Ralph and Ramon from purchasing egged her on at the holiday party with two extra shots of tequila.

As for the tale of the nude water skier, the event was the summer picnic of a manufacturing company. As always, the employer rented an area at the lake, provided food, and made a beach available. Oh, and one more thing—there was beer, lots and lots of beer. The drinking started about noon and by 4:00, everyone was having a rip-roaring time. It was about then, in fact, that Richie decided to water ski in the nude.

Fortunately, Richie was a really good water skier. Unfortunately, he was drunk enough to decide that dropping his shorts and doing a few passes as close to the beach as possible was a really good idea. And what talent! Richie even managed to drop a ski and scream at everyone, "look at me, look at me."

The scene was reminiscent of the old joke: "Q: What're a redneck's last words? A: Hey, y'all, watch this." Fortunately, Richie didn't die, but he also didn't make it to his next paycheck. But he at least left everyone else with a great story to tell for years to come—"Hey, Ernie, do you remember that time when Richie dropped his trunks and skied past everyone at the beach?" "Yup, sure do, what a great guy he was."

The "This Should Be in a Book" Tale of the Two Sales Representatives

Some companies seem to purposely invite problems related to bad judgment and alcohol. A number of them reward salespeople for their success. They name such persons to the "admiral's club," or something similar. Then they send those top performers to a congratulatory retreat or even a cruise, often without spouses. And, of course, they ply them with alcohol.

Why don't those companies also just throw in strippers and Chippendale dancers? Good grief, the above scenario is guaranteed to create some kind of good story, probably every year. And, in fact, it does just that.

On one of these events, Tammy and Sam, two young sales representatives from different parts of the country (both married and both among the top salespeople in the entire Fortune 200 company), close the bar at 2:00 a.m. on the last night of the retreat. Somewhere around that same time, Tammy and

Sam jointly decide that they simply have to have each other. They're kissing and cuddling as the bar closes and they not-so-quietly decide to look for a room so they can move to the next level of passion.

Immediately Tammy and Sam encounter a logistical problem. They can't go to Sam's room because he is sharing the room with someone else from his office. Fortunately, Tammy has her own room, but she is too drunk to remember which room is hers. All she recalls is that her room is somewhere on the 5th floor.

Sam and Tammy work their way up to the 5th floor, fall laughing out of the elevator, and kiss and hug their way down the hall. As they work their way down the corridor, they loudly try Tammy's key in every passing door. Their passion is quickly building and they haphazardly bump loudly into various doors as they try to figure out which one is Tammy's. Alas, if they only knew that Tammy's room is actually on the 6th floor rather than the 5th.

In any event, at about 2:30 in the morning, tired of searching for Tammy's room, Sam and Tammy have a mutual revelation. What do they need a room for? After all, they have the hallway.

And how does the employer come to know all this? Because four different people saw Tammy and Sam going at it in the hallway. Amazingly, none of these four spectators was actually in the hallway. Rather, they were watching through the little oval peepholes in their hotel doors.

Ultimately, the employer is left in a bind. After all, Tammy and Sam are two of its best sales representatives. Given that, the employer admonishes each of them and chooses to withhold their performance bonus due to their inappropriate behavior. At that point, Tammy threatens to sue. Her claim? Sexual harassment. When confronted with the evidence that Tammy sure seemed to be enjoying being harassed, Tammy responded by arguing that she had been too drunk to know what she was doing and therefore it wasn't her fault. A ridiculous claim? Of course. A bad idea by the employer in the first place? It sure was.

So Should We Banish Alcohol from Company Events?

While it's worth considering the banishment of alcohol at company events, that may be impractical. Certainly it makes sense to serve something other than beer at the company picnic. Be aware, however, that people will likely bring their own anyway. Further, there are business events where alcohol actually seems to be a business necessity. Our society largely sees such events as appropriate. In fact, a reasonable level of drinking can help people to enjoy each other's company more and create a better team environment. So long, that is, as the magic line of bad judgment is not crossed.

Team building aside, one great reason to consider banning alcohol at company events is the risk that can come from serving drinks and then allowing people to drive. Virtually every state has a law that permits legal actions, including criminal proceedings, to be brought against the server of alcohol, even if that server is a homeowner or an employer rather than a bar. Consequently, caution has to be exercised to avoid this potential serious liability.

Do You Know Better?

These state laws are called "dram shop" laws. Originally meant for bars, most now apply to any situation in which a host serves alcohol. Liability is not usually automatic. The question is whether the host should have known better than to continue serving alcohol to the individual in question.

Do We Have the Option of Serving Alcohol, If We're Careful?

Potential liability notwithstanding, alcohol is still being served by employers in a variety of contexts. Social mores continue to make that the norm in many organizations, from small businesses to large accounting and law firms. However, if you're going to serve alcohol to employees, be careful.

First, getting your employees drunk should not be your goal. Mixing in a little alcohol to allow for better social interaction is okay. Passing around shots to see who can drink the most is a really stupid idea. Remember you're an employer. Your fraternity days are officially over.

Second, watch what's happening during the event and see if any problems are being created. If someone has had too much to drink or if Wayne in HR is hitting on Melissa in marketing, feel free to intercede in the interest of good judgment.

Third, have a plan ready in case some people seem too inebriated to drive. And, in cases of doubt, don't take no for an answer. Have a taxi on call if needed, and force the issue where it is reasonable to do so.

Any Other Words of Wisdom?

Yes, don't be naive. People plus alcohol plus company function creates a potentially potent mixture. Plan ahead and take some reasonable steps to reduce the chances of a serious problem. You don't have to become a prudish, stick-in-the-mud employer. However, you also don't want to be foolhardy.

As for your managers and their various levels of judgment, do something to increase your chances of success. Improve your promotion practices, conduct pre-employment testing where appropriate, and train managers in leadership and other essential skills. At that point, the mistakes should decrease. Be aware, however, that mistakes of judgment will still happen—remember that people are people. Nevertheless, if you act to better your interests, other people will too.

CHAPTER 22

Sexual Orientation, Same-Sex Issues, and the "Because of Sex" Requirement

When most people hear the term "sexual harassment," it brings to mind a stereotypical situation: A female employee being harassed by a male co-worker or male supervisor. However, employers cannot afford to define sexual harassment by the common stereotype. Sexual harassment has been interpreted to include, as well as exclude, particular types of discrimination. You should know what types of discrimination are legally recognized as unlawful, as well as which types are not. With this information, your organization can make its own choices regarding its sexual harassment policy. Will your policy be in line with only what federal and local laws require? Or will its coverage go above and beyond the requirements of the law in your area? As discussed in Chapter 9, the latter option makes more sense in a healthy work environment, but that choice is up to you.

This chapter will assist your company in evaluating its policy and analyzing its risk. It will cover some types of sexual harassment that you may not have thought of, such as same-sex sexual harassment. It will also provide detailed information on sexual orientation harassment, a type of discrimination that, although not illegal under federal law, has received a lot of attention in state and local legislation. Finally, you'll be given suggestions for reviewing your company's sexual harassment policy with same-sex and sexual orientation harassment in mind to ensure that the policy is designed to cover these areas of potential liability.

Not a Laughing Matter: How Same-Sex Sexual Harassment Can Arise in the Workplace

Same-sex sexual harassment can be a gay female supervisor asking a female subordinate for sexual favors. However, that isn't a common occurrence. Same-sex harassment instead may be more commonly known in your workplace as "horseplay," "joking," "teasing or kidding," "fooling around," or "locker room talk." Let's examine the following scenario and consider whether the conduct is "roughhousing," or whether it rises to the level of same-sex sexual harassment.

Gay Doesn't Excuse

There are cases where a gay manager hits on a subordinate employee. Those cases raise the same issues of foolishness (i.e., quid pro quo, in many circumstances) discussed in Chapter 11. They should be treated in the same manner, which is usually pretty harshly.

Gary, a forklift operator at a construction site, is a quiet and soft-spoken man who keeps mostly to himself. He is a good worker who comes to the job site every day and performs his duties without question. Gary is not much of a partier and prefers the solitude of his apartment to a night out at Molly O'Shea's Irish Pub. Gary also has a crush on one of his neighbors, Brianna. If he arrives home promptly at 5:30 p.m. every weekday, he can usually run into Brianna and strike up a conversation as she's on her way to pick up her three kids at school. Therefore, Gary's never gone out with the guys after work.

Gary's co-workers are resentful of the fact that he never joins in with them and their happy-hour antics at Molly O'Shea's. They've recently begun teasing Gary about his lack of desire to go to the bar after work, and that perhaps he "can't hold his liquor like a man" and that "he's a girlie girl." After a particularly wild night at Molly O'Shea's, one of Gary's drunken co-workers sneaks back into the facility and spray-paints the particular forklift Gary always uses with abusive phrases in bright pink. The drunken co-worker also spray paints a picture of Gary in a dress in the men's bathroom.

Gary complains to management about the above behavior. The spray paint is cleaned up, but management brushes aside what happened as "horseplay." However, three of Gary's co-workers are upset that he reported the problem and they assault him in the parking lot after their shift one night. They drag Gary to his car, which they have vandalized with the pink spray paint, and pull a pink tutu over his head and around his waist. They also pull pink panties over his jeans, touching him inappropriately in the process. The whole time Gary is taunted with claims that he is a "wussy." Gary's co-workers tie him up and leave him in the parking lot, hoping the workers on the next shift will find him. Thankfully, a security guard notices Gary, rescues him, and sends him safely home.

It's hard not to feel sorry for Gary after what his co-workers did to him, but was this just mean-spirited horseplay, or do the actions of Gary's co-workers rise to the level of same-sex sexual harassment? In order to answer this question, we must first examine what same-sex sexual harassment is, and when and why inappropriate behavior will be categorized as same-sex sexual harassment.

What Is Same-Sex Sexual Harassment?

Same-sex sexual harassment occurs when the harasser and the victim are members of the same gender, and the victim can establish that the harassment was "based on his or her sex." Such harassment can constitute either quid pro quo sexual harassment or hostile work environment sexual harassment. Same-sex sexual harassment can occur between males and males and between females and females, regardless of the sexual orientation of either the victim or the harasser. It also can occur whether or not the harassment was based on sexual desire. The focus of the inquiry is on the conduct and the direction of the conduct. Here are the legal questions that arise:

1. Was the conduct unwelcome and based on gender?
2. Was the conduct related to a term or condition of the victim's employment?
3. Did the conduct create a hostile work environment?

Applying these three factors to Gary's situation, he probably has a claim of hostile work environment same-sex sexual harassment. Gary obviously didn't appreciate his co-workers' comments, because he complained to management about the harassment. Further, the comments were based on Gary's gender, or in this case, his co-workers' opinion that Gary lacked the "stereotypical" male attributes of enjoying partying, drinking, and spending time with other men in a bar setting. Therefore, Gary was harassed for being a male who was not "man enough" for the men around him.

Considering that the harassing conduct occurred over a period of time and involved a physical altercation, there may also probably be enough evidence for Gary to show that he suffered from a hostile work environment due to the severity of the behavior.

Why Is Same-Sex Sexual Harassment Unlawful?

For a period of time, it was unclear whether federal law actually made same-sex sexual harassment unlawful. After reading about what happened to Gary, it might be hard to understand why there was any hesitation. The difficulty lies in the purpose behind our country's laws against discrimination. Title VII was designed to prevent discrimination based on particular categories, one being a person's sex. Further, the understanding of the problem of sexual harassment when the law was passed was that men were harassing women. It never occurred to Congress or most courts that men could be sexually harassing other men. So while the teasing and taunting Gary experienced from his male co-workers probably qualifies as same-sex sexual harassment, inappropriate behaviors in the workplace between members of the same sex were for years not anywhere on the radar screen.

No Debates Then

Remember that Title VII was passed in 1964. Gays were not exactly stepping out of the closet in the 1960s. Consequently, issues of sexual orientation weren't the subject of many congressional debates.

The key to falling under Title VII's protection is this: the inappropriate behavior between persons of the same sex *must* be based on the victim's gender. Do you recall the story early in the book about the bisexual supervisor not being in violation of the law? That's because his come-on's were not based on sex—he was willing to come on to either sex.

So what does "based on sex" mean? Let's compare the following example to what happened to Gary:

Shelly is a beautiful and fashionable young woman who is always up on the latest trends. She is pursuing a fashion design degree but in her spare time works at a chic clothing store. Shelly loves her job, except for the fact that she has a co-worker named Jessica who doesn't do any work. Instead, Jessica is constantly primping in the mirror and trying on the expensive clothes the store carries whenever the supervisor leaves the store on break. Jessica also asks Shelly what Shelly thinks of the various outfits and which one looks best on Jessica. Jessica leaves the outfits she has tried on in the floor of the dressing room for Shelly to pick up.

Shelly, fed up with Jessica, asks her manager if she can work a different schedule to avoid Jessica. Jessica overhears Shelly's request. Hurt and upset, Jessica begins to treat Shelly very badly when Shelly's new schedule overlaps with Jessica's shift. Jessica insults Shelly's personal clothing choices, as well as the combinations Shelly selects for the store mannequins. Jessica also blows kisses at Shelly in a sarcastic way whenever Shelly leaves the store. When Shelly ignores her, Jessica points to her own buttocks and tells Shelly to "kiss it."

Shelly, feeling harassed and at a loss of what to do to make Jessica stop this behavior, files a claim of sexual harassment with the clothing store.

While Jessica's behavior is certainly inappropriate, it doesn't rise to the level of same-sex sexual harassment. Unlike Gary's situation, Shelly is not uncomfortable because she's being harassed about her sex. Instead, she's being harassed because she has a personality conflict with Jessica. Although some of Jessica's actions could be considered sexual in nature, the basis of the harassment is actually the animosity between the two women. Therefore, Shelly doesn't have a claim of same-sex sexual harassment.

In another case from a few years ago, the male president of a small company had an affair with one of his workers. According to the worker, she was forced into having the affair due to the president's power over her job. Ultimately, the affair ended when the president's wife found out about it. The president then fired the female worker with whom he had been having the affair. Does that sound like quid pro quo sexual harassment? Maybe, but it wasn't. The reason for the discharge was that the president's wife, *who owned the company*, ordered the president to fire the female employee. Consequently, the woman wasn't fired "because of" her sex. She was fired because the wife/owner was mad at the husband/president for having an affair.

Addressing Same-Sex Sexual Harassment in the Workplace

Going back to Shelly's case, the fact that she doesn't have a viable legal claim of sexual harassment should be irrelevant to the good employer. What happened in that situation was inappropriate behavior by Jessica even if it wasn't sexual harassment. Recall that Gary's ordeal with same-sex sexual harassment started out with teasing about not going to the bar after work. Animosity between workers can quickly escalate into sexual harassment if the employer is not mindful of what is taking place on the job site. To help your company remain vigilant about same-sex sexual harassment, consider doing the following:

1. Don't overlook complaints of excessive teasing, horseplay, or locker room antics in your workplace. As we have discussed, these sorts of situations may already be, or can quickly escalate into, same-sex sexual harassment.
2. Make sure that your sexual harassment policy is taken seriously and is

consistently implemented. Just because the situation doesn't meet your stereotypical "male/female" sexual harassment situation doesn't mean its not unlawful sexual harassment.

3. Update your sexual harassment policy to include same-sex sexual harassment as yet another example of inappropriate behavior. Educate your employees on same-sex sexual harassment. They can't report the offensive behavior as sexual harassment if they don't understand the broad ranges of conduct your policy covers.

4. Investigate all claims of sexual harassment in a timely, fair, and efficient manner. Remember that same-sex sexual harassment is focused on whether the conduct is based on sex and has nothing to do with the sexual orientation of the parties or whether sexual desire is involved. Also remember that, to be safe, your focus should be on inappropriate behavior, no matter how it arises.

Sexual Orientation Discrimination

Sexual orientation discrimination occurs when an employee is treated differently or harassed because of his or her real or perceived sexual orientation. This form of discrimination differs from same-sex harassment or sex discrimination because the conduct is based on the victim's sexual orientation, rather than his or her status of being male or female. To help illustrate the difference, let's look at the following example:

David is a male nurse who works the night shift at the local hospital. He enjoys socializing with his co-workers, the majority of whom are female. The female nurses find David very attractive and often talk about his clean-cut appearance and taste in designer clothing. One nurse, Amanda, is very taken with David and often talks about him with the doctors with whom she is assigned to work.

Dr. Anderson, who works with Amanda often, is tired of hearing the nurses swoon over David. He doesn't understand why the nurses are so interested in a guy that is obviously a homosexual. Frustrated by the nurses' "misplaced" attraction and his own dislike for homosexuals, Dr. Anderson begins making snide comments about David's sexual orientation whenever a nurse praises him. He also constantly asks David about his "boyfriend" and when he "is going to come out of the closet."

When Amanda overhears Dr. Anderson's remarks about David one day, she tells him to leave David alone. Dr. Anderson comments that Amanda should give it up because "that fag is never going to sleep with you." David is standing right behind Dr. Anderson and hears the entire exchange. David files a sexual harassment claim against Dr. Anderson with the hospital's Human Resources department.

Unlike the situation with Gary the forklift operator, Dr. Anderson is focusing on David not because he is male, but because Dr. Anderson perceives that David "is obviously a homosexual." Dr. Anderson's harassing remarks center on David's perceived sexual orientation, are clearly unwelcome, and are causing David to work in a hostile work environment. However, despite the troublesome nature of Dr. Anderson's conduct, such conduct would not be considered sexual harassment in many parts of the country.

But ... Isn't Sexual Orientation Discrimination Against the Law?

One answer to this question is "Yes." Another answer to this question is "No." The most correct answer is "It depends." The unlawful nature of sexual orientation discrimination depends on where the conduct takes place. Federal laws against discrimination do not include sexual orientation as a protected category. A large number of state discrimination laws do recognize sexual orientation as a protected category, but many others do not. To make matters more confusing, many counties and municipalities have also passed their own local ordinances to provide protection against sexual orientation discrimination. To determine whether your organization has a duty to provide protection from discrimination and harassment on the basis of sexual orientation, you must be aware of both state and local laws.

1. State Laws

As of the date of this book's publication, 17 states and the District of Columbia prohibit sexual orientation discrimination by private employers. The 17 states include California, Connecticut, Hawaii, Illinois, Maine, Maryland, Massachusetts, Minnesota, Nevada, New Hampshire, New Jersey, New Mexico, New York, Rhode Island, Vermont, Washington, and Wisconsin. Additionally, while no state law has been passed, at least one court in Oregon has found that sexual orientation discrimination is prohibited by Oregon's state constitution.

2. Local Laws

More than 180 cities and counties across the country prohibit discrimination on the basis of sexual orientation. If you are unsure whether local laws provide protection against sexual orientation discrimination, check with your state labor department or state fair employment office.

Finding Local Laws

One problem with local ordinances is that they can be very difficult to find. They aren't published in the same manner as state and federal laws. If you have an interest in identifying locations where sexual orientation discrimination has been made illegal, try checking the GLAD web site or the web site of the Human Rights Campaign Foundation (which has great search tool), or a publisher such as BNA or CCH, or data that can be provided to you by an employment law firm.

Other Causes of Action

Even if no state or local laws provide protection against sexual orientation discrimination, your company should still consider providing protection against this type of discrimination. Victims of sexual orientation discrimination may still be able to sue their employer or co-workers under a number of legal theories that are generally applicable in a majority of states:

- Assault
- Battery
- Invasion of privacy
- Intentional infliction of emotional distress

- Defamation
- Interference with an employment contract
- Wrongful termination
- Negligent hiring, retention, and/or training

Of course, the victim of sexual orientation discrimination must be able to prove his or her case under one of these theories, and not on the basis of sexual orientation discrimination itself. However, it is easy to see how the conduct associated with sexual orientation discrimination can fall into one of the above categories.

Let's take, for example, a lawsuit for defamation. To prove defamation, generally all a victim has to do is show the following: (1) an oral or written statement to someone other than himself, (2) that is false, and (2) that was understood to be about the victim or that harmed the victim's reputation.

Apply these three factors to the conflict between David and Dr. Anderson. Even if Dr. Anderson's behavior took place in a locale that doesn't recognize sexual orientation harassment, David may be able to sue Dr. Anderson for his defamatory comments. In addition, David will probably pursue a negligent hiring, retention, and training action against the hospital.

Law or No Law

Many employers are protecting gays against discrimination as a matter of policy even if the law applicable to them doesn't require such protection. A decent number of employers now even provide benefits to same-sex partners, and some states have passed law requiring such benefits.

With the various numbers of tort and negligence claims available to sexual orientation harassment victims, your organization should carefully consider whether to provide protection for this category even if state and local laws do not mandate such protection. Further, for all the reasons we have previously discussed, you're better off focusing on inappropriate behavior anyway, whether or not such behavior amounts to sexual harassment.

Muddying the Waters a Bit More: When Sexual Orientation Discrimination May Be Unlawful Under Federal Law

We've just discussed that sexual orientation discrimination is not prohibited under federal law, but that it may be unlawful under state or local law, depending on your location. However, due to some recent court cases, federal law is not completely down for the count on sexual orientation discrimination just yet. With just the right kind of sexual orientation harassment, a homosexual employee, or an employee that is perceived to be homosexual, may be able to bring a lawsuit based on the following two situations:

1. Where the harassers are motivated, either in whole or in part, by a belief that the homosexual employee was not conforming to stereotypical gender roles
2. Where the harassers offensively touch body parts of the homosexual employee that are associated with sexuality

The reason these two situations may qualify as actionable sexual harassment is this: The employee's sexual orientation harassment claim would still be disallowed because it's not recognized by Title VII as a viable claim. However, the above conduct may constitute plain old sexual harassment based on sex.

To illustrate the first situation, let's look again at Gary the forklift operator and compare his claim to David the nurse. Suppose that both Gary and David were homosexuals. Neither of them could bring a federal discrimination lawsuit based on sexual orientation harassment. However, Gary could probably bring a federal sexual harassment lawsuit because his harassers were motivated by a belief that Gary's behavior was not how men ought to behave. In contrast, David would probably still be out of luck. His harasser, Dr. Anderson, wasn't harassing David because of his failure to conform to the idea of the stereotypical male, but rather, because of his opinion about what he believed were David's sexual choices. Dr. Anderson never related his harassment of David to the idea that David failed to conform to masculine stereotypes.

Gary's situation also helps to illustrate the second situation where sexual orientation harassment may be actionable as typical sexual harassment. Recall that Gary was physically assaulted by his harassers, who pulled a pink tutu over his head and pink panties over his jeans, touching him inappropriately in the process. Where harassers engage in the offensive touching of body parts associated with sexuality, it may be enough to show that the conduct was based not only on the victim's sexual orientation, but on sex as well.

Obviously these concepts can be very confusing. Realize that we're once again trying to stick a round peg into a square hole. Consequently, the best advice is to be responsive to any claims of offensive behavior or harassment. For the sake of company reputation and positive working environment, no company should tolerate such inappropriate behavior in the workplace, whether directed at homosexual employees or not. However, from a legal standpoint, be sure to listen to complaints from employees for instances of gender stereotyping or offensive bodily contact. These factors could trigger liability under Title VII even if sexual orientation is the basis for the conduct.

Addressing Sexual Orientation Discrimination in the Workplace

Regardless of what discrimination laws are applicable to your company, you should consider protecting employees from sexual orientation discrimination. Sexual orientation discrimination can open an employer up to tort liability, as well as a regular sexual harassment claim if the harassing conduct involves gender stereotyping or offensive bodily contact. As we have discussed, a general way to encompass a prohibition on sexual orientation discrimination into your company's policies is to utilize a general policy against inappropriate behavior. This type of policy will also make the sometimes difficult distinction between same-sex sexual harassment and sexual orientation harassment less burdensome for your staff. Under a policy against inappropriate behavior, it doesn't matter on what basis a victim is being discriminated against or harassed—it's the conduct, not the cause, that triggers employee discipline.

CHAPTER 23

Customers, Vendors, and Other Nonemployees: Thar Be Dragons Here, Too

As originally created, Title VII focused on discriminatory acts by employers, employment agencies, and unions. Things have changed since 1964. Among the many ways that business is different now than it was then relates to what jobs an employer fills with actual employees, as opposed to temps, contractors, and the like.

Let's provide some history. In 1964, the average manufacturing company employed virtually everyone who was present on its site. That included the security guards, the cafeteria workers, the janitorial crew, and the vacation relief team. At least back then it was easy to tell who the employees were—one could assume that they included virtually everyone who was on the site.

In 2007, things are very different than they were in the 1960s. Now the guards are supplied by an outside guard service. The janitors come from a cleaning company. The cafeteria workers are provided by Joe's Sandwich Shop or by a national food service company. And the vacation relief team is now comprised of temps, who also appear in various other roles at the location.

Beyond these nonemployees, the average work site also includes contractors, vendors, consultants, the occasional re-engineered retiree, and a variety of other persons. However, one thing remains consistent—all these on-site characters are human beings, meaning they too might have an interest in things like sex. So is the employer responsible for their escapades too? The answer is usually, "yes."

But These People Aren't Mine!

You say they aren't yours, but sometimes they are. Ever heard of a concept called co-employment? It's what happens when you exercise too much control over a contractor, a temp, or a consultant. Even if that person is technically employed by someone else or is an "independent contractor," he or she becomes yours (and also theirs) for legal purposes. The Internal Revenue Service and others have issued detailed tests for analyzing when a person is an

---

Independence and the IRS

Here is a link to one explanatory page from the IRS on the independent contractor issue: http://www.irs.gov/businesses/small/article/0,,id=99921,00.html. There also exist formal IRS regulations on the topic. In addition, most states have passed their own laws and regulations dictating who is and who is not an employee. The state laws largely, but not entirely, are patterned off the IRS rules.

---

independent contractor and when he or she is not. The most crucial element of that analysis relates to the amount of control an organization exercises over the day-to-day work of the individual.

If the person ends up being yours under the above control test, he or she is likely to also be your employee for Title VII purposes. In other words, he or she can sue you. Similarly, his or her actions could create liability for you. And that includes in regard to issues of discrimination and harassment. For example, if a contractor sexually harasses your employee, a co-employment relationship over that contractor could lead to your having the responsibility for resolving the problem.

But What If I've Done Everything Right and They're Not Mine?

Unfortunately, liability might even arise if you have been careful not to unduly control a contractor or temp to the point of making him or her a co-employee. A number of courts and state laws have created liability for harassment even if the problems occur between one of your actual employees and nonemployees with whom they interact. Based upon current law, your best bet is to assume that you have responsibility for such problems whether you actually have a legal obligation or you don't. Certainly the implications of such harassment will affect you whether or not a legal duty arises.

To make things worse, you have reason to be concerned whether your employee is harassed by an outsider or whether it is your worker who decided to make inappropriate sexual comments to a vendor's representative, a summer intern, or the copy machine repairman. All these things happen with considerable frequency. Television sitcoms have even featured such scenes and, as we all know, TV is just a microcosm for reality (or is it the other way around?).

Liability for Customers

Customer issues can cause some of the biggest of problems. Let's picture how the harassment issue usually arises in this situation.

Wendy Robinson is a young, female salesperson who is trying hard to make it in this, her first sales job. Wendy, is earnest, hard-working, a bit naive, and very attractive. To get her started, you assigned her to work with Ronaldo Hernandez. Ronaldo does a good job of showing Wendy the ropes before he turns over three accounts for her to handle on her own. One of those accounts is with Framed Works, whose assigned buyer for your account is Franz Mikaels.

After a month of calling on Framed Works, Wendy seems to be making considerable progress in further developing the sales relationship between your company and Framed Works. What Wendy doesn't realize, however, is that the relationship is succeeding in part because Franz is hitting on her. While he has not actually asked her for a date or for sex yet, he has been doing what he refers to as "setting the table." Two weeks later, when Wendy meets with him "over a quick drink to discuss a new deal," Franz asks her if she is dating anyone and if she is interested in going to his condo for a while.

Wendy apologizes to Franz "for apparently misleading him." She then tries to orient things back to business. Franz, however, is not to be easily denied. He offers Wendy an increase in sales if she'll sleep with him. Wendy says she needs to think about that, then excuses herself and breaks off the meeting.

A week later, Ronaldo approaches you and says that the two of you need to talk. After closing your office door, he tells you that Wendy has reported the above facts to him. Fortunately, she is being professional and reasonable about the situation. Among other things, Ronaldo explains that he suggested to Wendy that she give him back the Framed Works account and he would get her a different account. Wendy's response to that offer, however, was to ask why she should be punished for the harassment created by the customer. In fact, Wendy apparently hesitated to report any of the harassment because she didn't want to get Franz in trouble or affect the relationship between your company and Framed Works.

So what do you do now? Fire the customer? Good grief, surely that can't be required under the law. It's not like you have a never-ending supply of good customers.

In fact, an employer may have to fire a customer to avoid sexual harassment. However, that usually happens in restaurants and bars, and typically there is only an individual customer involved in the problem. In situations such as Wendy's, there are better solutions. Remember, the legal requirement is to take whatever reasonable steps are needed to stop the harassment. Consequently, the best thing to do is call Framed Works to discuss the situation. Many small businesses may feel very awkward about this call to a customer, but in today's world, the call usually works without putting the customer relationship at risk.

One key to successfully resolving the above problem is determining who in your organization can best discuss the problem with the appropriate person at Framed Works. The answers to that question can be plentiful, including owner to owner, sales executive to purchasing executive, human resources to human resources, or a variety of other combinations. Consider the options carefully, but don't sit back and say it's not your problem. It is your problem, but the situation can usually be resolved without losing Wendy or causing a lawsuit.

Customer Relationships

Most customers, in fact, welcome a call. They are worried about liability too. Be sensitive for certain about the customer relationship, but realize that there is way to raise the issue properly and in a way that will protect both organizations.

But What If the Customer Doesn't Want to Be Reasonable?

Most of the time, the customer is as interested as you are in avoiding a legal mess. However, there are some customers who might not fully comprehend the problem, or a customer might believe the story that Franz has concocted rather than the description of the facts that Wendy has provided to you.

In situations that aren't easily resolved, it could be appropriate to ask Wendy to give up the Framed Works account. Hopefully that will be the rare case, and hopefully you can find a replacement account so that Wendy is not affected monetarily. If a major customer doesn't get it and firing the customer isn't the right move, however, you may need to find a creative way to make Wendy happy.

In certain circumstances, it may be appropriate to create some appropriate evidence to protect yourself. That approach usually arises in situations involving vendors, contractors, and temp agencies than it does customers. Such evidence is discussed in the action plan contained at the end of this chapter.

You May Have More Leverage over Vendors, Contractors, and Temp Agencies Than You Have over Customers

The interaction problem experienced by Wendy and Franz or something like it can arise in numerous circumstances. How about the temp that makes a sexual comment to your employee, or the employee that hits on a contractor, or even the vendor that just can't keep his sexist comments to himself when he is visiting your location?

Customers are usually the most difficult cases because you can't afford to lose your customers. Stated differently, the customer has the leverage and usually you don't. By contrast, your company is more likely to have leverage over vendors, contractors, and temp agencies. Consequently, if one of the employees of these outside parties harasses your worker, you can usually take a stronger stance. Often the best thing to do is tell the outside party to assign the problem child to a work site other than yours. However, do *not* tell the outside party to fire its employee. That decision is for the other party, not you, and if you cross that boundary, you might be back to the co-employment problem that was discussed earlier in this chapter.

Also, leverage doesn't mean you can do anything you want to do. If it is your employee that has harassed the temp or the contractor, telling the outside party to remove its employee from your site without doing more isn't going to keep you out of legal trouble. While a transfer of a temp in those circumstances may be a good idea, this shouldn't occur by your mandate. Rather, it should take place after an investigation, discussion with the temp agency, and discipline given to your worker, assuming that discipline is appropriate. Otherwise, you haven't done your legal duty—you have merely misused your leverage.

> ## Keep the Contractors at Arm's Length
>
> One practical problem related to contractors is that they often are on your site every day. Consequently, the walls break down and often the contractor employees think they're working for you. Do yourself a legal favor—don't invite the contractors and temps to the steak fry or to the holiday party. If you want them to be able to attend such events, have their employer offer the invitation.

A Plan for Investigating and Dealing with Alleged Third-Party Discrimination or Harassment

1. Realize That the Problem Does Occur

Employers tend to focus on the issues created by their own employees, sometimes to the exclusion of other issues. Granted, issues with temps tend to hit employers right over the head, but the knee-jerk reaction in such circumstances is often a problematic "fire the temp." By comparison to vendor-employee and customer-employee issues, blinders often blur the underlying concern. In situations that involve harassment, the smart employer doesn't focus entirely on the employment relationship, but the problem itself. While these cross-organizational issues might concern two companies, potential liability arises for each, and therefore the issues need to be addressed.

2. Don't Over-React, but Do Take Action

Where a third-party employee harasses your employee, it is easy to demand that the third-party employee be fired. But guess what—now *you've* made the discharge decision instead of having the actual employer do that. Certainly you should demand action when an outside employee does something inappropriate, but you should work through his or her employer in that regard.

3. Investigate the Issues, Involving the Third-Party Employer As Appropriate

Because the third party has a stake in this situation, it should be involved as well in dealing with these types of inter-company problems. While it may seem awkward, the investigation of this harassment or discrimination situation should be done by both employers. Depending upon the circumstances, they can investigate separately or together, but since each must get the full story, some level of cooperation makes sense. Only through a dual investigation can both companies get the facts they need to say that they have acted reasonably under the law.

4. Realize That Remedies May Be Different in the Context of a Third-Party Situation

Where a two-employer problem exists, the remedy isn't as simple as discipline/separation. As with Wendy above, the harassed employee may have a legitimate business interest in continuing to work with the second employer. Hopefully that employer will realize that Franz needs to be disciplined or transferred so he won't bother Wendy again. However handled, remedies in multi-employer situations get complex, and such remedies may need to be more creative.

5. Documentation (and Evidence) May Be Different in This Context As Well

You'll still want to document your investigation and remedy as you would in any instance of harassment or discrimination. In a multi-employer situation, however, there may need to be correspondence back and forth between the companies. Be cautious about that exercise—correspondence where each employer blames the other will come back to haunt both companies. Granted, there will be times when a firm but reasonable letter needs to be sent saying "you need to deal with your harasser," but cooperation creates a better defense and prevents a plaintiff from "dividing and conquering."

6. Exert Pressure If the Third Party Isn't Cooperating Effectively

As the above suggestions intimate, there are times when the other employer may not fully comprehend the need for meaningful action. Temp agencies are usually quick to remove a temp that isn't making the agency's customer happy. However, vendors and contractors as well as customers may make for a more difficult challenge. As stated previously, an e-mail or letter-writing battle isn't the best way to resolve such issues, although an appropriate and reasonable letter may be needed from time to time. To avoid creating problematic proof, however, phone calls and meetings are best. Two years from the date of the call, no one will remember the details, but e-mails and the harsh language that is in them seem to live forever.

Be Careful with E-Mail

E-mails are a potential legal disaster because they are often so casual and frank. In effect, we write e-mail like we talk, not like we would write a memo. Be cautious—if you are addressing an important issue in an e-mail, write it appropriately.

---

7. Don't End a Good Business Relationship over a Single Harassment Situation

The situation with Wendy and Franz obviously created an awkward situation, and that awkwardness can affect the two business entities as much as it does the two participants in the problem. Unless the other party completely refuses to cooperate in resolving the situation, however, don't let these circumstances cause an end to an otherwise positive business relationship. There is almost always a way to work these matters out.

8. Consider a Cooperation Clause in Your Contracts

Given how often these inter-company problems happen, one wonders why more contracts don't include cooperation clauses in which the business partners discuss how to address employee-related issues. Granted, contract clauses can create contract-oriented litigation. However, such provisions also can suggest that the companies have intended from the beginning to deal effectively with cross-organizational discrimination and harassment situations when they arise.

9. At All Times, Avoid Co-Employment Where You Can

While co-employment issues are not an overwhelming concern in the world of discrimination and harassment, the problems they cause in limited circumstances are just a minor blip compared to co-employment tax and benefit concerns. In context outside the discrimination and harassment arena, co-employment situations can create huge problems. Just ask Microsoft, which suffered through a $110 million co-employment problem. In short, pay attention—don't let their employees become your employees by exercising too much control. If a problem exists with another employer's worker, go back through that employer to solve the issue. With temps in particular, you should be a conduit of factual information rather than a decision-maker. Don't worry—95% of the time if you provide the facts, the temp agency will voluntarily solve the problem.

10. Get Help Where Needed

As should be apparent by now, the more parties one adds, the more complicated the situation gets. With Wendy and Franz, we had two people but also two employers. Things get dicey. Call a lawyer. They're not cheap, but the good ones will save you a lot of pain and anguish.

CHAPTER 24

Favoritism, Bullying, Nastiness, and Other Potential Supervisor Landmines

Employers who are concerned about all the harassment that has been addressed in this book may be wondering about one more potential issue—what about the office bully? Is he or she a legal problem too? After all, every office seems to have a manager who succeeds by bullying his or her subordinates. Sometimes, in fact, it seems that federal law must require every employer to have at least one such manager, so prevalent is the problem.

No Law to Retain Problems

Honest, there is no law requiring you to hire or retain at least one bad manager. There also is no law requiring that you hire or retain an office gossip, a problem employee, at least one worker who complains about everything, and at least six workers who don't come to work often enough. However, law or no law, it seems that every workplace has met all these obligations.

Fortunately for employers, the almost universal answer provided by the courts is that bullying, without more, is not a violation of law. Employers fairly consistently win those cases by relying on something called the "equal opportunity jerk defense." Our explanation is that the manager in question may indeed be a pain in the rear end, but if the manager is a jerk to everyone, he or she isn't discriminating and thus there is no viable legal claim.

However, the legally protected days of the bully manager may be limited. As of the date of this book, 12 states are considering legislation that would make it unlawful for a manager to bully his or her underlings. As discussed below, these statutes are very concerning, in part because the term "bullying" isn't amenable to a very clear definition. That, though, isn't likely to keep some states from passing such laws. Further, whether these state laws are enacted may be irrelevant—some courts (most notably the 9th Circuit Court of Appeals) already are finding a variety of creative ways to make "equal opportunity bullying" illegal.

Know the Law!

The states in question are purposely not listed. Proposing a law and passing a law are two different things. Be alert, however, to your state laws that affect employment. Talk with a lawyer or find some other means to update yourself about state and other developments.

Beyond bullying, this chapter also deals with the multiple problems created by supervisory favoritism, manager unfairness, and the age-old complaint about that "nasty, mean ogre that manages payroll." All of these situations create serious management concerns. Some even lead to potential legal liability.

The Limits of the Concept of a Hostile Work Environment

The word "harassment" and the term "hostile work environment" have been in the media for long enough now to confuse people about their real meaning. People complain that they have been harassed simply because they're forced to come to work on time. Others say they are victims of a hostile work environment just because their boss expects her subordinates to work hard.

While judges also occasionally get confused by the term, a hostile work environment in and of itself does not constitute a legal violation. To date, there exists no law stating that work must be a place that is both enjoyable and free from difficult supervisors. Instead, for a legal claim to exist, the problematic hostile work environment must relate to a protected characteristic such as sex, race, disability, or national origin. Anything else may be aggravating or frustrating, but it isn't against the law.

Unfortunately, not everyone understands the above limitation. Many well-trained and capable human resources professionals will tell you that a hostile work environment is illegal, without further defining the context of the term's applicability. Perhaps their error isn't that big a deal—a hostile environment can't be a good place to work, even if the hostility has nothing to do with protected characteristics. Nevertheless, it helps to sort out the illegal from the problematic, and a generic "hostile work environment" isn't a legal issue. Further, as we discussed early in this book, even a sex-based hostile work environment isn't illegal unless the actions underlying the hostility rise to the level of being severe and pervasive. Remember—Title VII isn't a code of civility.

What Constitutes an Equal Opportunity Jerk and Why He or She Isn't a Legal Problem

Let's take a real-life example. Mr. Johnson was a high-level manager in Florida for a leading stock brokerage firm. To put it mildly, Mr. Johnson had a "Type A" personality if ever there was one. He was both a screamer and a "ready, fire, aim" kind of guy. Unfortunately, Mr. Johnson's management style eventually led to the stock brokerage firm being sued over one of Mr. Johnson's decisions.

The reality is that Mr. Johnson fired Sue Smith, a female stockbroker, for legitimate reasons—her production numbers were too low. However, her sensitivity level was high, and she concluded that Mr. Johnson was a sexist. Based on that allegation, she sued him and his employer for sex discrimination in regard to the discharge decision. The case went to trial before the National Association of Securities Dealers. The hearing was, in a word, memorable.

Ms. Smith was the first witness to testify. Her testimony wasn't particularly impressive. When asked why she thought she was a victim of sex discrimination, all she did was point to Mr. Johnson and say that he didn't like women, that he felt women should be secretaries rather than stockbrokers, and that he was in general a sexist. Granted, all those accusations sound serious, but Ms. Smith provided no actual evidence to back her conclusions. Rather, she simply concluded that she was right and Mr. Johnson was wrong. In short, all was going well so far for the company.

Things got more complicated, however, when the plaintiff's counsel called his second witness—a former broker whom we'll call Ms. Sullivan. She too had been fired by Mr. Johnson. When asked at trial what she thought of Mr. Johnson, Ms. Sullivan was quite direct—in her words, "He's the biggest asshole I've ever met in my life." Wow! No mincing of words there, but did that end the deal? Of course not.

Ms. Sullivan began to tell stories about Mr. Johnson. Unfortunately for the company, she didn't stop for 45 minutes. The stories were vivid and astounding—and there was no way that Ms. Sullivan was making any of this up. Her last story in particular was telling about Mr. Johnson and his personal style.

At one point, Mr. Johnson had apparently gotten mad at Ms. Sullivan for losing an account. He screamed at her on the phone to "get [her] ass down to [his] office now." When Ms. Sullivan got to the office, Mr. Johnson slammed the door behind her and began to castigate her. As Ms. Sullivan put it, "He lost control—I watched his face go from white to red to blue to purple." In fact, Mr. Johnson got mad enough that he threw a pen at Ms. Sullivan and tossed a legal pad across the room. Later in the conversation, believe it or not, he launched a stapler at the wall. At that point, Ms. Sullivan had enough, and she walked out of the meeting. The next day, however, Mr. Johnson called Ms.

Sullivan back into his office and gave her a written warning "for leaving the meeting before it was over."

Good grief. What a jerk! So what else did she say about him? Well, that was it for stories, but at that point everyone in the courtroom was paying very close attention. The plaintiff's lawyer, feeling on top of the world at this point, had only one more question to ask: "Ms. Sullivan, having said all this about Mr. Johnson, you agree, do you not, that he discriminates against women in the workplace?" At that point, Ms. Sullivan hesitated, for 10 seconds or so. Under the circumstances, that short pause seemed like an eternity. Finally, Ms. Sullivan answered, stating "I don't think I can say that." The plaintiff's counsel, who had just been atop the ocean liner but now suddenly found himself in a life raft, meekly asked Ms. Sullivan, "Why can't you say that?" Her answer? "Mr. Johnson is a jerk, but, to be completely honest, he's a jerk to everyone, not just to women."

Ah, the quintessential equal opportunity jerk defense. And it worked. The three arbitrators correctly applied the law and decided in favor of the brokerage firm. In short, Mr. Johnson was a bad boss, but he wasn't any different to women than he was to men. So the company won. Remember—under discrimination law, an employer need not be a good employer or even a smart employer. Instead what it must be is a nondiscriminatory employer, and that is what Mr. Johnson was.

So If I Hire a Bully, I'm OK?

Well, to answer that question, maybe we should define what "ok" means. Technically speaking, you haven't violated any laws, but you also haven't done yourself a lot of good. First, those states that will eventually pass anti-bullying laws may get in your way. Second, you should read the section of this chapter below regarding the consequences of the difficult and unfair boss. These managers definitely cause problems, even if they aren't technically discrimination problems.

Finally, in cases where bad facts exist, courts create bad precedents. That is exactly what happened in the 9th Circuit in the case of *EEOC v. National*

Education Association. This case was described already in Chapter 8, but a short revisitation is justified in the context of bullying.

If you recall the *National Education Association* case, the problem centered around a male bully. The good news, however, is that the manager in question was broadly considered to be an equal opportunity bully, who essentially yelled at everyone alike. Further, his comments were not sexual. Despite all that, however, the 9th Circuit found that the company was guilty of sex harassment due to the disparate affect the boss's bullying had on female workers.

Frankly, the court's logic is suspect. It is quite puzzling to suggest that "sexual" harassment exists in circumstances where both sexes were abused equally and nothing sexual was said. Nevertheless, the court found that unlawful harassment occurred in this case because women were "more affected" by the bad behavior than men, relying upon a "reasonable woman" test to justify its holding. Questionable logic, indeed, but that's what happens when a court stretches to find a solution to a bad factual situation.

Going the Distance

Only the 9th Circuit has to date gone this far under federal law. There exist some similar state decisions, especially in California. Most jurisdictions have not and are not likely to follow the logic of the *National Education Association* case.

The Problem of Favoritism

Perhaps you don't have any bully managers. So let's instead discuss another problem—the manager who plays favorites. A sexual harassment situation may arise when a manager is sleeping with a subordinate, if that relationship is having a negative impact on other workers. To some courts, such favoritism is "based on sex" and therefore creates sexual harassment. In this current chapter, however, let's assume that no one is sleeping with anyone else—can favoritism still cause problems for anyone?

The answer, of course, is "yes." Employees often complain about a manager who plays favorites. And if a manager bases his favoritism upon unjustified

characteristics, like the cuteness of a female, the willingness of a male subordinate to play golf with the manager, or race or religion, a legitimate concern arises. The problem with favoritism, however, is that all managers play favorites, but often the "playing" is fully justified by legitimate business considerations.

Simply put, some employees are better workers than others. Where that is so, a manager may be prone to reward the better workers with better raises, more attention, and greater levels of trust. Is that favoritism? In a sense, yes, but that kind of "favoritism" is based on legitimate business considerations. Such favoritism should not only be legitimate, but if done properly, it could persuade less effective workers to improve their performance in order to receive greater raises themselves.

In short, favoritism based on legitimate business interests is not unlawful. However, favoritism based on golfing relationships, racial considerations, going to the same church, and other similar criteria can create both a morale problem and a legal problem. Simply put, work decisions, including rewards and assignment of tasks, should be based on business considerations. If a white manager favors white employees, or a black manager favors black employees, or a Catholic manager favors Catholics, discrimination issues can arise. Further, these managers aren't acting appropriately even from a business perspective. Business decisions should be determined by business considerations, not personal preferences based on personal characteristics.

Don't Make It Personal

Again we go back to training. Managers need to be aware that business decisions should not be impacted by nonbusiness-related personal preferences. Such preferences almost always sound like favoritism.

Difficult Managers Who Do Not Behave Illegally

As stated earlier, every work environment seems to have at least one difficult manager. Put into context, different managers approach management through different styles, and some are more directive and harsh than others. To make matters more complicated, difficult or even abusive managers can be effective in terms of results. Ever heard someone say, "He's a great manager because he always makes his numbers?" Well, making numbers is one criterion for evaluating greatness in a manager, but should it be the only one?

An abusive manager can make his or her numbers by intimidating subordinates. Almost everyone has had a manager who produces results but leaves bodies in his or her path. Unfortunately, many organizations don't consider the bodies, but focus on the numbers, thereby granting "great manager status" to persons who don't deserve it. In short, companies are too prone to focus on production numbers, to the exclusion of considerations such as turnover, employee satisfaction, worker empowerment, and respect for the individual. Granted, being too soft as a manager can be as problematic as being too hard. The key is in the balance. Dictatorships are efficient and often effective, but in the long run they will fail. Managers should understand that fact.

The good news, however, is that the dictatorial manager isn't doing anything illegal, even if the pending state bullying acts are passed. That said, these managers may be creating other problems. One such problem is a union campaign—in many such campaigns, the unhappy employees aren't actually looking for a union. Instead they are trying to solve the problem of the difficult manager. In addition, turnover and morale issues can become rampant due to difficult supervisors. Finally, a dictatorial management strategy also can lead to lawsuits, whether valid or not, simply because the employees see no other recourse for resolving their concerns.

Respect Matters

Union organizers themselves state that respect issues often carry more prounion votes than wage and benefit concerns. When employees vote in a secret ballot union campaign, they are in a sense deciding what they think of both their boss and their employer.

If Bullying Laws Get Passed, We'll Be Litigating Forever

Employment lawyers who worry about the future of their chosen field should wish upon a star that all the states will pass anti-bullying statutes. Not only will there be a tremendous increase in litigation, but all the cases will be inherently interesting. Bullying stories always make for great fun in front of a jury.

Beyond volume of litigation, a serious problem will arise from these future bullying cases. Can we really create a standard that will separate the legitimate cases from those that aren't? After all, that task has been extraordinarily difficult even in sexual harassment cases. And, not surprisingly, it will be even more daunting in straightforward bullying cases.

Presumably, the term "hostile work environment" could be used in these bullying cases. However, unlike sex and race cases, the term will now have no specific context. In sex and race situations, liability is assessed based on sexual or racial comments, graffiti, and the like. By contrast, in bullying cases, the issues will instead be addressed based on general behavior that typically has a legitimate management goal in mind.

Presumably, Mr. Johnson, our stockbroker manager, would be guilty under almost any bullying standard. However, that's the easy case. Let's look instead at two other potential circumstances.

First, what of the boss who loses his temper under legitimately stressful circumstances? Picture Quincy Jeffries, who is faced one day with getting out two large production orders even though two of his five machines are down for maintenance problems. To make things worse, three of Quincy's 10-person crew are out that day, for a variety of reasons. Quincy nevertheless has worked all day to meet an unmeetable deadline, with increasing frustration and pressure. At 4:35, just when the impossible seems like it might be possible, disaster occurs. Lauren Richardson, hurrying to beat the clock, accidentally runs her forklift into a large box of the product. Unfortunately, Quincy loses it on the spot—screaming at both everyone and no one, telling all the workers to "get their asses out of here," and coming as close to a stroke as one can come without actually breaking a blood vessel.

Is the above scenario a violation of the bullying law or not? Who knows? Assuming that a severe or pervasive standard is applied, this isn't a pervasive problem, but some courts or juries might find it to be severe. If so, won't a lawsuit arise somewhere every day, including to good people who have temporarily fallen over the edge for no fault of their own? The point is that most of us wouldn't consider Quincy to be a bully—he just had a really bad day. And a bad day, especially if followed by an apology the next morning, shouldn't create the basis for a lawsuit, should it?

Then what about Connie Alexander? In general, she's a good boss, but recently she's been having problems. Her marriage isn't doing well, she suspects that her husband is having an affair, and her patience is running thin. Further, the doctor is having a hard time balancing the medicine Connie takes to deal with her hormone imbalance. Consequently, for four months now, Connie has been touchy at work. She hasn't screamed at anyone and she hasn't "lost it." However, she has been difficult, often snipping at people for relatively small issues. In particular, her administrative assistant, Zeke, seems to be getting the brunt of Connie's impatience.

So at what point does Zeke get to sue? Is Connie's increasing stress and irascibility creating a "pervasive atmosphere" of bullying? Or is this just life as we know it, and could all of us be Connie at certain periods of time? If bullying laws pass, the questions above would be answered by juries, and that could be a shame in many situations. And think about this—"punitive" damages are usually based on "bad acts," and bullying seems to inherently be a "bad act."

Hopefully the states that are looking at passing bullying laws will think about all this. Chances are, however, that some of them won't. What will then follow could be good for lawyers, but hardly anyone else. Perhaps in the long run the workplace will be better due to anti-bullying laws, but there should be other, less litigious ways to reach that same goal. Training in leadership skills would be a great start, as discussed in Chapter 5.

CHAPTER 25

Training Requirements and Suggestions

By now we've probably said it enough, but let's go there one more time—*train your employees not to harass anyone*. Also, not to discriminate. And how to raise concerns about harassment and discrimination. And train managers how to respond to complaints. As well, train investigators of claims how to investigate. Then train managers how to manage effectively in the first place and you'll just about have it.

The most essential element of training comes from *Faragher*. To use the defense established there, that is, where a complainant has to come to you first instead of going to court, you have to tell people how to raise concerns. Beyond *Faragher*, the rest of the training goals come from the common-sense need to reduce your risk of claims arising in the first place. Otherwise, a few states have already started legislatively mandating harassment avoidance training. The most notable law comes from California, of course, but Connecticut and Maine have chimed in as well. Let's deal with these requirements first, then we'll offer some ideas on how to do effective training in general.

California, Connecticut, and Maine: Mandatory Harassment Training Requirement

In 2004, Governor Arnold Schwarzenegger decided it was important for California to make sexual harassment training mandatory. California joined Connecticut and Maine as the three states in the nation requiring that private employers train their managers on preventing workplace harassment, especially sexual harassment. The California law, Assembly Bill 1825 (A.B. 1825), goes beyond the relatively straightforward requirements of Connecticut and Maine by significantly regulating (many would say, over-regulating) the subject matter, quality, and delivery method of training. Even before this law, the California legislature made it a violation (since 1985) to "fail to take all reasonable steps necessary to prevent discrimination and harassment from occurring."

Training Is Central

Federal Sentencing Guidelines recommend training too: (1) All organizations, whether privately or publicly held, must provide all employees and managers with effective and periodic ethics and legal compliance training.—Section 8B2.1(b)(4) (2) Basic harassment and discrimination training is a central component of any ethics and compliance training program.

Case Law

Case Law: "[L]eaving managers in ignorance of the basic features of [employment] laws is an 'extraordinary mistake' for a company to make, and a jury can find that such an extraordinary mistake amounts to reckless indifference." (*Mathis v. Phillips Chevrolet, Inc.*, 7th Cir. 10/15/01)

The Details of the California Training Law
Who Must Comply with California's Sexual Harassment Law?

The California law applies only to employers with 50 or more employees or contractors. Employees include full-time, part-time, and temporary workers. If the entity employs or engages "fifty or more employees or contractors for each working day in any twenty consecutive weeks in the current calendar year or preceding calendar year" it is covered. As the regulations state: "There is no requirement that the 50 employees or contractors work at the same location or all reside in California."

The New California Law

Employers with 50 or more employees must provide at least 2 hours of interactive sexual harassment prevention training. Applies to all supervisory employees employed as of July 1, 2005.

Definition of "Supervisor" is very broad. New supervisors: Be trained within 6 months, with retraining for everybody every two years.

Who Must Be Trained?

California does not contain a definition of the statute's term "supervisory employee," but the Fair Employment Housing Act (FEHA) defines "supervisor" as any individual having the authority ... to hire, transfer, suspend, lay off, recall, promote, discharge, assign, reward, or discipline other employees, or the responsibility to direct them, or to adjust their grievances, or effectively to recommend that action ... if the exercise of that authority is not of a merely routine or clerical nature, but requires the use of independent judgment. Only supervisors located in California must receive the required training.

Who Can Conduct the Training?

Trainers "must have knowledge and expertise in the prevention of harassment, discrimination, and retaliation." The final California regulations now state that live training sessions must be lead by a "qualified trainer." A qualified trainer (QT) satisfies the requirements if, as an individual, she or he has demonstrated two qualities:

1. Through formal education and training or substantial experience, the QT can effectively lead in-person or webinar trainings; and
2. The QT is a qualified subject matter expert ("SME"). An SME is an individual who must have "legal education coupled with practical experience, or substantial practical experience in training in harassment, discrimination and retaliation prevention."

If the trainer meets the first requirement, but is not an SME, then an SME must be available to answer questions and provide feedback either during the training session, or within two business days (presumably, within two business days after the question is asked).

All trainers, even those who are not SMEs, must also be qualified to train about the following subjects:

- What are unlawful harassment, discrimination, and retaliation under both California and federal law
- What steps to take when harassing behavior occurs in the workplace
- How to report harassment complaints
- How to respond to a harassment complaint
- The employer's obligation to conduct a workplace investigation of a harassment complaint
- What constitutes retaliation and how to prevent it
- Essential components of an anti-harassment policy.
- The effect of harassment on harassed employees, coworkers, harassers, and employers

Can You Use E-Learning Training Programs, and How?

Yes, e-learning counts. The above knowledge and expertise standards also apply to those responsible for writing, reviewing, or approving self-study e-learning harassment training. Such training must be developed and approved by instructional designers, QTs, or SMEs. Instructional designers (that is, individuals with expertise in current instructional best practices) cannot develop a program on their own. Instead, they must develop the training content based upon material provided by an SME.

What Subjects Must Be Included?

The learning objectives of the training and education are to: (1) assist California employers in changing or modifying workplace behaviors that create or contribute to "sexual harassment," as that term is defined in California and federal law; and (2) develop, foster and encourage a set of values in supervisory employees who complete mandated training and education that will assist them in preventing and effectively responding to incidents of sexual harassment.

The following subjects represent a minimum curriculum that applies to all training programs, regardless of the training format, that are needed to meet these goals.

- A definition of unlawful sexual harassment under the FEHA and Title VII of the Civil Rights Act of 1964. In addition to a definition of sexual harassment, an employer may provide a definition of and train about other forms of harassment covered by the FEHA, and discuss how harassment of an employee can cover more than one protected category.
- FEHA and Title VII statutory provisions concerning the prohibition against and the prevention of unlawful sexual harassment.
- The types of conduct that constitute harassment.
- Remedies available for harassment.
- Strategies to prevent harassment in the workplace.
- Practical examples of workplace harassment, including but not limited to role plays, case studies, group discussions, and examples that the

employees will be able to identify with and apply in their employment setting.

- The limited confidentiality of the complaint process.
- Resources for victims of unlawful harassment, such as to whom they should report any alleged harassment.
- The employer's obligation to conduct an effective workplace investigation of a harassment complaint.
- What to do if the supervisor is personally accused of harassment.
- The essential elements of an anti-harassment policy and how to utilize it if a harassment complaint is filed. Either the employer's policy or a sample policy should be provided to supervisors. Regardless of whether the employer's policy is used as part of the training, the employer must give each supervisor a copy of its anti-harassment policy and require that each supervisor read and acknowledge receipt of the policy.
- Practical examples aimed at instructing supervisors in the prevention of harassment, discrimination, and retaliation. (This requirement is not mentioned in the regulations but is required by the express language of A.B 1825. Training programs should certainly include such examples.)

All the Forms of Harassment

"May I conduct a two-hour program and discuss harassment on legally protected categories other than sex?"

Thank goodness, yes. The regulations explicitly allow programs to explain "a definition of other forms of harassment … and [to] discuss how harassment of an employee can cover more than one basis."

What Training Formats May Be Used?

One requirement is common to all California training—interactivity. All training programs must be interactive and "shall" (not "may") include the following: (1) questions that assess learning, (2) skill-building activities that assess the supervisor's understanding and application of content learned, and (3) numerous hypothetical scenarios about harassment, each with one or more discussion questions so that supervisors remain measurably engaged in the training.

Requirements Particular to Classroom Training

Talk about regulating to the nth degree. Such training must be conducted in a setting removed from the supervisor's daily duties.

Self-Study E-Learning

There are two important restrictions in the use of self-study e-learning. The first restriction is that learners must have the opportunity to ask questions of a qualified person while taking the program. Thus, the program must provide a link or directions on how to contact directly qualified trainers or educators. These trainers or educators must be available to answer questions and to provide guidance and assistance on harassment training issues within a reasonable period of time after the supervisor asks the question, but no more than two business days after the question is asked.

The second major restriction is that employers must also ensure that students spend at least two hours taking the course. Although book marking functions are allowed, an e-learning program must contain some way to ensure that each learner spends the requisite amount of time actually taking the program.

Live Webinars or Webcasts

Live webinars, in theory, combine the advantages of classroom training (an instructor who can pose and answer questions in real time) without learners having to leave their offices. The key is to ensure that learners actually took the entire program, as opposed to answering their e-mails while the course played in the background. Therefore, those using webinars must document that each supervisor attended the entire training and actively participated with the training's interactive content, discussion questions, hypothetical scenarios, quizzes or tests, and activities. Good luck on figuring out how to do that, other than have a monitor present in each supervisor's office.

Tracking the "Every Two Year" Retraining Requirements

The final regulations confirm the availability of the training year tracking (TYT) method. Training year tracking may be used as an alternative to the "individual" training tracking (ITT) method. TYT allows an employer to designate a training year in which it trains some or all of its supervisors, and requires supervisors to be retrained by the end of the next training year, two years later. The training year need not coincide with a calendar year—it may be any period of 12 consecutive months.

Prior Training from Another Employer

The final regulations specify when a new supervisor may be able to count prior training received within six months of becoming a new supervisor to satisfy the new supervisor training requirements for her or his current employer.

How Do I Verify That the Training Occurred?

Employers must now track compliance by keeping records of its harassment training. The records must include:

- The name of the supervisor trained
- The training date
- The type of training
- The name of the trainer, educator or instructional designer

The records reflecting this information must be maintained for a minimum of two years.

Train Californians

Employers should continue to carefully audit which non-California supervisors "directly" supervise California employees—including those supervisors who do not reside in California. Although the regulations no longer require such training, it is highly advisable to train nonresident supervisors of California employees.

Four Legal Landmines and How to Avoid Them Through Training

There is a common misconception that compliance simply means "follow the law." It is much more than that. Indeed, companies that structure their compliance programs to meet statutory requirements may inadvertently place themselves at greater risk. The following four "landmines" illustrate how an effective compliance program entails much more than a narrow focus on the mandates of California's harassment prevention law (or similar such laws).

Landmine #1: Sex Only: Limiting Programs to This Single Topic

California's law is not just about sexual harassment! While the focus is on sex, the language of the bill affirmatively requires training on practical skills needed to prevent "harassment, discrimination and retaliation." It specifically leaves in place all existing requirements to train on other unlawful forms of harassment and discrimination (such as age, race, and religion). Training "may provide a definition of other forms of harassment … and discuss how harassment of an employee can cover more than one basis."

There is a serious danger that focusing only on "sexual harassment," if taken literally, may actually set employer training back 10 years—to the early 1990s. During those years, employer training efforts focused on sexual harassment prevention as an outgrowth of the case law following the confirmation hearings involving Supreme Court Justice Clarence Thomas. The obsession with "sex" left uncovered the serious problems associated with other forms of unlawful harassment. Racial harassment; harassment based on age, national origin or disability; and harassment associated with one's religious beliefs were not only illegal, but very significant workplace challenges.

An employer should ensure that its supervisors and managers understand their responsibilities under the organization's anti-harassment policy and complaint procedure. Periodic training of those individuals can help achieve that result. Such training should explain the types of conduct that violate the employer's anti-harassment policy, the seriousness of the policy, the responsibilities of supervisors and managers when they learn of alleged harassment, and the prohibition against retaliation. Comprehensive unlawful harassment training is so important that an employer may actually face a greater risk of liability and damages, including punitive damages, having conducted only sexual harassment training as opposed to no training at all.

Landmine #2: Providing Specialized Training Only to Supervisors in California Because the Law Does Not Apply in Other States

This may state the obvious, but California occasionally experiments with employment practices that are outside the national mainstream. To apply the California training statute solely to employees in California would be a major mistake for multi-state employers. First, the California statute makes explicit what has been an EEOC requirement for several years under federal law. This training needs to cover all prohibited forms of harassment and discrimination..

Second, the organization must consider the message sent to employees, judges, and juries in other states if training is limited to California. Imagine the following situation:

An employer with multiple locations across the country implements a robust training program for its California supervisors. A serious harassment incident arises in the organization's Dallas office. The allegations reference harassing behavior that was directly addressed in the California training program, but Dallas supervisors did not receive the same training. Imagine now that you are the plaintiff's attorney in this case, criticizing the employer's lack of reasonable efforts to prevent and correct workplace harassment. In this instance, a narrowly focused, localized training approach actually creates problems for the employer. Accordingly, one national training policy is highly recommended.

Landmine #3: Not Providing Training to Nonmanagement Employees Because the Law Only Covers Supervisors

All employees benefit and need training for at least three critical reasons:

1. Both managers and employees should be trained to better ensure the availability of an affirmative defense to harassment claims brought in federal court.

2. California Government Code section 12940(k) and federal law require employers to take "all reasonable steps necessary to prevent discrimination and harassment from occurring." Basic harassment prevention training for all employees is part of a reasonable step necessary to prevent workplace harassment and discrimination.

3. In the 2003 *State Department of Health Services v. Superior Court* decision, the California Supreme Court held that the Fair Employment and Housing Act (FEHA) does not allow the federal *Faragher/Ellerth* defense in harassment claims. Instead, for cases brought in state court, California employers may assert a different defense under the FEHA: the doctrine of avoidable consequences. This defense allows an employer to limit damages by proving that it took appropriate steps to prevent and address harassment.

According to the State Department of Health Services, to establish the avoidable consequences defense, a California employer must:

- Show that it adopted appropriate anti-harassment policies and communicated essential information to employees.
- Ensure a strict prohibition against retaliation for reporting alleged policy violations.
- Ensure that reporting procedures protect employee confidentiality as much as is practical.
- "Consistently and firmly" enforce anti-harassment policies.

None of these factors identified by the court are limited in scope to supervisors. The court further stated that in establishing the avoidable consequences defense, potentially relevant evidence includes "anything tending to show that the employer took effective steps" to encourage individuals to report harassment and for the employer to respond effectively. Clearly, this broader directive, in addition to the specific requirements listed above, strongly supports training for both employees and supervisors.

Landmine #4: Poor Quality: Thinking That Any Training Will Do

The law mandates that the training be of high quality and presented by "trainers or educators with knowledge and expertise" in preventing harassment, discrimination, and retaliation. If classroom instruction is used, the qualifications of the trainers must be established. Train-the-trainer programs may be appropriate, but the actual instructors still need to meet the knowledge and expertise requirements. Accordingly, human resources professionals and attorneys are specifically mentioned by the law as qualified trainers. These quality standards apply to both the trainers and those developing the training programs. If your organization is in doubt, it should consult qualified legal counsel to review the planned program.

Train Them All

Consider providing similar training to all supervisory employees nationwide. Doing so avoids inconsistency in training, and will help strengthen the company's defense to litigation against claims of inadequate or inconsistent training.

Mandatory Sexual Harassment Training Under Connecticut Law

The Connecticut Human Rights and Opportunities Act requires mandatory sexual harassment training under Connecticut law. Private and public employers with 50 or more employees must provide two hours of sexual harassment training and education to all supervisory employees, and to all new supervisory employees within six months of the assumption of a supervisory position. Like California, the training must be conducted in a classroom-like setting, using clear and understandable language and in a format that allows participants to ask questions and receive answers. Audio, video, and other teaching aides may be used to increase comprehension or to otherwise enhance the training process. In 2003, Connecticut's Commission on Human Rights and Opportunities issued an opinion letter stating that online courses will comply if the course "provides an opportunity for students to ask questions and obtain answers in a reasonably prompt manner." Thus live, online webinars, for example, would satisfy the commission's guidelines.

The content of the training must include the following:

1. A description of all federal and state statutory provisions prohibiting sexual harassment in the work place with which the employer is required to comply, including, but not limited to, the Connecticut discriminatory employment practices statute (section 46a-60 of the Connecticut General Statutes) and Title VII of the Civil Rights Act of 1964.

2. Definition of sexual harassment as explicitly set forth under Connecticut statutes.

3. A discussion of the types of conduct that may constitute sexual harassment under the law, including the fact that the harasser or the victim of harassment may be either a man or a woman and that harassment can occur involving persons of the same or opposite sex.

4. A description of the remedies available in sexual harassment cases, including, but not limited to, cease and desist orders; hiring, promotion or reinstatement; compensatory damages; and back pay.

5. A statement advising employees that individuals who commit acts of sexual harassment may be subject to both civil and criminal penalties.

6. A discussion of strategies to prevent sexual harassment in the workplace.

The regulations also encourage employers to discuss the following during the training:

1. Inform training participants that all complaints of sexual harassment must be taken seriously, and that once a complaint is made, supervisory employees should report it immediately to officials designated by the employer, and that the contents of the complaint are personal and confidential and are not to be disclosed except to those persons with a need to know.

2. Conduct exercises such as role playing, co-ed group discussions, and behavior modeling to facilitate understanding of what constitutes sexual harassment and how to prevent it.

3. Teach the importance of interpersonal skills such as listening and bringing participants to understand what a person who is sexually harassed may be experiencing.

4. Advise employees of the importance of preventive strategies to avoid the negative effects sexual harassment has upon both the victim and the over-

all productivity of the workplace due to interpersonal conflicts, poor performance, absenteeism, turnover, and grievances.

5. Explain the benefits of learning about and eliminating sexual harassment, which include a more positive work environment with greater productivity and potentially lower exposure to liability, in that employers—and supervisors personally—have been held liable when it is shown that they knew or should have known of the harassment.

6. Explain the employer's policy against sexual harassment, including a description of the procedures available for reporting instances of sexual harassment and the types of disciplinary actions that can and will be taken against persons who have been found to have engaged in sexual harassment.

7. Discuss the perceptual and communication differences among all persons and, in this context, the concepts of "reasonable woman" and "reasonable man" developed in federal sexual harassment cases.

Mandatory Sexual Harassment Training in Maine

In workplaces with 15 or more employees, Maine employers must conduct a training program for all new employees within one year of commencement of employment that includes, at a minimum, the following information:

- the illegality of sexual harassment
- the definition of sexual harassment under state and federal laws and federal regulations, including the Maine Human Rights Act and Title VII
- a description of sexual harassment, utilizing examples
- the internal complaint process available to the employee
- the legal recourse and complaint process available through the commission
- directions on how to contact the commission
- the protection against retaliation

Employers must conduct additional training for supervisory and managerial employees within one year of commencement of employment. This training includes, at a minimum, the specific responsibilities of supervisory and managerial employees and methods that these employees must take to ensure immediate and appropriate corrective action in addressing sexual harassment complaints.

Are Mandatory Training Laws Soon Coming to a State Near You?

It is difficult to believe that other states are far behind California, Connecticut, and Maine in making training mandatory, especially when some of those states already have statutes that encourage such training. However, since you're now convinced that training is a good idea anyway, maybe that isn't such a big deal.

Do State Mandatory Training Laws Create a De Facto National Standard?

As of this writing, only California, Connecticut, and Maine have statutes mandating workplace harassment training. Do the laws of these three states create a national standard? Only time will tell. However, proactive employers with any operations in either California or Connecticut would be wise to act as if the answer is a solid "yes."

Training As a Mandatory Part of the *"Faragher/Ellerth* Defense" to Workplace Harassment and the *"Kolstad* Defense" to Punitive Damages

During 1998 and 1999, the United States Supreme Court decided three cases that put employment law training on the agenda of any human resources professionals looking to avoid litigation. While the United States Supreme Court has since been relatively quiet on the subject, other federal courts and state supreme courts have taken the lead. These courts show an emerging trend that training may be an essential part of establishing an affirmative defense in harassment litigation or punitive damages in discrimination litigation.

Federal and state courts in many jurisdictions have held that training managers on preventing workplace harassment is an essential element in establishing the *Faragher/Ellerth* affirmative defense. These courts have held that merely having a harassment policy is not enough to satisfy *Faragher/Ellerth*. In addition, employers must show the following:

- training for the company's supervisors regarding harassment
- an express anti-retaliation provision
- multiple complaint channels for reporting the harassing conduct

Here are some thoughts on how to avoid or limit punitive damages through live interactive training:

Step One: Audit the organization's past harassment training efforts.

Step Two: Decide who will do the training. Regardless of whether the training is conducted with internal or external resources, live or online (or a combination thereof), California employers must remember the quality standards mandated by the statute, namely, that those who present the training must have "knowledge and expertise" regarding the prevention of harassment, discrimination, and retaliation. The two words in quotes, taken together, likely mean that trainers must know about harassment, discrimination, and retaliation in law and have practical experience dealing with such issues.

Step Three: Establish the training program—topics and timing. The California law requires a minimum two hours of sexual harassment training covering specific topics, including California law and remedies available to victims of harassment. Those are good areas for anyone to cover, but harassment avoidance, inappropriate conduct expectations, and ways to solve a problem are even more important.

Step Four: Decide who needs to be trained. The California statute requires training all supervisory employees. However, your goal should be to train everybody.

Step Five: Decide training delivery methods. Classroom training is best. However, the law allows other delivery methods if such methods are "interactive and effective."

Step Six: Draw up a training schedule. Newly hired employees or promoted supervisors should be trained. New employee orientation can easily include a videotape addressing discrimination and harassment terms.

Step Seven: Establish a procedure for ongoing training, especially in California but elsewhere as well.

Step Eight: Establish record retention procedures. Keep track of which supervisors and nonmanagers have taken and completed the training by creating and maintaining physical records, such as sign-in sheets. An employer that diligently trains all its supervisors with appropriate content in a timely manner, but cannot produce the physical evidence confirming it has done so, faces the possibility that it will be disbelieved by a jury, court, or administrative fact finder, and thus reap none of the benefits of its diligence.

Step Nine: Hand out simple reminder materials at the training sessions.

Step Ten: Make sure everyone attends. This training should be mandatory.

Select the Training Platform—Some Training Is Better Than Others

The decision regarding whether to conduct training using live instructors or e-learning training technologies will depend on factors such as the organization's goals, budget, and access to technology.

Advantages: In-Person Training
- Allows employees from various parts of the organization to learn from each other in an interactive environment.
- Builds teamwork along organizational or departmental lines.
- Provides instant feedback from trainer to trainees, especially when the trainer is a subject matter expert.
- Leverages employees' questions by allowing participants to learn from each other.
- Allows for "on the fly" changes whereby the trainer can adjust to the needs of a particular group during the presentation based on participant responses.

- May be easier and quicker to customize than technology-based training.
- May be more economical for small groups of employees.
- Trainers with significant authority or prestige can convey difficult concepts or convince participants about the importance of the subject matter (e.g., attorneys can often speak with authority on employment law issues such as harassment prevention and convince even those who initially do not "buy into" concepts).
- Courts have favorably mentioned live training in reviewing an employer's defenses to litigation, and there is more data to support the conclusion that live training changes the behavior that reduces litigation.

Advantages: Computer/Web-Based Training, Self-Study, or Asynchronous

- Allows large numbers of employees to be trained contemporaneously and quickly, even in remote locations.
- Can provide "just in time" training.
- More economical for training large groups of employees, especially when the expense of travel and time away from work are considered.
- Allows an individualized learning experience, at the learner's own pace.
- Because of the individualized learning experience, course length may be reduced while retention is increased.
- Requires that each learner perform tasks to complete training.
- Provides a consistent message without variation over the entire range of employees.
- Provides consistent evidence of training if training is an issue during litigation.

Advantages: Blended Solutions

Blended solutions, as the name implies, seek to combine the advantages of traditional classroom training and web-based training. Blended solutions allow expert trainers to communicate with learners online without either instructor or learner having to go farther than the nearest computer. Recent technological advancements have moved this type of training far beyond the traditional "webinars." Now learners can raise their "virtual hands" to ask real-time questions, teachers can give learners tasks to perform, and learners can even work in virtual groups to solve problems together. The primary advantages of blended solutions are as follows:

- Allows employees from various parts of the organization to learn from each other in an interactive environment, without travel costs.
- Builds teamwork along organizational or departmental lines.
- Allows instant feedback from trainer to trainees especially when the trainer is a subject matter expert.
- Leverages employee's questions by allowing participants to learn from each other.
- May be easier to customize than asynchronous technology-based training.
- Allows employees in remote locations to join in with other employees.
- Trainers with significant authority or prestige can convey difficult concepts or convince participants about the importance of the subject matter.
- Allows large numbers of employees to be trained more quickly than live training, even in remote locations.
- More economical for training large groups of employees, especially when the expense of travel and time away from work are considered.

Use Qualified Training Providers

Quality should be more than a buzzword when applied to the area of employment law training. As cases have frequently shown, improper training may be inadequate to provide the legal defenses allowed by the courts.

- Carefully review each outside trainer's skills and experience in providing the specific training involved. For computer-based training, quality means that the program must be based on content provided by legal experts with outstanding reputations. Be cautioned that training programs that are not legally sound may result in the employer being unable to establish a legal defense.

- Ensure that the training program is interactive and requires participants to engage in the learning process rather than being passive recipients of information. Passively receiving information means that participants will likely not retain key learning points. For example, using a story-based approach vastly improves retention, especially in computer-based training.
- If the training is provided from inside the organization, ensure that the latest training methodologies are used. Internal trainers should have significant experience with the legal subject matter (in-house counsel or human resources managers) and have gone through a "train-the-trainer" program.
- Ensure that the training focuses on the needed skills and is not a legal lecture. Detailed explanations of case law and statutes are more often confusing and counter-productive, especially when training employees and managers.
- Solicit the recommendations and views of other employers regarding the training provider.
- Review the experience the outside trainers might have in testifying or otherwise participating in the litigation process.
- Ensure that the topics covered in the training program are appropriate for the audience. For example, employees should receive training on preventing and reporting harassment, but they generally should not be made familiar with liability issues. Yet, these issues are important for managers.
- Use training providers whose material has been reviewed by attorneys experienced in labor and employment law issues.
- If using a mix of live and computer-based training, ensure that the message of both types of programs is consistent.
- Ensure that the training provider can track program completion.
- Evaluate the effectiveness of training by using written and performance testing, as well as on-the-job observations of supervisors.

- Discourage the use of pre- and post-training tests. These results can be used in subsequent litigation against the employer.
- If material has not been learned, retrain immediately. Decide in advance how the assessment will be used.

Training Costs: Pay Now or Pay (More) Later

Finally, don't get cheap, although don't buy a Ferrari either. It's far cheaper to train than it is to defend litigation. Bring in someone good, get the training done, sleep better at night, and be in a position to defend yourself if something bad happens. Don't be as dumb or short-sighted as some of your employees can be. Are you old enough to recall the Fram Oil Filter ad on television? It was a mechanic with an oil filter in his hand and a car with a burned out engine behind him. The buzz line was "Well, you can pay me now or you can pay me later." When it comes to training, buy the oil filter, and make it a good one.

CHAPTER 26

Beyond Sex: Race, Religion, and Many Other Forms of Harassment

Up to this point, we have focused primarily on the problems and issues associated with *sexual harassment* claims in the workplace. There are, however, a number of other categories on which a harassment claim can be based. These areas are either additional protected categories that are covered by Title VII of the Civil Rights Act of 1964 (such as race, national origin, and religion) or are covered under other federal laws such as the Age Discrimination in Employment Act ("ADEA") or the Americans with Disabilities Act ("ADA"). Courts have recognized that the legal standards applied to sexual harassment claims also apply to race, national origin, religion, and age. Courts are increasingly extending the same standards to disability claims.

Fortunately, the advice prescribed by this book is also applicable to these additional areas of potential liability. This chapter will provide you with a short overview of the additional categories on which a harassment claim can be based. The illustrations detailed below also should assist you in identifying what type of harassment you are dealing with when and if these issues arise among your employees.

Harassment Takes Different Forms

For years, almost all harassment claims were based on sex issues. Things are rapidly changing. While sexual harassment still leads the way, racial harassment and religious harassment are catching up.

Racial Harassment

Racial harassment occurs when an employee's or supervisor's improper conduct towards another employee is based upon the victim employee's race and the conduct in question creates a hostile work environment or interferes with the person's work performance. Once again, the severe and pervasive standard, with all of its vagueness, applies. Most cases involving racial harassment involve racial remarks and derogatory comments. More serious cases, such as the example discussed below, deal with racially expressive or intimidating behaviors.

In February 2007, the Equal Employment Opportunity Commission settled a case against AK Steel Corporation that dealt with extreme racially expressive and intimidating behaviors. In the lawsuit, the agency claimed that there was a hostile work environment at the company's Butler, Pennsylvania facility. This environment had allegedly included, since at least 2000, racially graphic graffiti, the displaying of nooses and swastikas in front of African-American employees, racial slurs, racial epithets, and the open display of Ku Klux Klan videos in employee lounge areas. The agency claimed that the graffiti contained direct or implied threats against African Americans, including instructions to "kill" them and a picture of bullets coming from a gun. This message also included a threatening insult towards African Americans. The company settled the suit for $600,000.

As evidenced by the above settlement, racial harassment claims can be particularly costly. Therefore, employers should ensure that their employees are not engaging in any types of behavior that could be considered racial harassment. Based on the obviousness of the problems in the above case, such vigilance would not appear to be a very hard task. However, employers must also be aware of more subtle or unusual circumstances of racial harassment, as illustrated by the following example:

Jay, a white concrete truck driver, is married to an African American woman named Gloria. Jay and Gloria have two children together, Mary and Elizabeth. Jay has always enjoyed his job until recently, when a new white employee, Matt, became his direct supervisor. Upon learning that Jay was married to an African American woman, Matt began to treat him differently than the other workers. Matt constantly complains about African Americans to Jay and asks him "How could you be married to one of those people?" Matt also told Jay he has never met an intelligent black person in his life.

Jay recently complained about Matt's comments to another supervisor, but apparently that didn't lead anywhere because Matt has continued to make similar remarks. In an effort to try to build camaraderie in the workplace, Jay offered to host a barbeque at his house for his fellow employees. When Jay invited Matt to attend, Matt stated he didn't visit people "in the black part of town" and that "it figures you would be serving barbeque. That's the only thing your kind of people eat." With these comments, Jay withdrew the invitation, and Matt immediately ordered Jay to go the plant manager's office and submit to a drug test. When Jay protested, Matt stated he had reasonable suspicion of Jay's use of drugs "because of the people you hang out with."

Although both Jay and Matt are white, Matt's behavior in the above encounters is based on race—namely, Jay's marriage to an African American woman. While this is not the sort of situation most employers would consider when imagining racial harassment, courts have recognized racial harassment claims based on associational discrimination. Consequently, employers must be careful to consider not only the more typical incidences of racial comments or remarks, but also racial harassment based on association.

National Origin Harassment

National origin harassment occurs where an employee's or manager's improper conduct towards a worker is based on factors such as a person's ancestry, birthplace, culture, linguistic characteristics, or surnames associated with a particular ethnic group. In light of the events of September 11, 2001, as well as recent debate in the United States over illegal immigration, national origin harassment claims are becoming far more prevalent than ever before.

Like racial harassment, national origin harassment is usually based on employees' derogatory comments, offhand remarks, and engagement in negatively expressed or intimidating behaviors. A majority of national origin harassment cases also include name-calling. For example, a number of cases involving Mexican-American or Puerto Rican employees involve the use of the names "Jose," "Chico," and "Taco," as well as the epithets "Spic" and "Wetback." Even if name calling has been accepted within your workplace as "joking," "teasing," or "locker room talk," this sort of behavior can subject your company to liability for national origin harassment.

Employers should also be aware that a case of mistaken identity is no defense in the realm of national origin harassment. If an employee harasses another employee based on a mistaken belief about that employee's origin, harassment still occurs because the employee's apparent national origin prompted the behavior. Courts have even recognized national origin harassment where the harasser is of the same nationality as the victim.

As always, be vigilant of your employees' conduct in the workplace and be responsive to complaints of name-calling. Also, if you employ an "English only" language rule, be sure that you can show this rule is necessary for business reasons. Tell employees when they have to speak English and limit the scope of such a rule only to business-related circumstances. If your rule prohibits employees from speaking another language even when they are on break, your rule is too broad and it may open the door to a national origin harassment claim.

On many occasions, supervisors complain about employees speaking a language that the supervisors don't understand. In work situations, this can be a legitimate concern if a job-related problem has arisen or can arise. Consequently, many employers whose workforce features employees whose first language is not English have begun offering English as a second language courses. In addition, such employers have encouraged managers to learn some aspects of a second language, usually Spanish.

On other occasions, it may be the supervisors who are too sensitive about the second language issue. They sometimes assume that the employees are talking about the supervisors in a language that the supervisors can't understand. Usually the supervisors are off base in their concerns, but facilitation of joint communication is always a good idea in these awkward circumstances.

The English Rules

For further guidance on English requirements at work, consult the EEOC's web site, which is www.eeoc.gov. The agency has produced a specific guidance document on these issues. The guidance focuses heavily on the issue of job-relatedness.

Religious Harassment

Like national origin harassment claims, religious harassment claims, especially those filed by Muslim workers, have increased since September 11, 2001. Like other categories on which a harassment claim can be based, religious harassment can be blatant and intentional, or simply the result of an environment that is intimidating to the employee. In either case, the employee must prove that the harassment was based on his religion. We will consider examples of both religious harassment that creates economic harm and that is based instead on a hostile work environment.

1. Religious Harassment Creating Economic Harm

Intentional religious harassment occurs when a supervisor or co-worker intentionally acts to affect the terms, conditions, or privileges of another worker's employment because of that employee's religious beliefs.

For example, John has recently converted to Judaism following his marriage to his new wife, Angela. Angela worries about John often because John has a very dangerous job—he works as a window washer in New York City. John spends his days suspended hundreds of feet above the streets washing and buffing the windows of office buildings.

John's boss, Buck, had always treated him fairly, that is until John's recent religious conversion. Buck is not overly religious himself, but he doesn't like what he has "always heard" about Jews. In addition, Buck has a Jewish neighbor near his house in the suburbs that is always blocking Buck's driveway with his "fancy cars." Buck decides that since John has recently converted to Judaism, he will probably be asking for a raise soon, and Buck "just isn't going to have operational costs driven up by a Jew."

Buck begins to tease John about everything from his religious conversion to giving up the bachelor life to get married, but eventually focuses his teasing by constantly referring to John as "the money-loving Jew." Buck threatens John, telling him that if he "opens his little Jew mouth to even think of asking for a raise," John will find himself flying through the air one day. Buck also ensures that he gives John the hardest jobs so he can be sure to receive criticism, making it harder for John to get a raise.

Buck is clearly engaging in intentional acts designed to decrease John's chances for a raise because John is Jewish. In these circumstances, John's employer could be liable even if it had no knowledge of Buck's actions because Buck has been given the authority, as the company's agent, to exercise discretion on behalf of the company. If Buck misuses that authority, as he has done here, the company is probably liable for religious harassment. Therefore, employers should train managers so that they will not blatantly display religious prejudice and ensure they know that any kind of harassment will not be tolerated.

2. Hostile Work Environment Religious Harassment

Religious harassment is analogous to sexual or racial hostile work environment-type harassment, where an employee shows that a reasonable person would consider the work environment hostile and the employee perceived it as abusive.

Ann is a highly successful campaign developer at a marketing company that specializes in promoting summer camps for children. Ann has worked with summer camp programs that focus on everything from sports to music to advanced musical programs for gifted children. Her current project is focused on promoting a summer camp for children interested in acting and musical theater.

Ann is sharing the lead development position on the project with Sharon, who works primarily with Christian summer camp programs. Ann and Sharon have never worked together before, and through their interaction on this project they begin to get to know each other. Sharon, who is a devout Christian, learns that Ann attended a Catholic church as a child but hasn't attended a church in many years. Sharon repeatedly asks Ann to attend her church, but Ann declines each invitation. After each time Ann declines Sharon's invitation, upon returning to her office she finds a pamphlet on Sharon's church or a handwritten Bible verse on a post-it note stuck to her computer monitor.

After several weeks of this behavior Ann confronts Sharon and asks her to stop leaving pamphlets and messages in her office and to stop asking Ann to attend church. The conversation turns into an argument and Sharon remarks that if Ann "would go to church and get in touch with God again" maybe she "wouldn't have so many personal problems." Ann walks out of the room and immediately tells her supervisor that she can no longer work with Sharon on the theater summer camp project.

In this circumstance, Ann has been subjected to a hostile work environment because she does not practice her religion in the same manner as Sharon. Sharon's actions, which she perceives as "well-meaning" and helpful to Ann, have actually made Ann feel intimidated and affected her ability to work with Sharon on completing the summer camp advertising project. Whether Ann has a legal case, however, is uncertain—a court will have to determine if Sharon's behavior is severe or pervasive. However, the employer need not focus on the legality of the situation, but the underlying problem. To remedy this sort of situation, an employer should take immediate action to stop the harassing or intimidating conduct and help create an environment in which both employees can continue to work productively and peacefully.

Religious harassment, whether intentional or unintentional, often involves extremely sensitive claims because of the importance that religion may play in an employee's personal life. It is often difficult for employers to balance the needs of employees like Ann, who want to be free from intimidation, with employees like Sharon, whose religion requires them to share their beliefs with others. These are often the types of situations where consultation with employment counsel would be wise before taking any action with employees.

No Preaching at Work

A few employees believe that they should have the right to preach to others at work and to seek to convert co-workers. The courts have consistently held that such is not the case. Informing an employee that he or she cannot use work time to proselytize is not harassment, no matter what the proselytizing employee says.

Disability Harassment

Disability harassment claims are relatively new, as federal courts have only recently begun to extend the protections against workplace harassment developed under Title VII of the Civil Rights Act of 1964 to the Americans with Disabilities Act. Courts have reasoned that since both of these laws contain identical language, persons with disabilities should be protected from harassment as well as discrimination. An employee who claims to have been harassed because of a disability must meet the legal standards applied to harassment claims arising under Title VII, as well as provide proof that they are in fact protected by the terms of the ADA.

In general, disability harassment cases are just like the other situations we have described above. Clearly, behavior such as teasing and name-calling because of one's disability is inappropriate and could amount to disability harassment. However, there also exist situations where disability harassment cases are slightly different from other circumstances. They often arise where an employer's behavior in response to an employee's disability walks the thin line between harassment and either (1) showing appropriate concern or (2) addressing poor performance issues.

1. Showing Appropriate Concern for an Employee's Disability

One major difficulty for employers in the context of disability harassment is the fine line between "harassment" and "showing appropriate concern." Under the

ADA, employers are required to engage in the "interactive process" with an employee once the employer has sufficient information to know that an employee is having problems performing his or her job because of a possible ADA-qualifying disability. Employers are required to limit their disability-related inquiries of their employees to job-related matters consistent with business necessity. These requirements, however, do not take into consideration the natural response of showing concern to another human being who is in distress.

A recent Pennsylvania case illustrates this problem well. An employee who suffered from anorexia and depression brought a disability harassment case against her employer. The employer was aware of the employee's conditions. In fact, the parties had discussed them openly at work. The employer had commented that the employee "looked pale," "looked horrible," "looked like she was going to pass out," "had blue lips," and that she "wanted her old [employee] back." These statements occurred over the course of about 15 months. The court, taking into consideration the open office environment and the personal relationship between the employee and her employer, found that the statements were more likely expressions of concern rather than statements of hostility. Therefore, the statements were not "severe" or "pervasive" enough to rise to the level of a hostile work environment.

2. Addressing Poor Performance Issues

Another major difficulty for employers in this area is addressing whether an employee's poor performance is the result of a disability, or rather, an inclination to avoid performing one's job duties. Consider the following example.

Elliot has recently returned to work after an extended vacation to Spain to "clear his head." Elliot has never enjoyed his job as a salesman for a plumbing supply company, and literally hates the sight of his cubicle after spending his days lounging on Spain's beautiful beaches. After two weeks back at work, Elliot tells his boss Anthony that he is "depressed." Alicia, one of Elliot's coworkers, overhears the conversation and tells everyone in their small office that Elliot is depressed and she can't believe he feels this way after taking time off to go on such a wonderful trip. Elliot's co-workers begin to tease him on a daily basis, saying that he went "loco in Spain" and to get over whatever is bothering him and "get with the program."

After some time passes, Anthony approaches Elliot about his job perform-ance, as Elliot has not sold a single piece of plumbing equipment in the month since he has been back from Spain. Elliot says that no matter what he does or how much medicine he takes, he can't seem to get over his depression. Anthony, recognizing that Elliot's condition may qualify as a disability under the ADA, asks Elliot what the company can do to help. Elliot requests addi-tional time off from work to help him battle his depression. Elliot also com-plains that Alicia and his co-workers' teasing is not helping the problem. Anthony grants Elliot an additional month off.

With his additional time off, Elliot decides to enter a rehabilitation center located in the Bahamas. It's a center that has been popular with celebrities lately, and Elliot's doctor is sure it will work for him. In the meantime, how-ever, nosy Alicia snoops on Elliot's work e-mail and sees a confirmation of Elliot's plane ticket purchase for the Bahamas. Alicia informs Anthony, who is furious and calls Elliot while he is gone, demanding his return to work and ranting that Elliot manufactured his depression and that he is just a "slacker." Elliot is not permitted to receive voice mail from anyone other than family while in treatment, so he is unaware of Anthony's concern until Elliot returns to work and runs into his very angry boss.

From the information Anthony received from Alicia, it clearly appeared to him that Elliot had faked a medical condition in order to garner additional time off for another vacation. However, this was not in fact the case, and Anthony's conduct (as well as that of Alicia and Elliot's other co-workers) could possibly constitute disability harassment if Elliot's depression qualifies him as a protected individual under the ADA. So what should Anthony have done? He should have gotten Elliot's side of the story before concluding that Elliot had cheated in regard to his leave.

Employees who may be protected by the ADA are definitely special cases for employers concerned about harassment issues. Be sure to always address blatant teasing or name-calling. Also handle with care issues of showing appropriate concern and addressing poor performance issues, as these circum-stances, if not handled carefully, present the possibility for harassment claims to arise. Nevertheless, if an employee has performed his or her job poorly, the employer is allowed to take disciplinary action on that basis. However, the situation should carefully be investigated before acting.

Don't Be Disabled by the ADA

Disability cases as a whole need to be treated sensitively. It is very easy to violate the ADA. That can happen by failing to accommodate a disability, by firing someone due to his or her disability, by treating someone as if they have a disability and they don't, and for other misdeeds. Talk with a lawyer before handling an awkward situation involving an employee's medical situation.

Age Harassment

The ADEA protects employees that are over 40 years of age against harassment on the basis of age. The standard for proving harassment under the ADEA mirrors that applied to claims brought under Title VII. Employees must show that they are protected by the statute because they are 40 years of age or older, they've been subject to harassment because of their age, the harassment unreasonably interfered with their work performance and created a hostile work environment, and their employer is liable for the harassment.

The majority of age harassment claims have been based on comments made by an employee's supervisor or co-worker. In order to invoke liability, these comments generally must be more than incidental remarks and must negatively affect the terms and conditions of the employee's employment.

For example, in a recent case in Texas, a court held that a single comment about an employee's age was clearly not sufficient to rise to the level of age harassment. Another recent case in Texas held that even several derogatory comments about an employee's age that occurred over a two-year period did not invoke employer liability because they were not pervasive enough to affect the terms and conditions of the employee's employment.

However, seven age-related comments made by high-ranking company officials concentrated over a two-year period were sufficient to show age harassment in a recent case from Puerto Rico. There, the employee, who was 49 years old when the comments began, was told by company officials that his health problems were due to his old age, that they preferred applicants with "youth and intelligence," and that his "gray hair must mean he's 60 years old." The employee was also told during a staff meeting to "be quiet" because he was "stale." The court determined that these comments occurred frequently enough for a jury to consider whether they rose to the level of a hostile work environment based on age harassment.

Employers should be concerned about both comments and behaviors that could amount to age harassment. For better or for worse, teasing due to age occurs with great regularity in our society, and much of the teasing is not meant to be harmful. At some point, the employer will probably have to step in and deal with the situations. While some employees may take pride in their age and boast about their experience or years in a particular field of work, not every employee who is over 40 likes this kind of attention. If unwelcome age-related comments or behaviors have occurred, or if a complaint is lodged about such comments or behavior, possible liability exists. In the age area, however, the courts will look at the overall picture of the situation to determine if the employee's work situation has truly been affected.

CHAPTER 27

The Relationships Among Discrimination, Harassment, and Retaliation

Perhaps at this point, you're thinking that even though people are people, and even though sex is a prevalent force in our society, you've got this harassment stuff mastered and all is well. Well, not so fast. There's one other problem that we haven't discussed yet at all that relates to harassment issues in the workplace. We now need to work our way through the messy connection between harassment claims and the world of unlawful retaliation.

What Is Retaliation and Where Does It Come from Legally?

Virtually every employment law statute in the United States has a provision in it prohibiting retaliation. Take Title VII, for example—when Congress passed a law to end discrimination, it also wanted to protect people who filed charges or raised issues of discrimination. It did that by stating that anyone who participated in the EEOC process or who opposed unlawful discrimination could not be retaliated against.

This prohibition against retaliation makes logical sense. If workers who complained of discrimination could be fired for complaining, the law prohibiting discrimination wouldn't be of much use. In a real world sense, Congress wanted to stop discrimination, and that wouldn't happen unless it also prohibited retaliation.

More Than Anticipated

Congress probably could not have foreseen how many retaliation cases would come to be brought under the employment discrimination laws. The percentage of such cases has risen steadily over time. That is true in part because in the early days of Title VII, most cases involved hiring or firing. Now numerous cases exist where the claimant is still employed by the company he or she is suing, such as harassment and failure to promote.

Retaliation Comes in Two Broad Forms

To make sure that it had the ground covered, Congress actually established two types of prohibitions against retaliation. The first comes from something called the "participation clause." The second is entitled "opposition retaliation." Both are relevant to the world of discrimination and harassment issues.

Participation retaliation was primarily intended to protect people who filed charges of discrimination with a governmental agency. Since then, it has been interpreted to cover other workers as well. Also protected, for example, is the co-worker of the person who brings a discrimination charge if that co-worker writes a letter or gives a statement in support of the charge. More surprisingly, even a person who is *not* trying to help the claimant is covered if he or she is retaliated against for activity involving the charge (or the later lawsuit).

In a very real case analyzed by the 11th Circuit Court of Appeals, a female worker was sexually harassed by several male co-workers. When the harassment concern was investigated, however, the males denied any wrongdoing and the company decided that it could not conclude that harassment had or had not occurred. Upset because, in her opinion, the company had done virtually nothing, the female worker sued. In the depositions of the male co-workers, all but one continued to lie about what they had done. However, one of the co-workers, whom we'll call Henry, apparently cognizant of the fact that he was testifying under oath, broke the wall of silence and told the truth.

In response to this scenario, the company realized that it had gotten the facts wrong, panicked, and settled the case for a meaningful amount of money. At that point, an upper-level executive wanted to know why the company had paid serious dollars to settle a case that he had understood was a weak claim. The executive was told that Henry's testimony had killed the company's case. The executive then reviewed the transcript from Henry's deposition, called Henry into the office, and fired him because of his testimony.

At that point, Henry brought suit against the company, claiming that he had been retaliated against due to his "participation" in the EEOC and litigation process. The company responded that Henry's claim was ridiculous, as he wasn't trying to help the woman who had been harassed. In fact, he was one of the harassers. However, the 11th Circuit concluded, probably correctly, that when Harry was fired "due to his testimony," he was covered by the participation clause. On the other hand, had Henry been fired for lying during the investigation, the company would have been ok. In those circumstances, however, it presumably would have had to fire the other harassers as well.

Fortunately, while the concept is intentionally broad, there may be some limits to the participation clause. In a case decided by the 7th Circuit Court of Appeals, a male worker claimed that his female manager had sexually harassed him by touching him with her breast. The claim was ridiculous—the only incident in question was clearly accidental and the reality was that the male worker was trying to get the female manager in trouble because he didn't like her. In response to the male worker's retaliation claim, which he filed after being fired, the court held that an EEOC charge brought in bad faith did *not* give rise to the protections of the participation clause. Significantly, however, the court said that a weak but good faith claim would be enough to be covered by the retaliation provisions of the law. That was the case because well-intended people should not be subject to retaliation, even if their claims are weak, but persons acting in bad faith should be outside the protections of the statute.

They Fabricate Sometimes

People do fabricate claims completely from time to time. Fortunately it doesn't happen that often. However, it occurs often enough that a good faith test is indeed sensible.

Many Harassment Cases Fall Under the "Opposition Clause" Rather Than the "Participation Clause"

In many sexual harassment cases, the employee who allegedly has been harassed doesn't file a charge of discrimination. Thus, he or she is not covered by the participation clause. Instead, that employee comes to management and raises an internal concern about alleged harassment. In doing so, the employee is protected against retaliation under the "opposition clause" of Title VII.

To "oppose" unlawful harassment or discrimination, an employee need only raise a concern internally about the allegedly bad behavior. Further, the employee need not show actual discrimination or harassment. Rather, all he or she needs to demonstrate to be protected against retaliation is that he or she "reasonably believed" that discrimination or harassment had occurred.

This lesser, "reasonable belief standard," is well intended. Congress and the courts don't want employees to be free game for retaliation just because they couldn't actually prove their case. So long as employees act in good faith and reasonably believe their complaint is valid, they are protected. This legal structure makes sense, but it can lead to some unusual results.

Back in the late 1980s, a high-level executive for a chain of convenience stores was driving through Hammond, Louisiana on a very hot day in August.

He was having a bad day, in part because the air conditioning in his car had broken down. Outside it was about 95 degrees and 98% humidity.

The executive stopped by one his company's convenience stores in Hammond and, in his opinion, got rude treatment from the clerk. The executive, in fact, went off the deep end, but, interestingly, not on the spot. Instead, he stormed out of the store and drove several blocks to the district manager's office. Immediately upon entering the office, he told the district manager to "go fire that fat, ugly bitch that waited on me." The manager, somewhat taken back, said he couldn't do that. He offered two explanations for his hesitancy: (1) "that worker is Mary, one of the best employees I have" and (2) "if I fire her for that reason, it would be discrimination." The executive responded that he didn't give a damn about any of that and if the manager didn't fire the clerk, the manager himself would be fired. At that point, the manager drove to the store.

When he got there, the manager asked Mary what happened. She stated that she didn't even know the executive, that things had been busy, and that she hadn't done anything wrong. The manager agreed, but then added, "Mary, he wants me to fire you, and he called you a fat, ugly bitch." At that, Mary broke into tears, as did the manager. And into the midst of this crisis, who should show up but the executive. And what does he do? Fires both of them.

First, who should have been fired in this instance? Correct, the executive. But that didn't happen, so let's go back to the law. Does Mary have a good case? Interestingly, no. She has to prove discrimination to win, but none of the three grounds available to her are going to work. Being fat doesn't count, at least under most discrimination laws. Neither does being ugly. And while being a woman does count, the executive's use of the word "bitch" isn't enough to show sex discrimination. Mary, in short, has no case, which seems patently unfair, but the law doesn't cover all wrongs.

Second question—does the district manager have a good case? This time, the answer is "yes." Why? Because his claim is for retaliation under the opposition clause. Fortunately for the manager, he doesn't have to actually prove discrimination, he just has to prove that he reasonably believed that there was discrimination.

> ## At Will
>
> Mary struggled to establish a case largely because of the "at will" rules. Many states still retain the "at will doctrine," under which an employee or an employer can end their relationship at any time for any reason. Of course, laws prohibiting discrimination and retaliation are major exceptions to the at will doctrine.

Fair, but Worrisome

Yes, fair but worrisome is a good way to put it. If a person is retaliated against due to raising a good faith concern about discrimination or harassment, they should be protected. The problem, however, is defining the term "reasonably believed." In one case, the U.S. Supreme Court held that one sexist joke is not the basis for a reasonable belief that harassment occurred, given that the definition of sexual harassment is that the behavior must be severe or pervasive. From there, however, we're not sure where the limits end and liability begins.

For companies, retaliation is a big problem. They should take action to prevent retaliation claims, without taking serious chances on what is and what is not "a reasonable belief." Otherwise, the risk is just too great. Set forth at the end of this chapter is a system for preventing retaliation claims. Before getting there, however, let's look a little more deeply at how retaliation and sexual harassment can come together in real life.

How the Retaliation Clause Affects Sexual Harassment Cases

Let's start with the easy case and a real situation. The general manager of an electrical utility company is an old-school kind of guy. Among his other odd ways, he invites a few work buddies into the main conference room every Friday at about 4:00 p.m. They open up a case of beer, cook up some popcorn, and put some pornography into the DVD player. Just working their way into the weekend.

This scenario occurs almost every Friday. The word is out among the office workers, but most of them don't care—they haven't been forced to view the videos and they generally prefer not having to deal with the managers anyway. However, one worker, whom we'll call Lisa, is put off by the knowledge that the managers are in the conference room watching pornography. Consequently, she files a charge of sexual harassment with the EEOC.

Does Lisa have a good case? In reality, the answer is "no." Certainly the general manager and his buddies are idiots and their behavior is inappropriate, but Lisa isn't a victim. She hasn't been asked to watch the videos, the managers don't talk with her about the porn, and she hasn't been directly affected by the behavior. In short, her sexual harassment claim, while well-intended, is weak.

However, after Lisa files her EEOC charge, the general manager gets really stupid. When the EEOC sends the charge to the company for response, the documentation comes to him, as the highest-ranking manager at the facility. When he reads the charge, he gets angry. He then calls Lisa on the phone and demands that she come to his office. When Lisa arrives, the general manager says, "Did you file this against me?" Lisa responds, "Yes, I did." The general manager then ends the conversation by saying, "Ok then, you're fired."

Is this retaliation? Absolutely. In fact, this manager is the poster child for how *not* to respond to an EEOC charge. The case that Lisa brought was settled for meaningful dollars and the manager was fired. What an idiot.

The key element of this story, however, is crucial to every employer out there. Very few companies would retaliate the way that the manager above retaliated against Lisa. Nevertheless, the retaliation provision in the law is dangerous to employers because a person who brings a weak discrimination or harassment case is just as protected against retaliation as the person who brings a great case. Thus, in many instances, a knee-jerk retaliatory action against a weak claim of discrimination or harassment provides the claimant with a gift: a really good retaliation case.

So what happens in a not-so-clear case? Let's assume that Kwanzi, one of your employees, complains that she is being sexually harassed by her manager. According to Kwanzi, the manager keeps saying suggestive things to her. Upon investigation, however, the reality appears to be that both Kwanzi and the manager are participating in the inappropriate behaviors. Apparently, they've been involved in a bit of flirting and teasing for at least six months.

Now, however, Kwanzi has started dating someone in finance and she wants the flirting to stop. Interestingly, the manager is amenable to that request, but he tells you that Kwanzi never told him that the rules had changed. In fact, she still occasionally says things to him that are semi-sexual in nature.

No Knee Jerks

As discussed in other parts of this book, one way to avoid a knee-jerk reaction is to prohibit any single person from having the power to fire someone without first discussing that possibility with the manager above them. Where a company has an HR function, the HR person should have to sign off as well.

It doesn't really look like we have sexual harassment here, in part because the behaviors seem consensual and the blame appears to be shared. However, you obviously have a problem to solve. You do that by laying down new ground rules between Kwanzi and the manager, and you warn him that his inappropriate judgment as a manager will lead to discharge if it continues. Everything seems to calm down until a month later when performance appraisals are given and Kwanzi gets a "needs improvement" mark on "cooperation and teamwork." Otherwise the appraisal is a "meets expectations" and Kwanzi's pay change is not adversely affected. Nevertheless, Kwanzi immediately claims retaliation for having raised a concern of sexual harassment.

Does Kwanzi have a good case? Answer: "no," but that may not matter. You have a problem. Probably more than any other claim, harassment allegations lead to issues of retaliation. For one thing, the employees involved often are still with the company and feelings have been hurt. Thus, conditions are ripe for a claim of retaliation.

In fact, Kwanzi's case is weak—whether or not she can show that the single "needs improvement" mark arose from retaliation, nothing meaningfully bad had happened to her. In general, the courts, including the Supreme Court, have required some type of materiality standard, primarily to avoid claims such as "he's retaliating against me—he's looking at me funny." Further, Kwanzi didn't file a charge with the EEOC or bring a lawsuit. Consequently, she's covered under the opposition clause rather than the participation clause, and thus she has to show a reasonable belief that she was sexually harassed. Under the above facts, it isn't very clear that she can make that showing.

The key point here, however, is that it may not matter whether Kwanzi has a good case or not. The employer has a problem. Granted, that problem gets much bigger if Kwanzi takes you to court, but the problem exists even if she doesn't do that. You now have to deal with the situation of the employee who is raising a claim against you and working for you at the same time. Some suggested ways to do that appear at the end of this chapter.

The Reality of Retaliation

One more warning about retaliation—some managers actually do want to retaliate against employees who accuse them of discrimination or harassment. That obviously was the case with our porn-addicted general manager of the electric utility. However, other managers also are capable of some form of harassment. Even some high-level executives, used to the concept of "corporate loyalty," question the requirement of nonretaliation. As one such executive put it, "if the employee brings a suit against the company that writes her paycheck, isn't that some form of corporate treason?"

Treason? Wow—whatever you don't do, don't shoot the employee who brought the claim. In fact, don't retaliate at all. There are better ways to approach the problem. There also are ways to deal with another retaliation-related issue—the employee who becomes more interested in his or her claim against the company than he or she does in getting work done.

For better or for worse, once an employee brings a claim, he or she has taken an action that has implications for the working relationship. Assuming that we can keep the managers from retaliating, can we also keep the employee focused on work? Regrettably, sometimes the answer is "no." Some employees who bring claims seemingly lose interest in succeeding at work and instead focus their energy on their claims. Some even take on a victim mentality and almost invite discharge so they can bring a claim of retaliation. Other claimants, of course, take a more constructive approach, but a real sensitivity arises when claims are made by a present employee against a current employer.

To complicate things even further, there are plaintiffs' lawyers who suggest to people that they file a weak charge just so they can subsequently fall within the retaliation laws. Remember that under the participation clause (as opposed to the opposition clause), weak charges are protected so long as they are brought in good faith. The line between "weak" and "good faith," however, is anything but clear. Consequently, some claimants file charges primarily to fall within the protections of the anti-retaliation laws even if they really don't think that discrimination exists. Good luck in managing those folks moving forward.

EEOC Sensitivity

The EEOC also is very sensitive to potential retaliation issues in cases where an employee still works for the employer he or she is filing a charge against. The charge form itself includes a discussion of retaliation.

A Plan to Prevent Retaliation Claims

Retaliation issues sound like a total mess, don't they? Indeed they can be. So, given that reality, let's create a system to get you through these problems.

1. Include an Anti-Retaliation Provision in Your Non-Discrimination Policy

Remember the law states that an employer must not discriminate *and* must not retaliate. Knowing that, an employer's policy should include both an anti-retaliation provision and an anti-discrimination provision. The anti-retaliation provision is simple to write:

> The Company prohibits retaliation against any employee for reporting, filing, testifying, assisting, or participating in an investigation, proceeding, or hearing conducted by the Company or a federal or state enforcement agency. Employees should report any retaliation to a supervisor, any manager, or to [insert name of appropriate contact]. Any complaint will be investigated in a timely and reasonable manner. If a report of retaliation is substantiated, appropriate disciplinary action, up to and including discharge, will be taken.

2. When a Concern or a Complaint Is Raised About Discrimination or Harassment, Consider the Practical Problems That Could Arise from Retaliation

When a concern or complaint is raised in circumstances where the complaining employee is still working with the company, you should immediately assess the practical side of the situation. Ask yourself this question—given the nature of the complaint and the people involved, is there a chance that retaliation could occur? If the answer is anything close to yes, evaluate your options. As discussed below, you may need to move somebody or take other proactive steps. Simply "hoping for the best" is not an effective business strategy. Do something where something needs to be done.

3. Immediately Educate Managers About the Issue of Retaliation

Your policy may be clear as to the expectation of nonretaliation, but immediately make sure that any managers involved in the situation at hand are aware of that policy and what it really means. As stated previously, managers sometimes don't realize that the law requires that they turn a blind eye to what they might consider an unjustified or even a bad faith claim of discrimination. Once the complaint is raised, no matter what the context, a meeting needs to occur regarding the management expectations moving forward.

4. Involve Human Resources in Any Decisions Moving Forward

In cases where retaliation has occurred, one missing component is often the involvement of human resources. A human resources professional should be giving advice as to future decisions about the complaining employee. That professional is inherently more likely than the operations manager to be neutral and to be trying to avoid potential claims of retaliation. No significant decisions about the complaining employee should be made without approval from human resources or some other neutral person.

5. Tell the Complaining Employee That He or She Should Report Any Concerns About Retaliation

It helps to tell the complaining employee in advance that you don't want retaliation to occur. Be straightforward and explain that the complaining employee should report any concerns regarding retaliation. Also tell the employee that he or she needs to continue to perform his or her job. If retaliation issues occur, however, you want the employee to come back to you so that they can be addressed.

6. Consider Separating the Employee and the Manager About Whom He or She Is Complaining

The most likely person to retaliate is the manager who is accused of discrimination or harassment. As a result, if concern of potential retaliation exists, consider separating the employee and the manager. Once that is done, the employee has to show that some other manager decided to retaliate, and that is harder to prove. In some cases, it is better to move the manager than the subordinate, but often that is difficult from an operations standpoint. If so, ask the complaining employee if he or she would be interested in moving to avoid retaliation. Often the individual will answer in the affirmative. And in some situations, a required transfer may occur just because no other viable option exists. Where that is the case, however, make sure that the transfer is not, in fact, a demotion or some other form of adverse employment action.

7. Be Cautious in Making Adverse Decisions but Do What You Need to Do from a Business Perspective

In these difficult circumstances, many employers often choose not to discipline the complaining employee due to fears of retaliation. Bending over backwards to some degree is understandable, but the filing of a claim does not give the employee license to ignore the employer's rules or to quit performing to legitimate expectations. Be cautious, but don't treat a complaining employee better than you would someone who hasn't complained.

8. Consider Possible Creative Solutions

Don't be afraid to think outside the proverbial box. Creative solutions include facilitating discussion among the concerned parties, seeking outside resources to help, considering a severance package, formally mediating the matter, and creating a "go to source" for the employee and the manager if things get awkward.

9. Get Legal Counsel

Retaliation cases are very difficult to handle. Get help if you need it. Lawyers can tell you where you are in comparison to a court's likely expectations. They also may have some practical suggestions for you given their experiences in handling similar cases for other employers.

10. Always Ask the "Magic Question" Before Firing the Complainant

Try as you may—in some cases, the complaining employee may do things that cause him or her to get a bad review, be disciplined, or get fired. Before you take any step like that—ask yourself the magic question: "Would we be taking this action if we had never heard about this claim of harassment or discrimination?" If the answer is clearly "yes," things should be ok. If the answer is "no," you're taking a big risk. If the answer is "we're not sure," call your lawyer and ask for help. In court, a retaliation claim is analyzed by evaluating "causation." Did the complaint lead to the discipline or discharge that followed? Knowing that to be the law, you should ask that question before the judge or jury does.

CHAPTER 28

The Progressive Employer: Combining Respect, Diversity, and Harassment Avoidance to Make a Better Workplace

If there is one chapter in this book that every employer, large or small, should read, it's this chapter. Ironically, of course, this is the last chapter of the book. However, what's in this chapter wouldn't make that much sense unless you've read at least some of what came before it in this book.

If you've read the proceeding 27 chapters, you should realize by now that the law on discrimination and harassment is complex. You also should understand that try as you might, things may still go wrong. When the employer's obligations focus on the actions of human beings, stuff is going to happen. Consider the options—dating disasters among your employees, sex talk that everyone incorrectly thought was consensual, and subconscious issues of discrimination. If those things can lead to liability, what chance do you really have to avoid problems?

And let's make the forecast even more gloomy. In assessing potential liability, juries and sometimes even judges don't actually evaluate discrimination. Instead they focus on fairness, whether they admit that or not. Some cases lead to plaintiffs' verdicts even though no discrimination exists. Because the situation was handled less than effectively by management, juries have concluded that discrimination occurred even if the only wrong was a bad decision or a not very effectively handled situation.

Runaway Juries

Most juries actually do a pretty good job, despite all our criticism of them. However, the fear factor is the runaway jury. Perhaps not surprisingly, the dangers of juries are somewhat geographical in nature. Berkley and Oakland, California are problems for an employer. San Diego and Orange County aren't bad. In Florida, hope you get sued in Jacksonville, not Miami. And on and on throughout the country.

With Dangers All Around, What Is the Best Course of Action?

What do you do to best protect yourself? Well initially, train, train, and train some more, as we have discussed now on several occasions. In addition, get some effective legal help. Don't spend dollars on litigation if you can better spend them on avoiding litigation. Further, put systems in place that are discussed throughout this book—no knee-jerk reactions, involve human resources or at least another manager in decisions, create effective policies that rely, in part, on common sense, and work to rid yourself of ineffective managers.

But all of what we've already covered relates in some way to discrimination and harassment concerns. Let's go farther. If you really want to be a "favored place to work," you need to be the unusual employer. It's not about money as much as it's about building a brand. And, in the case of being a good employer, the brand is based on fairness, a progressive outlook, reasonable compensation and benefits, effective communication, employee empowerment and loyalty, solid "change management" strategies, respect for the individual, and diversity. Let's consider each of these goals individually.

Fairness As an Employment Concept

So what is fairness? Who knows—bias being what it is, fairness usually depends on individual perspective. What is fair to you may be ridiculously unfair in someone else's eyes. However, there are components of fairness that should exist in every workplace, to which we all should agree.

True or false—no one should ever be surprised to be fired? True, of course, at least absent the stubborn fool who can't see the light right in front of him. But what does this "fairness" mean in real life? Well, before someone is fired, they had to do something pretty bad that, more often than not, violates a policy. If an employee decides to bring a gun to work, he or she should hardly be shocked to be fired. Otherwise, with respect to less dramatic performance concerns, employees deserve something that might be called "due process." To the good employer, that means offering "notice of the problem" and "a fair opportunity to improve."

And what's a fair opportunity to improve? Many employers give someone 30 days. But is that really fair for an employee of 20 years, particularly if no

---

The PIP

The length of a "PIP" (performance improvement plan) should depend upon the length of the worker's employment and whether the employee already has received notice of the problem. For short-term employees, 30-day plans are fine. For an employee of 25 years who has never before received a bad appraisal, 90 days or more should be considered.

---

prior warnings were provided? Juries and judges both can smell a set-up, where no prior warnings exist for years, then in 30 days the file is literally papered in detail. The better answer is to give honest but tactful feedback throughout the course of employment. If that occurs, no one really can say that they were surprised to be fired, and that should be your goal.

A Progressive Outlook Makes a Difference

"Progressive" doesn't mean either granola-headed or based in California. It means paying attention to the relationship with one's employees. The old-school management philosophy of "firm but fair" is outdated. Some form of employee empowerment makes sense, as discussed below. Managing people effectively, with skill and leadership, is absolutely crucial.

Being progressive also means being tuned into the employment world around you. Smart employers realize, for example, that Generation X'ers are different from Boomers. And Generation Y is different from Generation X. That isn't to say that you need to offer psychoanalysis or Myers-Briggs tests to everyone. However, you need to realize that people are different, that generations vary in broad terms, that one management style isn't effective to everyone, and that progressive employers are open to new ideas.

Generational Differences

As of 2007, there are four identifiable generations in the workplace. They are all different in one respect or another. Don't be naive to that, but don't vary your policies by generation either. The differences show up mostly in dealing with people issues and understanding an employee's expectations.

Fair Compensation and Benefits

To be an effective employer, you don't have to be the highest-paying employer in your geographic territory. Wages depend on skill, industry, geography, and availability of manpower, among other factors. Within one's geography and industry, however, an employer should be within reasonable distance of the pay leader. Otherwise, recruiting and retention become a serious challenge.

As for benefits, the same concept exists, but with one additional watch-out. Beware the "take-away" in regard to benefits. Every time health insurance premiums go up and employee contribution rises, someone says "they've screwed us again." That isn't to say that increases in insurance premiums are inappropriate. What it does mean is that those increases need to be accompanied by education about why such a change is occurring. It also means that unnecessary takes-aways should be avoided, and that rules and policies should not be written based on the misdeeds of one or two bad employees. If you have two workers who dress inappropriately, don't write a three-page dress code—go deal with those two workers.

Effective Communications

Employers and employees by nature need to communicate. Some do, some don't. Those who do sometimes do it well and sometimes do it not so well. In light of this inconsistency, how about a plan?

Think of communication as broadly happening at three levels. The first is where the employer must provide information down the ladder, to the employees. The second assumes that, on at least some occasions, the employer and the employees must share and discuss situations. Finally, the employer has to obtain information from employees in order to make effective decisions and be aware of workplace concerns.

All employers communicate from top to bottom, but many do it poorly. Often the communication is by memo or e-mail. How personal is that? Another option is the large group meeting. Not a bad idea, really. However, most employers conduct large group meetings primarily to offer bad news, that is, it's time for another reorganization. Maybe you also should consider having large group meetings to pass out good news from time to time. One way to do that is to have such meetings on a regular basis—perhaps quarterly, as a sort of "state of the business" address. Further, don't unduly sugarcoat bad news or overstate good news. Employees are smarter than you think.

As for sharing ideas and discussing issues between manager and employees, that isn't likely to happen in large group meetings. The atmosphere simply isn't conducive to discussion. Instead, discussion is more likely to occur in small group meetings. Some of those meetings need to be conducted by the direct manager. Others can be facilitated apart from the manager, but that can't happen too often or the manager will be effectively removed from the information chain.

Use Your Intranet

Intranets, used properly, can help with communication. Include data about the company and ensure that people have access to news information, policies, and other helpful data. Employees like to know what their employer is doing at locations other than where they work.

Finally, and perhaps most importantly, managers have to obtain information from employees, lest they not know what is happening in the workforce. Unfortunately, it has gotten more and more difficult to accomplish this last piece of the communication pie. In large part, the reason for this problem is e-mail. Simply stated, some managers just don't talk to employees any more. Instead, they e-mail or text message. Both forms of electronic communication have their legitimate place, but neither is very personal (yet, at the same time, e-mails are personal enough to include insults and rudeness that would rarely be offered verbally). In any event, by not talking directly to each other, crucial pieces of communication are missed, such as "How are you doing today?," "Did you have a good weekend?," and "What's been happening so far today?" Minor though they may seem, these types of questions lead to short personal discussions that help bridge the gap between manager and employee.

There is a lesson to be learned here. Get away from the computer from time to time. Go talk to somebody. Get out of your office for an hour or two per day. As some employers advise their managers, "supervise by walking around." It will make a difference over the course of time.

Employee Empowerment and Loyalty

Empowered employees are happier and more loyal employees. If the employee is permitted to be part of the solution, he or she is more likely to support the business plan and the operation. Why simply institute a new attendance policy without seeking input from the employees? Those who are involved in the process may well help sell the change to their co-workers. Further, and this comes as a surprise to old-school managers, employees sometimes have very good ideas.

That isn't to say that empowerment is the right approach to every situation. There are some problems that require a higher-level approach. There also are situations that require confidentiality until later in the process. Nevertheless, empowerment works in numerous situations. Granted, it isn't as efficient as a dictatorship, but it sure is more effective.

Consider the Concept of Change Management

As most of us know, change is inevitable. As we also know, most people hate that reality. For whatever reason, very few people embrace change and many people accept it only by kicking and screaming through the entire change process. And the problem is that change seems to occur faster in business than in any other area of life. Failure to deal effectively with change could lead a business to serious problems. Similarly, adapting effectively to change could lead to tremendous business success.

The question therefore arises—how do you get employees to change? The answer, unfortunately, is complicated. One thing, however, is clear—they will never likely change as quickly as you want them to change. The reality is that most managers, when change is required, effectively say "jump." In essence, if change requires a move from point A to point B, managers suddenly recall their high school geometry, that is, the shortest distance between A and B is a straight line. Thus the manager's expectation is as follows:

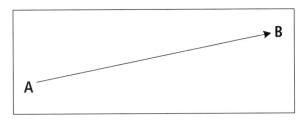

Unfortunately, many employees are incapable of moving so far, so fast, with so little information. In fact, even lower-level managers may be unable to make such a change. Where absolutely required, the point A to point B jump is fine, but it may not be worth the fall-out that may occur later. In short, where time permits, a stepping stone approach is the better way to accomplish change.

Stepping stones, however, aren't enough. The latitudinal lines in the image above represent education and discussion. The longitudinal lines represent change. With each step up comes education and discussion. With time, change is accomplished more effectively than otherwise would have been the case. Even then, some employees will whine, digress, and fight the change. At some point, they may leave, but that won't necessarily be a bad thing. More difficult is firing the employee who simply can't adapt, but that may be necessary as well from time to time.

Change Brings Uncertainty

There exist numerous psychological studies regarding people and change. Read some if you're interested, but feel secure in knowing that many people don't like change. Some employees detest it. In fact, some very unhappy people will continue to work in a job they hate because changing jobs is, for them, a worse alternative.

Respect for the Individual

This one should be easy by now. We've really been discussing it for the entire book. Whether framed as nondiscrimination, nonharassment, or simply respecting people for who they are without the need for stereotypes and biases, the concept leads to better practices and better decisions. The issue can sometimes be stated as simply as saying be open-minded, not closed-minded. Small-minded managers tend to stereotype, often to the point of foolishness.

Even if not intended, closed-mindedness can appear to be discrimination in the eyes of employees. Further, managers who view the world too narrowly lose perspective. The world of employees is a complex place, as discussed further in the section below on diversity. Being a good leader means respecting individuals and realizing that what works for one person may not be effective for another.

Diversity in the Workplace

Finally, the progressive employer should climb aboard the diversity train. For medium and large-sized employers, that may mean establishing a diversity program. For small employers, it means understanding the concept of diversity and getting managers to be open to the benefits of diversity.

Before we discuss the concept of diversity and how to build a plan, let's make sure that we're defining diversity correctly. Many people struggle with the definition. Is diversity about race? Well, yes, but only in the same way it is about sex and about growing up in New York City versus the small town of Live Oak, Florida. Diversity is really about differences, and the purpose of employing diversity as a business model is to gain from those differences rather than ignore them.

One problem with virtually all cultures in the past is that those persons who were "different" weren't accepted as part of the culture. A crucial aspect of diversity is recognition of the error in those ways. Instead of rejecting differences, you want to learn from them and reap the benefits of looking at the world (as well as distinct business issues) through a number of different sets of eyes. If indeed "two heads are better than one," then using diversity to one's advantage in crafting business solutions should be a no-brainer.

Why push for diversity? Well, let's start by looking at your customer base. It's not 1955 anymore. Whatever sex, color, ethnic background, and age you are, chances are that you're selling to or interacting with people who are different from you. Not only may they look different, they may act different, go to a different place of worship, eat different foods, and come from a different country. If your response to these differences is to back away, you're hurting your own business. Instead you should be welcoming of the differences and support this diversity, because the world in which we live isn't about to change course and become less diverse.

When it comes to dealing with people who are different from you, you ultimately have two broad choices. You can build walls or you can build bridges. Which choice you make is up to you, but the better model for business is to embrace the diversity while using the other tools discussed in this chapter to get all those different types of people to row the boat in a direction that will lead to success.

To be candid, diversity, like respect for the individual, is not the most streamlined of business models. It is far more efficient to have one person make the decision than to seek input from people of differing backgrounds. Given the diversity of the world market, however, the better decision is likely to be that supported by a broader-based analysis. In short, it's worth giving up some efficiency to improve the future course of the business.

Becoming More Diverse

How diverse is the U.S. in 2007? Very diverse, and getting more so by the day. Whites ultimately will no longer have majority status in a few years. Open your eyes to your customers—they may be a very diverse group.

Now then, we were going to offer up a business plan to support our new commitment to diversity. Frankly, that could lead to a book of its own, so our plan is going to be just a start rather than a full business model. Here is a quick list of 10 things to consider:

1. Think openly—broad-based decisions are better than ones that are derived from a narrow perspective.
2. Promote diversity—push for it as a policy, but don't frame it as affirmative

action or even about race or sex (except to use those as examples of differences).

3. Work to find and support diverse candidates. The world's a diverse place and good candidates are available. Go find them and, once they're on board, do the right things to retain them. If need be, expand the base of your recruiting by including diverse colleges and other sources that might provide different candidates than are currently available to you.

4. Educate your managers about the benefits of diversity and work with them to think broadly in analyzing their business options.

5. Train employees about respecting differences and, more importantly, learning from those differences.

6. Foster a public perception of openness and inclusion. The company that successfully achieves diversity should do so openly. Tell the public about what you're doing, from advertising to support of locally diverse events.

7. Help to expand the pools of diverse candidates. That might mean doing some things that aren't immediately going to return your investment, such as supporting kids in troubled schools or pushing for more women to get involved in the sciences. In the long run, your support of diverse goals will come back to benefit you.

8. If you're big enough to do so, assess your numbers in regard to diversity, but don't create a quota system or get involved in "reverse discrimination." Saying that you want more diverse candidates before filling a job is fine. Stating that this is a job for an African-American female constitutes race and sex discrimination, even if the underlying notion is well-intended.

9. Address diversity at all levels, not just at the lower rungs of the company. Diverse management teams also tend to make for better decision-making, and they show your support for the concept of diversity.

10. Take credit for your efforts. If you're pushing to support diversity, most of your consumers will respect what you're doing.

The appendix of this book includes talking points regarding diversity as well as a schematic of all the things that should be considered in a diversity program. There also exist a wealth of diversity research and materials that apply to the business world. Go educate yourself about the benefits of diversity. At the same time, don't get caught up in the world of making race- or sex-based decisions. Stating that you are hiring this manager because he is black constitutes a violation of Title VII in the same way that saying that he is the right choice because he's white.

It isn't that hard to become a diverse and progressive employer. However, if you don't pay attention to those issues, you won't get there. Step back periodically and analyze where your organization is and where it needs to go. Then good luck getting there. There will be bumps along the way, but progress will be made if you apply the effort and focus to move the ship forward.

Glossary

AB 1825: California statute mandating training for managers related to avoiding sexual harassment. Smaller employers are exempt but should consider similar training anyway to avoid potential liability.

Actual damages: A successful claimant in a discrimination or harassment case is entitled to damages for actual losses, such as lost pay and benefits.

ADA: The Americans with Disabilities Act, a federal law intended to prevent discrimination against persons with disabilities. The law has been interpreted to also prevent harassment against such persons.

ADEA: The Age Discrimination in Employment Act, a federal law intended to prevent discrimination against persons age 40 and above. There is a limited exception for certain high decision-makers and policy-makers. Certain states protect age generally rather than limiting their laws to those above age 40.

Adverse employment action: An action or decision by an employer related to discrimination or retaliation. In many circumstances, a court will not find liability for a petty action, such as moving an employee's desk or coaching him or her. "Adverse," however, may not be limited to actions that are directly related to pay.

At-will employment: A doctrine that means an employee may leave a job at his or her will and an employer may terminate an employee for any reason as long as the termination is not unlawful or discriminatory.

BFOQ: A bona fide occupational qualification related to a protected characteristic. Most relate to age, such as age limits on pilots and firefighters. A few relate to sex, such as prison guards. BFOQs are not favored in the law.

Change management: A practice or strategy in which employees are encouraged to and taught how to react to change in a positive manner and to deal with change effectively.

Charge of discrimination: A formal government complaint filed by a person claiming discrimination. Such a charge can be filed with the Equal Employment Opportunity Commission, a federal agency, or a similar state agency.

Comparative risk: Evaluating an employment decision by analyzing the risk of making such a decision as compared to risk of failing to make such a decision. In some instances, a discharge of a problem employee is less risky than keeping that employee in the workforce.

Compensatory damages: A form of damages that can be recovered by a successful claimant in a discrimination or harassment case. Compensatory damages can include "pain and suffering."

Harassment and Discrimination

Consensual behavior: Behavior that could be considered harassing except that both parties consent to the behavior. This can include anything from teasing to dating.

Discrimination: Treating one person or a class of persons differently from another person or class of persons due to a protected category, such as race, sex or disability (among others).

Disparate impact: Sometimes referred to as "unintentional discrimination," disparate impact can occur when an employer uses a tool, rule, practice or policy that creates a statistical or other negative impact on a protected group.

Disparate treatment: Often referred to as "intentional discrimination," disparate treatment essentially involves treating a person less favorably because of a protected characteristic.

Diversity Initiative: Recognizing that differences exist among people, from race to geography to culture and education, and that such differences may have a positive impact on business rather than a negative impact.

Document retention: A system of both keeping and discarding documents at set periods of time. Some document retention timetables are legally mandated.

EEOC: The Equal Employment Opportunity Commission, a federal agency charged with administering and enforcing the federal anti-discrimination laws.

Equal employment opportunity: The concept of providing employment and other decisions on a non-discriminatory basis.

***Faragher* defense:** A Supreme Court-created means of protecting an employer from liability for certain types of sexual harassment based on training, proper policies, and responsiveness to problems.

FCRA: The Fair Credit Reporting Act, a federal law that requires that background checks be done in a certain manner involving disclosures and explanations.

Fraternization: Employees who are involved in a relationship that goes beyond work and, in many cases, beyond friendship. Particularly problematic if it occurs between a manager and a subordinate of that manager.

Gender stereotyping: Basing behavior toward a perception of what one sex or the other does, thinks, or should be doing, e.g., women shouldn't work in a manufacturing environment; men should be macho, but woman should be less aggressive.

Good faith investigation: A legal requirement incumbent on an employer in response to a situation involving harassment or, in some cases, discrimination or retaliation.

He said, she said situation: A circumstance where one cannot determine who is telling the truth between an accuser and the accused. Usually an employer can make (and is entitled to make) a credibility decision, but on rare occasions such decisions are difficult due to a "he said, she said" situation.

Hostile work environment: A scenario where an unreasonable environment is created at work due to unlawful harassment.

Idiot: What your manager is when he or she asks a subordinate for sexual favors.

Job-relatedness: A standard through which employment decisions, from hiring to firing, are based on criteria related to the job.

***Kolstad* defense:** A Supreme Court created means of protecting an employer from punitive damages for discrimination if managers are trained to make decisions in a nondiscriminatory manner and proper policies are put in place.

Legitimate, non-discriminatory business reason: The burden on an employer in a disparate treatment case, i.e., the employer must articulate a basis for its decision related to legitimate business reasons.

Love contract: A formal or informal agreement used where two employees, often managers, are dating. The agreement underscores the consensual nature of the relationship and educates the parties on what to do if things go bad.

Negligence: A standard applied where an employer or agent of an employer has a duty to act reasonably to someone else, including the public.

Objectivity: Making decisions based on legitimate, objective criteria, such as years of experience, education, skills, or quality of work.

Opposition retaliation: A legally-protected situation where an employee raises a concern about perceived discrimination. To be protected, the employee must reasonably believe that the situation is, in fact, one involving discrimination.

Ostracization: A scenario that may occur after an employee raises a concern about discrimination or harassment. If co-workers won't talk with or deal with the employee, ostracization has occurred.

OWBPA: The Older Workers Benefit Protection Act, a federal law requiring certain actions on the part of the employer in circumstances where a person over 40 is asked to waive his or her right to bring an age discrimination claim.

Participation retaliation: Unlawful retaliation against an employee because he or she filed a charge of discrimination or lawsuit, supported someone else who has filed a charge or lawsuit or has been involved in such a charge or lawsuit.

Performance improvement plan: A "PIP," i.e., a period of limited duration, such as 30 or 90 days, in which an employee must improve his or her performance or suffer consequences for not having done so.

Pretext: A concept in which an employer's apparently legitimate reason for a decision is rendered not legitimate through proof that the reason is fake, false, or not genuine. Often lack of consistency and inconsistent evidence are used to show pretext.

Prima facie case: The initial burden of one bringing a discrimination claim, usually involving a showing that one is protected by the law, is qualified for a position, was rejected for or fired from such a position, and that others of a different classification were treated differently.

Protected characteristic: A characteristic covered by an anti-discrimination law, such as race, sex, national origin, and age.

Punitive damages: A form of damages that can be assessed in a discrimination or harassment case. Punitive damages are assessed in order to punish the employer for its illegal actions.

Quid pro quo: A type of sexual harassment where a person with authority over another worker demands sexual favors in exchange for a work-related benefit or who carries through on a threat because his or her request for sexual favors was rejected.

Reasonable person standard: The standard through which most courts determine if sexual harassment exists, i.e., whether a reasonable person would conclude that the behavior in question was severe or pervasive in nature.

Reasonable woman standard: The standard through which a few courts determine if sexual harassment exists, i.e., whether a reasonable woman would conclude that the behavior in question was severe or pervasive in nature.

Retaliation: Taking action against an employee for having raised a claim or concern of discrimination or harassment.

RIF: A program or decision in which a workforce is cut by eliminating workers or positions.

Sensitivity training: A formal or informal course intended to educate an employee (usually a manager) about the importance of complying with antidiscrimination or anti-harassment laws.

Severe and pervasive behavior: The level of harassing behavior that must exist before a situation rises to the point of a violation of the law.

Statistical disparity: A set of circumstances where there exists a difference between one group and another, related, for example, to hiring, salary, promotions, or some other type of employment action.

Statute of limitations: The time period in which one must bring a legal claim.

Subjectivity: Making decisions based on non-objective factors, such as attitude, fit, feel, and judgment. Such factors combined with a statistical disparity can create a disparate impact claim.

Summary judgment: Providing a judicial judgment in favor of one litigant over another, without the need for trial, usually due to a failure of the other party to establish a claim after the conclusion of discovery.

Title VII: The federal law that prohibits discrimination in employment based on race, sex, color, national origin, and religion.

Unlawful harassment: Harassing actions based on a protected category that rise to the level of being severe and pervasive or which constitute a quid pro quo sexual harassment situation.

WARN: The Worker Adjustment Retraining Notification Act, which requires that an employer give certain notices to employees and others in specific types of reductions-in-force involving 50 persons or more.

Welcomeness: The concept that certain inappropriate sexual behavior is not unlawful because the recipient of the behavior invited or consented to that behavior.

Zero tolerance: The concept that an employer will not permit *any* type of action of a certain nature, such as violence or sexual harassment. A potentially dangerous way to define a prohibition because it can create a discharge for relatively innocuous behavior.

Talking Points: The Elements of Diversity

A. Internal Analysis

1. Fostering an environment of openness and inclusion

Diversity is recognition of the value inherent in human differences, from cultural to racial to religious variations among us. Diversity also focuses on the concept of inclusion. Historically, companies have not done a good job of including a diverse group of people into their ranks. That has been short-sighted and sometimes the result of discrimination. From a business perspective, the value of diversity comes from recognizing the need to learn from each other, to accept the differences among us, and to realize that differences can be used to develop an organization's strength.

2. Addressing issues from the top down

Diversity initiatives do not work effectively unless they are recognized and marketed from the highest executive level. To be successful, a diversity program must be supported at the top of the organization.

3. Diversifying the boardroom

To establish a culture of diversity throughout an organization, a company should include its board of directors as one target of its diversity program. Credibility comes from a desire to diversify at the director level. Diverse candidates are available at the board level but it may special effort to locate them.

4. Eliminating obstacles

There are obstacles to attaining diversity. These obstacles range from personal biases to work systems that inadvertently preclude diversity. For example, a recruiting system that relies on word of mouth from current employees will limit diversity efforts if the current workforce is not already diverse. A whole range of obstacles needs to be evaluated and eliminated for a diversity program to be successful.

5. Training managers and others

Many managers do not understand diversity. They often view it as affirmative action, which is something that diversity is not. To understand the concept and realize its value, managers must be trained about diversity and the values that it promotes.

6. Utilizing diversity as a part of a decision-making model

A company should make recognition and achievement of diversity a goal in its decision-making processes, from hiring to customer marketing. However, there are significant legal risks within the concept of making diversity part of

a company's decision-making model. For example, classifying job openings as male, female, black and white is illegal. Careful planning makes these risks less problematic.

7. Mentoring and development

Diversity cannot be achieved unless diverse candidates are sought. In some instances, geographical availability or other market factors limit such candidates. Plans need to be made to reach out to diverse candidates, to develop ways to find them and, where they are already on board, to mentor those persons.

8. Recruiting vs. retention

Too many companies focus their diversity program on recruiting. Retention also should be a focal point. Retention requires support and the elimination of obstacles. Support includes mentoring, performance development, and effective feedback. Elimination of retention-related obstacles includes steps such as providing day care and "parent tracks" to avoid losing new parents of either sex.

9. Assessing the numbers

To a degree, diversity can be measured in numbers. However, to speak solely of statistics regarding race and sex is misleading—diversity is broader than such limited demographics. Further, focusing expressly on "affirmative action-type numbers" can be legally risky. Quotas, for example, are illegal in almost every context. However, goals and recognition of the need for diverse candidates is legal and admirable, as is seeking out diverse recruits.

10. Taking credit for what one does

Most employers that have implemented diversity programs have neglected to take sufficient credit for their efforts. Recognizing the achievements of the corporation will make further efforts at obtaining diversity easier to implement. Further, if an employer's success in diversity is publicly recognized, that will open marketing opportunities and recruiting markets that were previously difficult to enter or obtain.

B. External Analysis
1. Expanding the breadth of recruiting

To obtain qualified diverse candidates, organizations must actively seek out such persons. That may entail recruiting at historically black colleges, establishing relationships with female and Latino professors, connecting with community organizations, and advertising in creative and diverse manners.

2. Finding the candidates

Candidates can be found in numerous ways. However, waiting for candidates to simply show up on the doorstep is *not* one of those ways. Creative recruiting is required, from internships to connections with specific schools and community programs, to various other methods of outreach.

3. Decision-making in hiring

There are times when one should consider diversity as a factor in a hiring or promotion decision. However, nonqualified individuals should not be hired no matter what diversity they would bring to the table. Further, companies should avoid quotas, as discussed above. That said, diversity and the value it brings to a corporation should be considered as a factor in the decision-making process, in the same manner that a good academic record may be considered. Be careful, however, not to make a decision that is actually based on characteristics such as race or sex.

4. Convincing the candidates

To more easily obtain diversity, it helps to have some diversity. Minority candidates, for example, tend to go where others like them have succeeded already. However, corporations must start somewhere if they do not already have such persons on their payrolls. To convince diverse candidates of a company's intentions, diversity programs that include internships and mentoring need to be developed and expressly discussed in the recruiting process.

5. Supplying the candidates through early intervention—school participation, internships, sponsorships

In many cases, there are, unfortunately, too few diverse candidates with necessary qualifications. Sometimes that means that the employer is looking at too small a field, for example of colleges from which it recruits. On other occasions, there simply are insufficient numbers of certain candidates in certain fields (for example, female chemical engineers). In these instances, firms should take the long view and reach further down the educational system to help develop such candidates, such as getting involved in high school and even elementary school programs. Do not underestimate the publicity and practical effects of such outreach. True commitment to diversity means a commitment to helping to increase the pool of available, qualified candidates.

6. Fostering a public perception of openness and inclusion

The company that successfully achieves diversity should do so openly. The public should be told of the company's values in a variety of ways, from advertising to support of local events to relationships with schools and communities.

7. Connecting with the community

Quality candidates can come through recommendations from non-traditional sources, including community organizations. Connecting with the community also can create marketing and other opportunities. Community involvement has few downsides besides cost, and the cost of community action is often less than one would have imagined.

8. Supporting the community

Corporate support can range from volunteer programs to involvement in schools to participation in community events. "Community" can range from a small town to a nation.

9. Assessing the numbers

As discussed above, assessment of a program's results is smart. However, an undue focus on numbers, particularly to the point of establishing quotas, is legally dangerous. Assessment of numbers is safer for a company that falls within the ambit of the OFCCP, as such companies are required by law to establish goals if they are underutilized in certain demographic areas.

10. Taking credit for what one does

As previously stated, most employers that have accepted the value of diversity have neglected to take sufficient credit for their efforts. Legitimately but properly recognizing the achievements of the corporation will make further efforts in obtaining diversity easier to achieve. And, if an employer's success in diversity is publicly recognized, that will open opportunities and recruiting markets that were previously difficult to enter.

On the next page you'll find a schematic of ways to implement diversity in an organization.

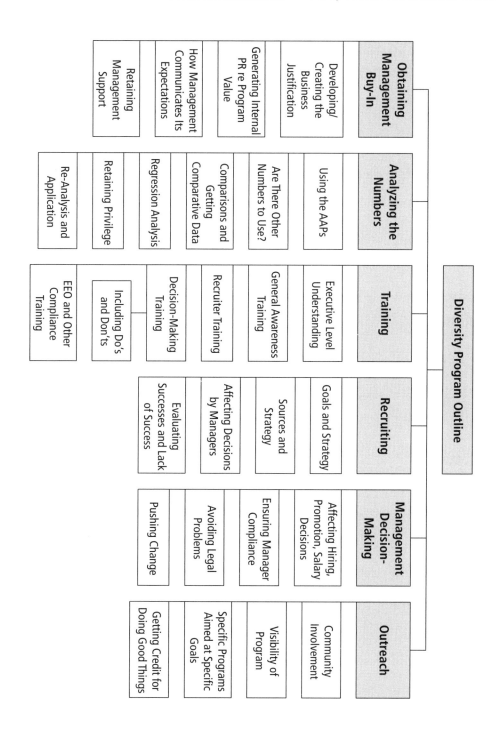

Diversity Program Outline

Obtaining Management Buy-In
- Developing/Creating the Business Justification
- Generating Internal PR re Program Value
- How Management Communicates Its Expectations
- Retaining Management Support

Analyzing the Numbers
- Using the AAPs
- Are There Other Numbers to Use?
- Comparisons and Getting Comparative Data
- Regression Analysis
- Retaining Privilege
- Re-Analysis and Application

Training
- Executive Level Understanding
- General Awareness Training
- Recruiter Training
- Decision-Making Training
- Including Do's and Don'ts
- EEO and Other Compliance Training

Recruiting
- Goals and Strategy
- Sources and Strategy
- Affecting Decisions by Managers
- Evaluating Successes and Lack of Success

Management Decision-Making
- Affecting Hiring, Promotion, Salary Decisions
- Ensuring Manager Compliance
- Avoiding Legal Problems
- Pushing Change

Outreach
- Community Involvement
- Visibility of Program
- Specific Programs Aimed at Specific Goals
- Getting Credit for Doing Good Things

Index

A

Abusive managers, 236–244

Accusers, interviewing, 138

Affairs. *See* Office romances

Affirmative action programs, 26

After-effects of harassment

    challenges to employers, 173–175

    recommended actions for, 175–180

Age discrimination

    avoiding in workforce reductions, 38–42

    mandatory retirement rules and, 32–33, 37

Age Discrimination in Employment Act, 14, 37, 277–278

Age harassment, 277–278

AK Steel Corporation, 268

Alcohol at company events, 206–211

Alcoholism, 206–207

Allison Gas Turbine, 76

Alternative work arrangements, 149

Americans with Disabilities Act, 15, 274–277

Antidiscrimination laws (U.S.), 9–15. *See also* Age Discrimination in Employment Act; Title VII

Anti-harassment training. *See* Training

Anti-retaliation provisions, 288

Appraisals, 23

Appropriate concern for disabilities, 274–275

Associational discrimination, 269

Attorneys
    calling for assistance, 53, 234
    selecting, 57
    as trainers, 167, 262

Attorneys' fees, 14

At will doctrine, 284

Audits, 57

Automatic liability
    for harassment, 106, 111, 119
    as higher standard for managers, 204

Avoidable consequences doctrine, 255

B

Background checks, 46

Bad judgment by managers, 204–206. *See also* Inappropriate behavior

Bad press, 165

Baker, Jim, 164

Baker Hostettler, 169

Ball of credibility, 206

Baskerville v. Culligan International Co., 81

Believability of actions, 22–24

Benefits, 297

BFOQs, 32–37

Bisexual defense, 67

Blended training solutions, 262–263

Body language, 146–147

Bona fide occupational qualifications (BFOQs), 32–37

Breakups, 183–189

Bullying laws, 243–244

Bullying managers, 236–244

Burlington Industries v. Ellerth, 105

Business Judgment Rule, 144

Business necessity, 25

Business planning for diversity, 302–304

C

California anti-harassment training law
    compliance challenges, 253–256
    major requirements, 246–252

Carr v. Allison Gas Turbine, 76

Change management, 299–300

Civility standards, 85

Civil Rights Act of 1964
    early Title VII cases, 11–14
    passage of, 10–11, 63–64

Civil Rights Act of 1991, 78

Civil rights law development, 10–16

Class action lawsuits, 3, 25

Clinton, Bill, 82, 164

Closed-mindedness, 301

Coaching, 116–117

Co-employment, 226–227, 234

Color discrimination, 13

Coltran case, 144

Common sense, 17, 54, 85

Communications, 297–298

Comparative risks, 56–57

Compensation, 48, 296–297

Complaints, 125, 130, 136

Concluding harassment investigations, 139–142

Connecticut Human Rights and Opportunities Act, 256–258

Consensual behavior
    lack of complaints versus, 112

leading to harassment claims,
183–189
welcomeness versus, 77
Consistency
of position on harassment, 127
pretext and, 21, 23–24
of responses to harassment claims,
145–146
Constitution (U.S.), 10
Constructive discharge, 173
Cooperation clauses, 233
Corroborating evidence, 147–148
Costs of harassment claims, 2
Court cases
*Baskerville v. Culligan International
Co.*, 81
Burlington Industries v. Ellerth, 105
Carr v. Allison Gas Turbine, 76
Coltran, 144
EEOC v. Harbert-Yeargin, Inc., 133
*EEOC v. National Education
Association*, 74, 239–240
Faragher (see *Faragher v. City of Boca
Raton*)
Griggs v. Duke Power, 27
Harris v. Forklift Systems, 81
*Holman v. Indiana Department of
Transportation*, 67–68
Kolstad v. American Dental Association,
131
Mathis v. Phillips Chevrolet, 247
Media General Operations, 90
*Paula Jones v. William Jefferson
Clinton*, 82
Reed v. Shepard, 75
Scarberry v. ExxonMobil Oil Corp.,
132–133
*State Department of Health Services v.
Superior Court*, 255
Co-workers, harassment by, 110–117
Creative remedies to harassment, 160

Creative remedies to retaliation, 291
Credibility of witnesses, 143–150
Curricula for harassment training,
249–250
Customer preferences, 33–35
Customers, harassment involving,
227–230

D
Damages, 131–132
Dating. *See also* Office romances
employer policies on, 192–193,
199–201
leading to harassment claims,
182–189
potential risks of, 193–198
Decision days, 159
Defamation, 222
"Desperate Housewives," 109–110
Dignity, 51, 300–301
Direct discrimination, 18
Disabled persons, 15, 274–277
Discharges
Coltran rule, 144
constructive, 173
disadvantages to companies, 165
discrimination in, 48–53
as excessive response, 87–88, 146, 152
severity of behavior and, 153, 154,
160–161
Disciplinary actions
appropriateness of, 153–156, 173
communicating to accused, 140
describing in anti-harassment policies, 124
excessive, 87–88, 152
for fraternization policy breaches, 201
for high-level managers, 163–169
legal requirements, 152
proactive, 156–160
Disclosure, 100

Discrimination
  avoiding in discharges, 48–53
  avoiding in hiring, promotion, and
    pay, 44–48
  avoiding in workforce reductions,
    38–42
  common sense regarding, 17
  continuing presence, 59
  development of laws against, 10–16
  historical basis, 9–10
  legal definitions, 18–19
  pretextual reasons for, 20–24
  proving disparate treatment, 19–20
  reasons for claims, 3
  sexual orientation, 219–224
  societal influences, 4
Discriminatory errors, 43–44
Disparate impact, 18–19, 24–29
Disparate treatment, 18–19, 19–24
Diversity, 301–304
Documentation
  of follow-up activities, 179
  of harassment complaints, 136, 138
  importance, 55
  of responses to harassment claims,
    138–139
  retaining, 56
  of third-party harassment, 245
  of witness credibility, 148–149
Double standards, 4–5
Dram shop laws, 209
Dress codes, 36
Drinking at company events, 206–211
Drug testing, 46–47
Due process, 295

E
EEOC v. Harbert-Yeargin, Inc., 133
EEOC v. National Education Association,
    74, 239–240
Effective communications, 297–298

E-learning programs, 249, 251
Electronics policies, 97–98
E-mail messages
  discrimination in, 51
  examining in harassment investiga-
    tions, 137
  in-person communication versus, 298
  legal risks of, 233
  sexually oriented, 93, 94, 95–96
Emotional firing decisions, 50
Empathy for after-effects of harassment,
    176–177
Employee assistance programs, 176
Employer responses to co-worker
    harassment, 115–117
Employer standards for sexual harass-
    ment, 86–89
Empowerment, 298–299
English-only rules, 270–271
Equal Employment Opportunity
    Commission, 13–14, 271
Equal opportunity bullying, 236,
    237–240
Equal Rights Amendment, 12
Evaluations, documenting, 55
Excessive disciplinary actions, 87–89,
    152, 155–156
Exit interviews, 51
Expert witnesses, 78–79
ExxonMobil Corp., 132–133

F
Facilitating discussions, 157–158, 178
Facts, documenting, 55
Fair Credit Reporting Act, 46
Fair Employment and Housing Act, 247,
    249, 255
Fairness, 28–282
False information, 141, 158–159
Faragher v. City of Boca Raton
  case described, 100–102

employer defenses under, 120–127,
132, 259–260
as guide to training, 246
negligence standard for liability, 106,
112–114
Favoritism, 196–197, 240–241
Federal courts, 67
Federal sentencing guidelines, 246
Filter software, 95
Financial penalties, 165
Firewall software, 97
Firings. *See* Discharges
Fit, 29, 45
Flight attendants, 33–34
Flirting, 192, 285–286
Follow-up
to harassment investigations, 141,
159–160
on harassment's after-effects, 175–180
Fram, 265
Fraternization policies, 199–1201

G

Generational differences, 296
GLAD web site, 221
Good faith beliefs, 144, 145–146
Gossip, 194, 200
Griggs v. Duke Power, 27

H

Harassment, prohibited types, 267. *See
also* Sexual harassment
Harrah's Casino, 36
Harris v. Forklift Systems, 81
Height, 19
Higher standards for managers, 204
High-level managers, harassment by,
163–169
Hill, Anita, 2
Hiring. *See also* Quid pro quo harass-
ment
avoiding discrimination in, 44–48

demanding sexual favors in, 100–102
diversity in, 303
for management positions, 205–206
*Holman v. Indiana Department of
Transportation*, 67–68
Home Depot, 28
Homosexuals, 219–224
Hooters, 34–35
Horseplay, 214, 215
Hostile work environments
difficulty of defining, 115, 237
employee dating leading to, 195–196
excessive discipline for, 86–89
Faragher defenses, 120–127, 132
identifying, 52–85
quid pro quo harassment versus, 120
religious harassment in, 272–274
requirements for, 106, 107
Hot pants, 33–32
Human resources departments
followup to harassment interventions,
173, 175
interventions with office romances,
185–186
involving in retaliation cases, 289
sexual harassment awareness, 60–61
Human Rights Campaign Foundation,
221

I

Inappropriate behavior
assessing levels of, 153–156, 172
describing in anti-harassment policies, 124
employer definitions, 86–89
NLRA protections, 89–91
by nonemployees, 226–234
Inappropriate nicknames, 22
Inconsistencies, 21, 23–24
Independent contractors, 226–234
Indirect discrimination, 18, 19–24

In-person interviews, 146–147
In-person training, 261–262
Instructional designers, 249
Intent in discrimination, 18
Interactive training, 250–251, 264
Internet, avoiding abuse of, 93–98
Interviews
    with harassment witnesses, 137–139
    notes from, 47
    remote versus in-person, 146–147
    small talk in, 29
Intranets, 298
Investigation reports, 139–140
Investigations
    concluding, 139–141
    conducting interviews, 137–139,
        146–147
    importance, 129–134
    interference with, 150
    investigator appointment, 133–135
    paid leave during, 198
    policies for, 125, 126
    pre-interview actions, 135–137
    of romantic breakups, 187
    of third-party harassment, 231–234
IQ tests, 27

J
Jefferson, Thomas, 8
Job-related criteria for hiring, 45–46
Johnson Controls, 35–36
Jones, Paula, 82
Judaism, 261–262
Jury trials, 12, 78–79, 294

K
Kolstad v. American Dental Association, 131

L
Labor unions. *See* Unions
Languages, 270–271
Layoffs, 38–42

Leadership training, 205
Lead exposure, 36
Lewinsky, Monica, 164
Live training, 261–262
Live webinars, 251, 255
Local laws. *See* State and local laws
Locke, John, 9
Loss prevention managers, 134
Love contracts, 201–202

M
Maine anti-harassment training law,
    258–259
Managers
    bad judgment by, 204–206
    bullying, 236–244
    favoritism by, 240–241
    training of (*see* Training)
Manager/subordinate romances,
    187–188, 200
Mandatory anti-harassment training
    California law, 246–256
    Connecticut law, 256–258
    Maine law, 258–259
Mandatory retirement policies, 32–33,
    37
Married couples, 192–193
Mathis v. Phillips Chevrolet, 247
May, Misty, 5
Media General Operations case, 90
Men's jobs, 27–28
Microsoft, 234
Miller Brewing Company, 87–88, 152
Minor offenses, 87–89, 146
Mistaken identity, 270
Motives, examining, 148

N
Name-calling, 270
National Labor Relations Act, 48, 89–91
National origin cases, 13, 270–271
National training policies, 254

Negligence standard, 106, 107, 111–114
Nicknames, 22
9 to 5, 60
9th Circuit Court of Appeals, 74,
    239–240
Nonemployees, inappropriate behavior
    by, 226–234
Nonmanagement employees, anti-
    harassment training, 254–255, 258
Nonresident supervisor training, 252
Nonverbal communication, 146–147
Nudity, 208

O
Objectivity, 28–29
Obscenity, 72
Office romances
    appropriate discipline and, 160–161
    as common occurrence, 182–183, 191
    employer efforts to regulate,
        192–193, 199–202
    potential risks of, 193–198
    as quid pro quo harassment, 102–105,
        186, 194–195
Older Workers Benefit Protection Act,
    40–41, 42
1-3-5-3 rule, 1178–179
Online training, 251, 256, 262
Opposition retaliation, 282–283
Ostracism, 174–175

P
Paid leave, 198
Participation retaliation, 280–282
Patience with underperforming employ-
    ees, 50–51
Paula Jones v. William Jefferson Clinton,
    82
Pay equity, 48
Penalties. *See* Disciplinary actions
Performance appraisals, 23
Performance improvement plans, 295

Performance problems, disabilities and,
    275–277
Personal e-mails, 98
Personal preferences, 241
Pervasive behavior, 83
Pilots, 32
PIPs, 295
Planning for diversity, 302–304
Policies
    employee dating, 192–193, 199–202
    as harassment defense, 106, 121, 122,
        124–126
    Internet, 97–98
    re-establishing, 158–159
    reviewing, 122
    simplifying, 54, 91–92
    training in use of, 250
Political correctness, 153, 154–156
Pornography, 93–98, 284–285
Preaching at work, 274
Pre-employment tests, 25–26, 27, 46–47
Preferential treatment, 196–197
Press coverage, 165, 166, 167
Pretextual problems, 20–24
Prima facie cases, 19–20
Prison guards, 32
Proactive discipline, 156–160
Productivity, 194
Progressive outlook, 296
Prohibited categories of discrimination,
    14–15
Promotions, 44–48, 205–206. *See also*
    Quid pro quo harassment
Proselytizing, 274
Protected, concerted activity, 89, 91
Protective policies, 35–37
Provocation cases, 74–75
Psychologists, 167
Publicity, 165, 166, 168
Public policy, discharges and, 52
Punitive damages, 131–132

Q

Qualified trainers, 248, 256, 263–265
Quality of training, 255–256, 263–265
Quid pro quo harassment
    Faragher and *Ellerth* standards,
      105–107
    hostile work environment versus, 120
    office romances and, 102–105, 186,
      184–185
    overview, 99–102

R

Race discrimination, 11–12, 62–64
Racial harassment, 268–269
Rape cases, 75
Reasonable behavior, 72–74
Reasonable belief standard, 282–283
Reasonable person test, 84–85
Record keeping, 261
Recruiting, 44–48, 303
Reductions in force, 38–42
Reed v. Shepard, 75
Re-establishing policies, 158–159
Rehabilitation Act of 1974, 15
Religious discrimination, 13
Religious harassment, 270–274
Remote interviews, 146–147
Renegade supervisors, 164
Reporting harassment, 125
Reports of investigations, 139–140
Respect, 51, 300–301
Retaining documents, 56
Retaliation claims
    avoiding, 288–291
    office romances and, 198
    with sexual harassment, 284–287
    types, 280–284
Retirement, mandatory, 32–33, 37
Retraining requirements, 252
Reverse discrimination, 303
Robots, 5

Runaway juries, 294

S

Salaries, 48
Same-sex sexual harassment, 214–219
Scarberry v. ExxonMobil Oil Corp.,
    132–133
Schwarzenegger, Arnold, 246
Scripts for coaching, 117
Security managers, 134
"Seinfeld" case, 87–88, 152
Self-selection, 28
Self-study, 251, 262
Sensitivity training, 163–169
Separating individuals, 149, 157
Separation agreements, 38–42
Serial harassers, 169
Severance agreements, 161
Severe or pervasive behavior
    actions qualifying as, 82–85, 153
    excessive measures against, 86–89
    overview, 81–82
Sex discrimination
    customer preferences and, 33–35
    development of laws against, 62–64
    early Title VII cases, 12
    as protective policy, 35–37
    vulnerability to claims of, 27–28
Sexism, 238
Sexual favoritism, 196–197
Sexual harassment
    application of Title VII to, 61, 66–69
    by co-workers, 110–117
    Faragher defenses, 119–127
    following consensual relationships,
      183–189, 194–197
    jury trials for, 78–79
    origins of legal protections against,
      59–64
    policy suggestions for, 91–92
    quid pro quo, 99–107

reasonable and welcome behavior,
    72–77
retaliation with, 284–287
same-sex, 214–219
sensitivity training for, 16.–169
societal influences, 4–5
stereotypical view, 213
Sexual harassment claims. *See also*
    Investigations
    defined, 130
    importance of investigating, 130–133
    potential disruptions from, 1–3
    reasons for, 3–4, 6–7
Sexual orientation, 219–224
Shop talk, 90
Showing appropriate concern for dis-
    abilities, 274–275
Similarly situated workers, 21
Slush words, 49
Southwest Airlines, 33–34
Spam filters, 95
Spouses in workplace, 192–193
State and local laws
    antidiscrimination, 15
    California compliance challenges,
        253–256
    California's anti-harassment training
        rules, 246–252
    Connecticut training rules, 256–258
    employment, 56
    Maine's training rules, 258–259
    on reductions in force, 41
    on sexual orientation discrimination,
        220–223
State Department of Health Services v.
    Superior Court, 255
Statistics, 26
Stern, Howard, 5, 110
Stewart, Potter, 72
Stupid statements, 21–22
Subconscious discrimination, 3

Subjectivity, 28–29, 45
Subject matter experts, 248
Supervisor/subordinate relationships,
    187–188, 200
Supervisor training, 247–248

T
Take-aways, 297
Targeted selection questions, 46
Targets, executives as, 168–169
Temporary workers, 226–234
Tennessee Supreme Court, 174–175
Tests
    pre- and post-training, 265
    pre-employment, 25–26, 27, 46–47
Third-party harassment and discrimina-
    tion, 226–234
Thomas, Clarence, 2
Three-way discussions, 178
Time for healing, 178–179
Timely responses, 126–127, 134
Title VII
    anti-retaliation provisions, 280
    applied to sexual harassment, 61,
        66–69
    early cases under, 11–14
    passage of, 63–64
    purposes, 59, 61
    severe or pervasive standard, 81–85
Training
    California compliance challenges,
        253–256
    California's mandatory rules, 246–252
    Connecticut mandatory rules,
        256–258
    as harassment defense, 123, 125–126,
        259–261
    for harassment investigators, 133
    Maine's mandatory rules, 258–259
    for management skills, 205
    methods compared, 261–263

overall importance for managers, 53–54
as protective remedy, 156–157
quid pro quo harassment, 105
sensitivity, 163–169
Training year tracking, 252
Transfers, 149, 290

U
Uhrich, Gale, 67
Uncertainty from change, 300
Unions
NLRA protections, 89
race discrimination by, 12
as response to abusive management, 242
Unpaid leave, 198

V
Vendors, 226–234

W
Wages, 48

Waiver of claims, 40, 41, 42
Wal-Mart, 3
Webcasts, 251, 256, 262
Welcomeness concept, 74–77
Witnesses
credibility, 143–150
interviewing, 137–139
investigators as, 133, 134
Women as harassers, 100
Women's jobs, 27–28
Worker Adjustment and Retraining Notification Act, 39–40
Workforce reductions, 38–42
Workplace romances. *See* Office romances

Z
Zero tolerance policies
overzealous interpretations, 88–89, 155–156
use of term discouraged, 92, 125
varying contexts for, 153